SURVIVING OFF

OFF-GRID

Decolonizing the Industrial Mind

Michael Bunker

Surviving *Off* Off-Grid

For free articles, sermons, and downloadable audios:
www.lazarusunbound.com

For information on Michael Bunker, or to read his blog:
www.michaelbunker.com

For Michael Bunker's Podcast: www.audiobunker.com

To contact Michael Bunker, please write to:
M. Bunker
1251 CR 132
Santa Anna, Texas 76878

Surviving *Off* Off-Grid

Decolonizing the Industrial Mind

by

Michael Bunker

ACKNOWLEDGMENTS

I want to thank the Lord Jesus Christ for his longsuffering and mercy; my family for their love, strength, help, and forbearance; the people in our Christian community for their support, courage, conviction, and patience with me; Stewart and Elder David Sifford for pushing me to finally publish a book for the first time in 9 years, and for your editing assistance and suggestions; my "friendslist" for their financial support, prayers, and help; and to all my readers at A Process Driven Life blog (*www.michaelbunker.com*), I thank you for reading my occasional scribblings. I would also like to thank Nick at *www.off-grid.net* for publishing an early version of the online book. I do thank you all with all my heart.

TABLE OF CONTENTS

FORWARD

This book was designed to be not only a platform for the teaching of Off Off-Grid living philosophy, but to fill a huge gap in both the "Survival", and "Off-Grid" information base. Catering to the "back to the land" movement; the "alternative energy" movement; the "homesteading movement", and a half a dozen other movements, authors, experts, and scholars have offered up a plethora (or maybe it is a smorgasbord) of books and other materials; some really good, some not so good, but virtually all with a single over-riding philosophy -- that "independence" can be had by half-steps, by learning a few techniques, by the pre-placement or stockpiling of industrially produced goods, and by shifting our "dependence" from one industrial supplier to another – all without fundamentally changing the foundations of how we think and live.

Independence is not a word without meaning. It cannot be an empty mantra, or a shadow without reality. Shifting our dependencies, or temporarily delaying their consequences, is not going to offer us a successful "survival", or even living, philosophy. There are a lot of really good "survival" and "off-grid" materials out there (and I do buy them), but there are almost no materials that challenge (or even explain) the fundamental pre-suppositional errors behind the cult of dependency. The One-World Cult of *modern industrial consumerism* is not dismantled, explained, or even challenged in most of the materials that are marketed to folks who tend to show signs of having had quite enough of it. It is our opinion that the lack of a cogent and consistent philosophy – one that challenges the ascendency and reign of the consumerist status quo - has left the enemy of true Independence in possession of the field of battle. It is our intention to offer a philosophy that, whatever may be said of it, stands *Contra-Mundum* (against the world), and against the prevailing foundational philosophy of industrial consumerism, thoughtless consumption, and the dependence on systems that are contrary to our own best interests. Maybe we have failed... maybe we have succeeded. There can be no doubt that the pantry of survivalism is full of stuff, techniques, tactics, materials, technologies, and alternative providers. What our pantry lacks is the honesty and the wisdom to question absolutely everything, because... who knows... maybe the Emperor, after all, truly has no clothes.

This is not a "how to do" book, though there is some of that in it. This is a "how to think" book. By definition, since most people love the world the way it is (maybe they'd like some cosmetic changes), it isn't for most people. Released into the world it challenges, and the philosophy it rejects, it is bound to be more hated than loved, more rejected than embraced. With all that said, it humbly offers another viewpoint, another completely different idea of life, and it is a call to consider again the old foundations and the old paths. It is designed to fundamentally challenge the way things are, and the religious, social, and cultural maxims that got us to where we are. It may make your head spin, or it may make you angry, but it will have been successful if it makes you think. "Survival" cannot be a temporary *Pyrrhic victory*, or pretty stitches on a mortal gash. If survival is to be real, it must result in salvation, which makes it all the more important that we question everything.

INTRODUCTION

If you pay attention to the news, there seems to be much trepidation and worry in the world today. Western Civilization looks to be coming apart at the seams - economies around the world are crashing, there are massive job layoffs and bank failures, and governments are printing and spending trillions of pretend dollars to try to stem the tide of collapse. There is a palpable nervousness in the air, and it seems that most people are just trying to pretend as if nothing permanently serious is going on.

For over a century the Western Democracies have seen unprecedented growth and relative success and have been the envy of the whole world when it comes to standard of living. Now, if one dares look closely, it appears that there is a change coming – and *that change is making a lot of people really nervous.*

But... have we been here before? Is there a time in history that we can look to in order to learn what is likely to befall Western society in the coming years?

URBANISM AND SUBURBANISM, THE MODERN ROME

Towards the end of the 4th century, Rome, the capital city of the Western Roman Empire was a metropolis of more than a million inhabitants. Most of the citizens of Rome were purely urbanites, people who had never known any other life and whose families and households had lived in the city for generations. The agrarian skills and trades that had allowed people to survive and thrive for thousands of years around the world had been almost completely lost by the city-folk in Rome, and, much like today, city dwellers looked down their noses and sneered at people who actually had (or chose) to work in the soil and with their hands to provide the necessities of survival. What a change this was from earlier epochs, particularly when we look at the Greek empire 500 years or more before Christ. Although much of the Hellenic world was urban, and although the Greek empire had some of the most marvelous cities ever built, the Greeks understood the slavery and deception of the city, and had a high regard for agriculture and the rural life. Of the Greeks, the great historian Will Durant said, *"The freemen of the countryside tend to look down upon the denizens of the city as either weakling parasites or degraded slaves."* Unhappily, in the fullness of time, the Greeks went down a road that is now well-traveled. They blazed that road for the Romans who were to come after them. *"In one century,"* Durant tells us, *"Athens moves from household economy – wherein each household makes nearly all that it needs – to urban economy – wherein each town makes nearly all it needs – to international economy – where each state is dependent upon imports, and must make exports to pay for them."* From freedom to dependence in just ONE CENTURY. Because of this dependence on imports and exports, when the Spartans destroyed the Athenian fleet of the Hellespont, starvation followed in the cities of Attica. But... enough of Greece; we're talking about Rome...

The Romans seem to have skipped the step where they highly respect farm life and look down upon city dwellers. Romans took to city life like a fish to water. People who arrived in Rome from the "country" or from the provinces were considered to be backward bumpkins compared to the cosmopolitan and progressive people of the eternal city.

Do you think of Rome as an ancient and unrefined city? Are you one of those people who think that because something existed long ago, it cannot have been better than what exists today? The city of Rome had running water, a sewage system, baths, mausoleums, temples, night clubs, restaurants, pubs, shops and even shopping malls. Many of the homes had air-conditioning, milk delivery, and indoor plumbing. Students attended the city's many schools and universities. Writers and artists worked by commission for religious leaders, politicians, and wealthier citizens. Specialization thrived. The Roman urbanites became bees in a massive hive. Most of the residents lived in apartments, walked to their jobs on cobblestone and brick streets lined with flowers and topiary, and lived their whole lives within the boundaries of the city. Many Romans had never even seen a farm nor did they possess any practical agrarian survival skills. Like the Greeks before them, they did their jobs, consumed, lived - and they let the government and the merchants mind the future. What could go wrong?

JIT = JUST IN TIME

The city was provisioned in much the same way that large cities are today. Away from the city there were clay and stone excavations, gold mines, tin and lead mines, metal forges and factories. Large granaries and warehouses in the harbor city of Portus, south of the city on the Tiber River, stored grains for daily transport for the *JIT* supply of Rome. An advanced system of transport and supply kept the city well stocked from every direction. Highways and roads, advanced even by modern standards and some still operating today, allowed for goods to be transported to Rome from all over the known world. With ease a middle-class shopper in Rome could, in a relatively affordable way, buy spices and fabrics from Asia, clothing and tools from local artisans or from the Middle East, and food from as far away as Western Europe.

Most of the citizens of Rome were employed in jobs that were made necessary by the massive amount of consumption by the citizens of the city. It was not uncommon for a wealthy Roman citizen to employ as many as 50 full-time paid workers, some whose day might consist solely of polishing candle sticks or sweeping floors, or carrying things from one place to another. Others worked in factories, shops, thermal bath houses, restaurants, accounting offices, in the business trades, or in the city's many venues of entertainment. Constant wars and conquests provided the means for a constant inflow of money and material for expansion and for the maintenance of jobs and a stable economy. Whereas the Greeks had built their prosperity on

11

Mediterranean trade via its vast network of foreign colonies and trading partners, the Romans supported their economy by conquest and the sword. It is true that Rome had massive slums - areas of poverty and degradation inhabited mainly by slaves and the poorer classes, but it also had very wealthy districts with upscale shops and boutiques.

The Romans, after centuries of living the urban life, had little or no concept of how their food was grown or produced. If you asked a Roman how sustainable his existence was, he might reply, *"Rome is the eternal city. It has always been here, and it will always be here. Whatever I will ever need is available in the shops and the stores".* You have to admit, seeing Rome would have been something to behold! If you asked that same Roman citizen from whence his water came, he would have likely shrugged and pointed to the aqueducts. To the Roman it seemed that freely accessible and plentiful water had always just *been* there. Eleven towering aqueducts, technological marvels built over a span of more than 500 years, brought cool, clear, potable water into the city from dozens of miles away. Underground pipes brought running water into, and provided air conditioning for, the houses of those able to afford it. Huge buildings and structures, built by both paid and slave labor loomed over the city streets. The imposing Roman Coliseum, capable of seating 50,000 spectators, was a marvel of engineering and construction. The Coliseum had stood for over 300 years and was the site of gladiatorial contests, executions, animal hunts, savage battles, and other public spectacles. In a marvel of engineering that matches anything done in entertainment today, the Coliseum could even be filled with water for staged mock sea battles... with full sized ships complete with crews! Construction was a way of life in Rome, and, much like in our present cites, construction meant jobs and it gave a sense that things were always going to get bigger and better.

But, at the turn of the 5th century, even though the Romans did not know it and could not have conceived of it, the end was very, very near. The thought of disaster would have seemed implausible to a

Roman. Rome had not fallen to an enemy army in 800 years, and even though cultural and social memories and historical awareness were much greater back then, it seemed as if Rome, the eternal city, would indeed continue on for centuries more.

The Roman juggernaut was both hated and feared by friends and neighbors alike for hundreds of years and it could be said that, much like America in the early 21st Century, world opinion had ceased to be favorable for the lone Western superpower. By the end of the 4th century many of the barbarian tribes had begun to unite against domination from Rome. The Visigoths had moved into the Eastern Roman Empire to escape persecution and subjugation by the invading Huns. Led by Alaric, the Visigoths and other barbarian tribes now found themselves subjects of Rome, and from the Romans they suffered from persecution, high taxes, government intervention and corruption, and forced conscription. Uniting together against Rome, the barbarian armies on several occasions besieged Rome and in the year 410 the Eternal City - that shining, wicked, prosperous, arrogant city that sits on seven hills - fell to the barbarian hordes. The destruction of Rome was unthinkable, but the unthinkable happened. Rome indeed fell. Most of the people starved, died of disease, or were killed during the siege, but hundreds of thousands of refugees fled into the countryside as Rome was sacked and burned.

What was life like in the city before the fall? During the sieges of Rome by Alaric (there were three in all) starvation and disease killed tens of thousands of people, and the city descended into a maelstrom of bloody violence, robbery, and even cannibalism. The Roman leaders continued to hold the spectacles and gladiator battles during the siege in order to keep people's minds off of their miserable condition, only now, instead of being satisfied with the destruction, death, and dismemberment of criminals, slaves, and political and religious prisoners, the people demanded that the bodies of the dead be given to them for their meat. The Romans ate each other. In a scene that has been repeated many times throughout world history - city and suburb dwellers, angry, starving, and without any practical skills or means of support, devolved into pitiless beasts when the JIT means of provisioning dried up. Once absolutely certain that nothing could go wrong, and looking down on those who made their productive living from the soil, when the means of production and distribution of mass-produced foods were destroyed, the people became animals, they died like animals, and/or became the food for animals and men.

Europe now descended into a period that is in our days called the Dark Ages. It was indeed dark, not because Rome had been some kind of beacon or a shining light, in fact, Rome had always been morally dark, brutal and nasty, blood thirsty and murderous. The Dark Ages were called "dark" because the elements that fallen man had come to regard as "progress" were all destroyed at the same time and in a sudden and magnificent fashion. The light of "civilization" was put out. The vacuum created by the fall of Rome was filled by power hungry priests, monks, and Popes, and, because of the ignorance of the people, un-Biblical superstition would reign for nearly a thousand years. Where once the mind and heart of men had been entertained and anaesthetized by *bread and circuses*, now man would once again earn his bread by the sweat of his brow, and fertilize his crops with his blood. He would be ruled over, in turn or in concert, by marauding bands and armies, religious charlatans, and a carnivorous aristocracy and nobility that would make the dark ages live up to their billing.

A hundred years after the sacking of Rome farm animals grazed in the now crumbling Coliseum. How is that for irony? Adults and children looked at the towering aqueducts and the fabled city streets and marveled at the technologically advanced society that must have created them. They couldn't even image it. Another hundred years after that, people were chiseling rocks and stones out of the walls of the Coliseum in order to build rudimentary stone buildings for housing. Many history students look at Roman ruins and believe that the destruction they see is solely the result of time and the elements, but in reality many of those structures were disassembled or torn down piece by piece for the base materials in them that could be had and used for the bare maintenance of life. Modern cities will likely face the same fate. Students today are taught that the destruction of Rome caused a great leap backwards in technology and knowledge, but wiser and more spiritual minds know that the so-called "advancement" of Rome was actually a work of God designed to show forth his manifold wisdom in its eventual destruction. It was a divine object lesson, a real-time example of what not to do and how not to live. The historians of Rome had not discerned the patterns in previous civilizations that should have alerted them to Rome's fate. The theologians were busy with issues of power, prestige, art, and money – and thus had neither the time nor the knowledge to understand what God's Word had to say about Rome. The Philosophers either could not or would not see the logical fallacy of a society built on the necessity of consumption and conquest. No prophet could be heard in the hustle and bustle of cosmopolitan Rome.

The technological feat that was classical Rome was actually a huge deception, a monstrous hologram of success and achievement. Rome was a city powered by human blood, coercion, and foreign domination (as any huge city or state must be). The success of Roman life came on the backs of slaves and conquered peoples, and was upheld by the use of crushing tyranny and the usurpation of God-given freedoms. Like in any major metropolis, the maintenance of the city of Rome required massive amounts of taxes and human investment. True wealth, created by the hard work and creativity of productive people who tilled, planted, harvested, milled, mined, constructed, etc. was expropriated at the point of a sword and by threats and very real violence. Taxes, as they are in any nation, were acquired in myriad ways, but all of those ways rested on the threat of imprisonment, death, or worse... the Coliseum.

In a sublime irony, the so-called "advancements" of Rome (those accomplishments that allowed hundreds of thousands of people to live in an artificially built and unsustainable society, separated from the means of production) actually served to cripple and mentally enslave the people who became addicted to city and suburban life. People moved out of the countryside and into the cities and suburbs for many reasons, but most went to Rome because:

1. Agrarian life had become difficult due to the continuous hardships imposed by the constant warfare always required for the maintenance of the big city-states; Roman civilization required conquest, conquest required armies and wars, armies move through farmland and destroy and steal everything in their paths. Oppressive taxes were bad enough, but the knowledge that your entire crop (along with your sons and sometimes your daughters) might be "requisitioned" by the next passing army was too much for many to bear. If everything was being stolen or destroyed in order to maintain the comfort of Rome... why not move to Rome? Such is the morality and philosophy of a life of plunder.

2. Rome had assumed an almost mythic status. Country-folk were considered backward and ignorant. Knowledge was in Rome. Success was in Rome. Advancement was in Rome. Enlightenment was in Rome. Rome, as a woman dressed in red, had become the beautiful and seductive harlot of the world, and fallen man was easily enticed to go in unto her.

3. Greed and Covetousness. It was said that Rome was the richest city in the world. God had commanded man to live simply and to be satisfied with food and raiment. He had taught men not to seek riches, but, as always, the carnal mind is able to rationalize any behavior.

To be frank, greed is the primary reason most people end up moving to the city. The carnal mind knows that country life is hard, and that there is no safety net. In the country you work and you pray, you plant and you water, and you look to God alone for the increase. City life provides a buffer zone between man and God. Specialization mitigates the immediate risk of failure, and provides an insurance-like effect when God's judgment causes or allows failures or disasters. In the country, if your crop failed, you alone were responsible and you were exposed and open before a sovereign God to whom you owed obeisance and service. But if you lived in a city and disaster struck, you could always just get a job polishing furniture or sweeping out kitchens. Risk could be spread out and shared in a Babylonian fashion.

The city-dweller is almost never survival or preparedness minded. Why should he be? His job is to perform his individual task and let others worry about the details of survival. The advent of specialization fractured the mind and caused man to focus on pieces of the puzzle instead of the whole picture. The urbanite doesn't allow himself to be concerned with whether or not the grocer has food or the peddler has supplies because during good times those things are not his concern. His mind is to be focused on his daily specialized tasks and the rest of the brain is allowed to atrophy. Subtly, his mind fragments. He can no longer think in "wholes". Everything has its compartment, and most things are someone else's business. Governments and the prophets of urbanization provide entertainments to keep the mind numbed and fractured and always new trinkets and wonderments appear to keep the soul anaesthetized. New products must always appear on the shelves in order to stave off boredom and angst – and the manufacture of eternally useless baubles serves to maintain an ever increasing need for jobs, employment, and economic growth. Survival and preparedness, once an unconscious way of life and a God-given instinct for the continuance of the race and for motivation to productive work, became nothing more than a hobby for enthusiasts and a pacifier for worry-worts.

MODERN SOCIETY AND THE MYTH OF MITIGATION OF THREATS

Today, the idea of corporate (conglomerate) mitigation of the threat of disaster or judgment is the foundational idea behind industrial and urban society. Our world now functions on the premise that if people become more specialized and come together to create a global corporate economy (a prosperity machine), nothing bad can happen here in the new global Rome. Like the Romans, we haven't learned anything from history. Modern urban society serves to take the mind off of the truth of the absolute sovereignty of God, and off of man's responsibility before this sovereign God. Another sublime spiritual irony is that, had man remained within God's declared will as to the manner and means of life and living, he would have not been so susceptible to the massive and destructive threats that face him today... and at the same time, having remained within God's will, he would be less likely to be facing wrath as a result of his rebellion.

It is an unhappy reality that it often takes massive and devastating economic interruptions in order to get people to think about doing things they ought to have been doing all along. It is a sad commentary on humanity that it often takes the fear of a second great depression to motivate people to learn the lessons of the first great depression. It is a sign of the human condition that most people, most of the time, will not do that which seems uncomfortable for them in the short run, even if it means that doing so will spare them the unbearable in the long run. This book is for the few who are willing to look at facts the way they are, and not just the way that people want them to be.

THE 80/20 RULE - AND WHY I BELIEVE THAT IT IS OVERLY OPTIMISTIC

In every field of endeavor in which I have ever engaged, especially while I was back "in the world" (serving the world, acting in concert with it as a cog in its machinery), there existed what was called an 80/20 rule. Many of you may have heard of it. The 80/20 rule is flexible and it changes based on context. There are innumerable different situations or genres, but in general it goes like this...

You may say that:

20% of the people do 80% of the work, while 80% of the people do 20% of the work.

20% of the people are producers, while 80% of the people are consumers.

20% of the people provide 80% of the benefits that sustain society, while 80% of the people provide 20% of the benefits.

Many years ago I was in a survival related course, and the instructor used the 80/20 rule. He said that 80% of the people are "victims, just waiting to happen", while 20% of the people are rarely victims because they are intelligent, engaged, aware, and responsive. Well, I am going to go on the record as disagreeing with the 80/20 rule in this case. I do not believe that anywhere near 20% of the people are producers, workers, or survivors. I believe 20% is overly optimistic in virtually any situation, and it most certainly is overly optimistic when it comes to survival. In reality, most of the people you know (likely including you), if examined in a historical context, are not now *viable or sustainable,* meaning that they would not survive even a short amount of time after a systemic failure of the JIT industrial/consumer life support grid that is our world today. I call this industrial-consumer life support system - *the perpetual 72 degree consumer womb.* If a situation was to arise where people were forced, even for a very short amount of time (say weeks or months) to live exactly as their great-grandparents or ancestors lived, they would die off in massive numbers in very short order.

An example: when rural electrification was underway during the depression of the 1930's, if a huge systemic disaster had wiped out the entire electrical system in America for a whole year, there likely would have been zero deaths that could be directly attributed to the power outage. So our base number is zero. By contrast, a similar unexpected and systemic loss of electrical power across the whole of America today would likely lead to deaths in the millions (more likely the hundreds of millions) if the outage were to last for a single year.

Industrialism coupled with modern consumer capitalism has created generations of *non-viable people* (people who are unable to survive outside of the artificial womb of JIT life), each generation more non-viable than the one before it, each peopled with individuals who cannot and would not survive even the mildest of interruptions in goods or services without massive government outlays and government rescue programs. We need look no further in our history books than Hurricane Katrina in Louisiana in 2005, or more recently, Hurricane Ike here in my state of Texas, to see how absolutely necessary massive government interventions (with funds and material) are to the short-term survival of modern man. In every case during the last several decades where massive disasters have been recorded, there has always been (however weak and/or slow it may appear) an outside source of stability that was ready and able to jump in and provide aid and comfort to support those who are otherwise unable to survive and support themselves. When hurricane after hurricane punished Florida and the American eastern coast in 2004, aid poured in almost immediately from the rest of the country and around the world. What happens when the response is not immediate? When Hurricane Katrina (historically not the biggest or most devastating storm) destroyed most of New Orleans, we saw the almost instantaneous devolution of that society and saw the monstrous result of carnal people being stripped of the support structure that has become necessary to sustain them. Even those who did survive well enough, who did not riot, who did not loot, who did not kill or rape – these were bolstered and supported by the knowledge that help was coming, and with the understanding that if they could hunker down and wait it out, they would soon be returned to their former state of dependency on the system which sustains them. But what if help doesn't come?

I am going to make a statement that might shock some people, and you would do well to ruminate on it for some time...

I believe that if tomorrow there were some sort of massive and comprehensive systemic disaster, resulting in a loss of JIT goods and services and a loss in available grid electrical power and water, and if that disaster (whether man-made or natural) caused a scenario where omnipresent paternal government could not or would not be able or willing to send any appreciable aid for a long period of time, that fully ½ or more of the population of the United States (or of just about any country for that matter) would die in less than a year. 150+ million deaths in less than a year, just in the United States; and I believe that my prediction is probably on the conservative side. But Rome never thinks she can fall...

Think about that. Most people who read that might scoff or deny that such devastation could be possible. Like the Romans in 410 A.D., they cannot conceive that any such thing could ever come to pass, nor can they even begin to quantify the difficulties and realities of what will occur when such a thing *does* come to pass. If Americans today were forced, without warning, to live for just 1 year exactly like their ancestors lived 150 years ago (and for the 6000 years before them), the greater part of them would die in a very short amount of time. This is exactly what I mean by "the perpetual 72-degree consumer womb". This is the very definition of a system that is not-viable, that is unsustainable. Most modernists are likely to disagree with me, because most modernists do not have any idea what life would be like (even on a very short term level) without the government sponsored artificial womb that has been created for them and in which they now live. In a remarkable departure from the historical experience of hundreds of billions of people who lived before our age, for the entire life span of virtually everyone who reads this, there has been a system in place to support and provide for all those who are unable or unwilling to take care of and provide for themselves and their families. Now be sure to understand me. I do not mean to say that people are unwilling to "go to work". If it has proven anything at all, our age has proven that men and women are willing to do all manner of dehumanizing and mind-numbing work, so long as they believe that they are not to ever be made *uncomfortable.* I am saying that most modernists are unable or unwilling to provide and support for their families outside of the comfortable but unsustainable JIT system that has put everyone within it at risk. We are several generations removed from the last generation that had to "make it" off the land without a safety net or an artificial system which piped in their food, water, electricity, and whatever else was necessary for their "survival". Even the term *Survival,* as it is most commonly used today, implies "lasting" or "making it through" to a time or place where the artificial womb of government or industry supplied material comfort and safety is in place. Most survival instruction and materials are predicated on the idea that survival means "to persevere until help comes or until 'normalcy' returns", which means that this type of survivalism assumes an eventual return to the crippling and atrophying way of life that put people at risk in the first place. Now, in and of itself, in the short run there is nothing wrong with this type of survival, if it is necessary and if it works. The problem is that so long as we deny that our current system of life and living is unsustainable, we will refuse to move towards a more realistic and honest system of life and living. Today, whether one agrees with it or not, every person who lives dependently on the system of JIT supply and security of this modern urban culture, is in daily peril of that very likely and impending reality where the system itself collapses and is either irreparable, or it cannot be restored to its former condition.

SO WHY THIS BOOK?

This book is not really a "how to" book. There will be some "how to" and plenty of "why to", but this book was not designed to be a manual on Survival. This book is about decolonizing and defragmenting the corrupted and atrophied mind and teaching people another way to think.

DECOLONIZATION

What do we mean by "decolonize"?

Every colonial power admits that there are certain things that it must accomplish when it colonizes a formerly independent and free people. The colonial power must first convince its new subjects (by warfare, or punishments, or education, or by whatever means are necessary) that they must change their former way of life and living. It is not enough that the people be forced to act differently, but, in the long term the newly colonized people must be taught to *think* differently. They must be reprogrammed. Their minds must be colonized.

Remember, please, what you have learned. A free and independent agrarian people can be conned into dependency and slavery in less than a century. This can only happen if the people are taught to think differently. Colonialism, whether good or bad, is designed to make a people change the way they think and operate so that they can become valuable and beneficial resources to the foreign colonial power. In order to make a successful and thriving agrarian people (the American colonies prior to the War Between the States) accept that industrialism would bring them both prosperity and unity, the minds of the people had to first be subjugated and colonized. There is a long story of how this colonization of the mind came to be, and it is a subject that could fill a whole book in itself, but it is inarguable that this colonization of the American mind took place. As Will Durant said, Greece went from self-sufficient, sustainable family life to international dependency on imports and exports in one hundred years. The same thing happened in the American colonies. During the Industrial Revolution, thousands of years of history and successful living were thrown out, the baby with the bathwater. Over a period of 100 years, the Agrarian mind was overthrown and the industrial and urban mind was developed in its place. Independency was replaced with dependency. Individuality was replaced with a horrible fake of the same name. The whole mind was fragmented and compartmentalized so that the man or woman could be forced into specialization – like an ant or a bee in a colony. People were robbed of their concept of "wholes" and instead were sold on the virtue of "parts". Survival became someone else's business. Marketers and salesmen applied to the baser desires of greed and covetousness to convince people that their old lives were hard and unprofitable, but in the Brave New World they would have gadgets and fun and free-time, and *leisure*. The family was fractured, and each member became replaceable. Even the definition of "family" was altered.

SIN IS CODIFIED AND MAN ATTEMPTS TO REIGN IN GOD'S STEAD

It is our opinion that urban-industrialism (and the inter-connected/inter-dependent world required to support it) is responsible for most of what is wrong with the world. Ok, sin is what is wrong with the world, but industrialism is the coalescence of all that sin does and can do in the world. It is distilled sin, in that it perpetuates and allows all that man imagines, and therefore, in industrialism nothing is restrained from man that he might imagine doing:

> *And the LORD said, Behold, the people is one, and they have all one language; and this they begin to do: and now nothing will be restrained from them, which they have imagined to do.* (Gen 11:6)

Now this makes industrialism the modern tower of Babel (the place, by the way, after the Noahic flood, where we find this process of agrarianism to urbanism first prominently displayed). It is the one language of the world, and it is the result of the carnal man saying, *"Go to, let us build us a <u>city</u> and a <u>tower</u>, whose top may reach unto heaven"*. Of course the city is *urbanism* and the tower is *industrialism*

Ok, so if you disagree with that and are unwilling to even consider it, then you have no reason to read further or to investigate the solutions provided for you in this book. Your system (urban industrialism) already reigns and is already out there on the plain of Shinar and you may go get your fill of it. If, however, you agree with (or want to investigate) what I have said, then Agrarianism is God's survival alternative. We believe that disconnecting from the current system is necessary for our spiritual safety, our physical well-being, and for our eternal good.

THE GRID

The connection that ties people into this modern Babylonian system is the system we call "the grid". That grid consists of physical and spiritual connections and services that intertwine us with the world, and cause us to rely on the world system instead of on God. There is a huge difference between utilizing some aspect of the world system, as necessary, for the purpose of further separating from it (much as you would, if you were in a small boat, push off from a dock in order to gain speed to separate from it), and loving the world by being tied to it - so do not let naysayers and illogical barkers convince you that if you believe in separation that this separation must be complete, total, and immediate - else you are a hypocrite. Let dogs bark. You just go on about the business of being obedient. Dogs defend what they love - never forget that. A barking dog is just defending his first love.

It is ridiculous and stupid for anyone to assert that because, at any particular time, we are still connected in one way or another to the grid, that we are hypocrites or that we are in precisely the same position as someone who is completely and utterly dependent on the grid. It is such an illogical assertion that it barely merits a response. Unhappily though, it is the argument that world and grid lovers use the most when trying to defend worldliness. They will look at the Amish and they will say, "Ha! Some of the Amish use cell phones or diesel generators! Ha! They are just as worldly as me, and they are hypocrites!" No. They are 99% less dependent on the system than you are. They are almost certainly not dependent on that cell phone or that diesel generator, and they almost certainly will not die if they have to go without it – since they have spent centuries learning how to live and survive off of the grid. So, like I said, the "hypocrisy" charge is as inevitable as it is stupid and illogical. Again, never mind barkers because they are just defending what they love.

Ok, as I was saying... this world "grid" system is most perfectly represented by the electrical grid. In the electrical grid, everyone is tied together and reliant on some mega-corporate (or fascist state/corporate conglomerate) system to provide them with power (This is not the section where we discuss electrical power; we are just using electrical power as a parable). Now, the trick for the industrialist is to provide *sooooo* much power, and at such a *seemingly* low cost, that people will go out into the corporate industrial stores and buy tons of once needless stuff that can be plugged eternally into wall sockets. Each one of these things in and of itself uses only a nominal amount of power, but each is designed to accomplish several things:

1. To cumulatively provide huge amounts of money to the power company.

2. To make us daily MORE dependent on the power company for the maintenance of a certain "standard of living". For example, if you require coffee in the morning, and you are a typical American, you are probably dependent on one or more machines to provide you with that morning java. So, you send a love offering to the power company every morning, along with most other Americans, in order to start your day like they do in the coffee commercials.

3. To make us daily less viable as creatures dependent on God alone for our provision, safety, happiness, and well-being. In other words, each generation is increasingly less and less able to survive without the comforts and conveniences provided by ubiquitous grid power.

4. To enslave us to our baser lusts. The system itself is designed to provide proxies for all that God would have for His children. The grid-system provides a perpetual 72 degree womb where every carnal need is met instantly by the world system.

After fallen man discovered the ability to create electrical power and to channel it down long power lines to each individual dwelling, the marketing arm of Satan clicked into business. Daily, more and more power gulping systems and gadgets are provided which take mankind farther and farther away from the way that God has ordained that His people live.

The Bible tells us what the job of man was before the fall:

And the LORD God took the man, and put him into the garden of Eden **to dress it and to keep it.** (Gen 2:15)

And this was the job of man after the fall:

Therefore the LORD God sent him forth from the garden of Eden, *to till the ground from whence he was taken.* (Gen 3:23)

We are to work with our hands (1 Thess. 4:11), in the ground/soil (Gen. 3:23), and to be content with food and raiment (1 Tim. 6:8). The lie of the industrial grid system is that if you will enslave yourself to your baser lusts (for comfort, leisure, entertainment, sin) then you will not have to labor in the soil. That is basically the gist of it. That is why your parents always told you to go to a worldly college to get a degree... so you wouldn't have to dig ditches. The world hates the idea of working in the soil, because that is what God has decreed for man. The world hates the idea of working in the soil because it reminds us that one day our mortal man must return to dust. Anyway, I digress... please forgive me...

So this grid system is a tool of the world for the enslavement of the minds and hearts of the people. Once again, if you will never agree, you may go your way... like the urban Romans before Alaric you are free to trust in man and in the world. Your system is out there and you may go have your fill of it. If, however, you still agree or you are at least considering what I am saying - we can move on to the next step.

GETTING OUT

Going "off-grid" looks, at first, like an overwhelming task. It is the giant in the land that keeps us from going in and taking the good land that God has promised us. The modern grid life is easy and relatively cheap (when you consider that you are already in it, and enslaved to it, and that it might cost you more to get out). The flesh loves air conditioning and microwaves and hair dryers and such things. All the junk we plug into outlets is designed to please and anaesthetize our flesh. That is why the *grid in our hearts* is so hard to get rid of (1 John 2:15-16, Matt. 13:22). The first task in getting off-grid is to fall out of love with these things - to realize that they enslave us and they are poisonous to our souls and to our hopes of freedom and of eternal life. It is necessary that we learn to see things as they really are, from a historical perspective and not from a modernist one. ***Not that going off-grid could ever save us, but be assured of this one thing: living for the flesh will certainly damn all those who serve and idolize it.*** Think of going off-grid as going into a lifeboat from a sinking ship. You may not be saved if you go off the ship, but you will surely die if you don't. We have to fall out of love with these things that pamper and cater to the flesh to the detriment of our eternal and physical safety and well-being. We have to look at things with a true and pure eye and we must evaluate the true purpose and need of things (Matt. 6:22). We must convince ourselves that most of these things (the stuff of the world that enslaves us) are poisonous to our well-being. Then we can more easily toss them. Those things that are conducive to off-grid living, or that can be used to our benefit, or that can be used to help us on our pilgrimage OUT of the system - we can retain for a time. The next step is to train ourselves to go without unneeded, unsustainable things, and train ourselves in older and better ways of doing things, which is to say... we need to learn to live like our ancestors:

> *Thus saith the LORD, Stand ye in the ways, and see, and ask for the old paths, where is the good way, and walk therein, and ye shall find rest for your souls. But they said, We will not walk therein* (Jer. 6:16).

Don't be one of those people who say "we will not walk therein". God has said that the old paths are better than the new ones. That is a fact declared from heaven. Learn it and love it.

28

The next step is to practice and begin to live the things that we say we believe. This is the first real step on the *Pilgrim's Progress*. Step out and start to practice and live a different kind of life – a life lived on the narrow path (Matt. 7:14). Sell all of the junk you don't need and begin to procure those things that will help you to live off-grid... which means you need to sell almost everything you own. Best to get used to it, since you won't take any of that stuff to wherever you go after you die anyway. It is completely counter-cultural to get rid of stuff and start to make do without, but it is one of the most liberating things you will ever do.

This book is about a whole new way of thinking and a whole new philosophy of life (maybe new for you, but old when examined historically). It is a paradigm changer and it is also a spiritual road map to simpler and Godlier living. It is designed to challenge everything you think about the world around you, and to offer alternatives to modern maxims and accepted shibboleths. In fact, truth be told, there is nothing new here at all. This is, of all things, a history book – a time machine - through which you may become acquainted with your own ancestors and their simpler, more sustainable, more successful and holy ways of life.

I pray it succeeds in whatever way the Lord would choose to use it.

CHAPTER 1
DEFINING TERMS

WORDS MEAN THINGS

Advanced communication, the use of words and sentences, separates man from the lower animals. Man is able to use a multitude of creative and descriptive words, and this wonderful ability of communicative speech is a gift of God to aid us in our understanding and our living. Words, and the proper use of them, allow us to come to agreement, or to understand where we differ, and they help us perceive how very important our agreements or differences may be. It is said that the only hope we have of ever coming to agreement with one another is if we share the same information and if we understand that information in similar ways. Words allow us to identify concepts, thoughts, and ideas, and enable us to communicate our understanding of those things to one another. Even the word "communication" has the word "commune" as its root, because we use words to commune with one another - and with our God. Discussion or discourse is the primary form of communion between man and man, and prayer is the primary form of communion between man and his God. Communion requires communication, and communication requires that we have some agreement and understanding as to the meaning of the words we choose to use.

Unhappily, words today, like most things, have lost their real value. Conversation has devolved into "talking", and talking seems to have its value in *quantity* (the sheer number of words) rather than in their *quality* and in our mutual understanding of the words used. Most conversation today is light and meaningless, and most modernists are able to have long and drawn-out "talks" where almost nothing is learned, decided, or actually communicated. As the total number of words has increased - true meaning, understanding, and communication has decreased. It is quite common today for two people to have an entire conversation where both parties leave the conversation believing that they are like-minded and that they agree, when in reality they have in no way come to any real agreement at all. Sure, they have agreed using words, not realizing that they have each held different interpretations and definitions of the words being used. Nowhere is this tragedy more prevalent than in religious circles. Religious words have become stripped down and systematized until most of the world's religions and denominations, some with patently opposing beliefs and understandings, have chosen to use the same lexicon, and have come to believe that they actually agree on the fundamental or principle elements of "faith" because of the similarity or likeness of the words being used. Some of the most important words that frame and define who we are as a people have completely changed meaning in the last 100 years. In the American system, the words of the framers of the United States Constitution have been twisted to the point that in many instances they are now understood to mean the exact opposite of what was intended by the original writers according to their own writings. Different political and cultural parties choose to adopt meanings for identical words that are often in diametrical opposition. In the most recent American presidential election, one party ran on a platform of "Change", as if "Change" means anything specifically without context or explanation. When asked to state the nature of the "Change" they said, "Change we can believe in". Nice. The other party ran on a platform of "Security" and "Freedom", after having spent their time in office making their countrymen less secure and less free. *All Politicians, like all Clowns, are liars.* Unhappily, in the "world" out there, words don't mean anything anymore, and every political party trades and benefits on two realities of our age: 1. People are historically ignorant, and can be made to believe anything without facts and, 2. Words (and facts) can be twisted to mean anything you want them to mean.

But... words *do* mean things.

Ok, so why all the emphasis on defining words? Because, this book is about *SURVIVAL,* a word that means drastically different things to different people. During times of stress and trouble, survivalism grows and thrives, and the importance of communicating what we mean by such an important word is multiplied. In attempting to communicate, it is not as critical that our use of a word follows accepted or cultural norms (although that certainly would be preferable) as it is that we share the same definitions. So long as we agree on the terms, we can communicate. If we share the same definitions, then we are able to commune in the arena of ideas and we are able to discourse more honestly about the how and the why of living... even if we disagree on the solutions.

Now, I must say here - as an aside - that this book and the ideas in it are very challenging to read, and they are very challenging to write. First, they are challenging to read because they run so contrary to the accepted thinking and the prevalent presuppositions of the day. Second, they are difficult to write for a few reasons. I want to address those reasons here so that the reader will have fair warning and an understanding of the challenges I have faced in writing this book.

I am a committed Christian (and YES, I understand that the word *Christian* is one of those words that no longer holds any real descriptive meaning or definitive power, and it is one that must be properly defined. I have done so elsewhere at great length, but do not have the space to do so here), and I understand that many of those who need the practical information that will be found later in this book, and who want to learn more about *Off Off-Grid living,* are not Christians. I have, however, been challenged by the difficulty of trying to present my philosophy without offending those who operate according to a fundamentally different worldview. I have determined within myself to just tell it how I see it and from my own particular point of view. It would be impossible for me to present my philosophy of living removed from the spiritual and religious foundation for that philosophy.

I have been asked, "Who is your intended audience?", and I can honestly answer, "Everyone". I have not made the assumption that anyone who reads this is already a true Christian, even though I have, in all of my writings, placed (or founded) my whole philosophy and worldview on my understanding of what Christianity is and what it requires. It is, of course, not my intention to exclude anyone. Facts and truth are, in and of themselves, exclusive enough. In fact, I have determined that in order to be fair, I must be willing to insult everyone equally, and I include modern "christians" and modern feel-good, comfortable "christianity" (which I reject wholly and not in part) in my condemnation of the world and the current world system. I know that this book could be written from several different angles. It could be written as a secular book, and the advice and counsel would be just as valuable (though temporal). It could be written from a Christian perspective with all separatist convictions tempered or removed in order to not offend worldly "christians", and I believe it would still have some value. In fact, if I were willing to do these things, it would probably sell more copies and maybe even make money, but I have rejected that counsel. The facts in the book are true whether you reject or accept my overt and sometimes offensive Christian Agrarian Separatism. I would have been a traitor to my conscience and a rebel to my convictions if I had tempered the book at all. I ask, therefore, that the reader simply read this book as the exposition of a new (actually quite old, but new to most folk today) philosophy and worldview, maybe written from a worldview with which you disagree, and that the reader glean what he or she can from it. You can learn from me, even if you hate my opinions. In my life I have read dozens of books (as Jimmy Buffet would say, "about heroes and crooks"), which describe and even proselytize for other religions and philosophies. I believe my God wants me to fairly examine and judge His claims, and I felt it necessary to do so by reading many philosophies and religious opinions with which I do not agree. I merely ask for that same courtesy, and that you read the material fairly and openly, and judge it for what it is.

Ok, let us get to these definitions, shall we?

SURVIVAL

The dictionary defines the word **survive** as "to remain alive after the death of someone, the cessation of something, or the occurrence of some event." Further, it is to "continue in existence or use", to "get along or remain healthy, happy, and unaffected in spite of some occurrence; to live through affliction, adversity, or misery."

At its very root, to survive is to live through or beyond some thing or occurrence. This definition, though technically proper, is entirely too bare and empty for our purposes here. It is stripped of any spiritual truth, or any philosophy or context of living. It is far too subjective for me, for if I have survived one avalanche only to be crushed by the next one – have I survived or not? To merely survive temporal occurrences in a life that is remarkably short and fleeting is hardly, to me, a philosophy worth embracing. Sadly, the modern concept of "survival" is wholly based on this empty philosophy. When you read of survivalism or survival today, it generally has this overall meaning – to live through an event, or events, no matter what the cost.

Now, if we say that our philosophy is *to live no matter the cost* - then we must conclude that that cost may include our immortal soul and our eternal happiness. Would it ever be a good deal to trade our immortal soul and our eternal happiness for temporal and fleeting survival? Does anyone truly survive this carnal world? In my worldview, they do not. To anyone who values law and morality, and particularly to the Christian, this definition of survival is inadequate and even dangerous. You see, if I were to begin to write or teach without properly defining what *I* mean by survival, I would do you a disservice, and I would feed into some scary and dangerous concepts that really have no place in the life and philosophy of right thinking people.

So I have chosen here to give you a working definition of what I mean when I speak and write of *survival* and *survivalism.* So long as we both are clear that this is what I mean when I use these words, then we are able to proceed in our discourse with understanding.

Survive - To persevere. To do all that is within my power to persist in my Christian duty, to maintain my Christian witness, to protect and defend all of my human and Christian obligations, to keep my hand to the plow, and to continue to live obediently as long as God chooses to sustain my life and ministry. <u>To stand.</u> (**Eph 6:13** Wherefore take unto you the whole armour of God, that ye may be able to withstand in the evil day, and having done all, to stand.)

My goal is not merely to continue to live at all costs despite the situation or danger that exists around me. Life is transient and passes so very quickly. My goal is to persist in my duties, to continue in obedience, and to live my life in such a way that, by the grace, mercy, and sustenance of God, I am able to stand and resist the dangers and follies of the world, the temptations of the flesh, and the wiles of the devil. My goal is to continue dutifully at my station; to stand against the tyranny of absorption into, and syncretism with, the world; and to hold fast to the old and narrow paths wherein is found the good and righteous way. My way is not the way of the world, and I do not value cohesion and intercourse with any system which is contrary to the direct statements of my God. Were I to live for a thousand years in the way the world has defined as acceptable, I will have failed to truly survive. Were I to perfectly avoid all danger, peril, and consequence, and in doing so glorify the Prince of this World (the devil) and his temporal and earthly reign, I will have failed to truly survive. I cannot say that I want to survive at all costs. I cannot say that "pulling through" is worth betraying my Master. I cannot believe that looking, dressing, and acting like the world is worth the evil that accompanies that mentality. I wish to survive *to the Glory of God,* regardless of what men say. The Bible says that *"whosoever will save his life shall lose it: but whosoever will lose his life for my sake, the same shall save it"* (Luke 9:24). This saying is a perfect paradox for the worldling or the modern survivalist, but for those who understand how to properly define *survival,* this saying makes perfect sense and is not paradoxical at all.

If we will survive, we must lose our lives. What can this mean?

"There is a way which seemeth right unto a man, but the end thereof are the ways of death" (Pro 14:12). Let us stay here for awhile and consider this. If it is true that the carnal man embraces a way that *seemeth* right unto him, and if it is true that the bulk of carnal men are at enmity with God (Rom. 8:7) and are pursuing a way that seems right unto them, then it must be true that the general and accepted way of the world is a way that seems right unto the world... but it is the way of death. There is no true survival in that way. We must, then, be counter-cultural - *Contra-Mundum*. True survival must presuppose that godly men go a different way than the way of the world:

> *"Enter ye in at the strait gate: for <u>wide is the gate, and broad is the way, that leadeth to destruction</u>, and many there be which go in thereat: Because strait is the gate, and narrow is the way, which leadeth unto life, and few there be that find it"* (Matt. 7:13-14)

Honest men and women without guile must operate on different principles, and their way must actually look and be different from the way that leads to death. This is a maxim, and all of our understanding of survival must rest on this maxim.

The way or philosophy of living that you find defined in this book may seem ancient or anachronistic (some might even call it "backwards") but it is a way that has been proven through the centuries. In every era or region where men and women have lived simply and according to the principles of God, righteousness and holiness have thrived. As the Bible says, in order to return to true godliness and a truly Biblical way of living, we must return to the old paths and the old ways. You will find this principle verse repeated in all my writings wherever you find them:

"Thus saith the LORD, Stand ye in the ways, and see, and ask for

the old paths, where is the good way, and walk therein, and ye shall find rest for your souls. But they said, We will not walk therein." (Jer. 6:16).

This principle is critical if we are to understand right living and true survival. Repentance is the God-given ability to understand that our current path and trajectory is wrong and perilous and will lead to disaster if we continue in it. Repentance is turning from that wicked way and returning to a successful way trod only by brave and hardy souls. The prophets of worldliness, urbanism, and industrialism have every interest in keeping consumers (lemmings) on the path that at its end must lead to destruction. There is profit in it for them. The prophets of industrialism and consumption have every interest in defaming and rejecting any call to repentance of spirit and of life. The prophets of today have a vested interest in teaching people that consumption is godliness, separation is of the heart only, and that holy and godly living is only an internal precept and not an actual calling. I understand this, and so should you. I understand that our call to true survival will not ever be popular, and few will ever heed it. But it is a holy calling nonetheless, and it is our duty to proclaim it.

In summation, when God took His people from Egypt (a type of slavery to worldliness and worldly wisdom) to the Promised Land, He promised that if they obeyed and followed His prophet (Moses), they would prosper and *survive*. No one believes that this promise meant that they would live carnally on this earth forever. Whether they stayed in Egypt or left for Canaan, they were eventually going to die. Survival, then, was the God-given protection and inclination to leave the world and the dominion of the Pharaoh of Egypt, in order to live simply and in a holy way (worship) under the authority of God alone. It should be said here that almost all of the Israelites loved the world too much, feared freedom too much, and never entered into the Promised Land. This is our model and "type" for separation from the world system. Survival is the process of trying to live obediently no matter what giants seem to be in the land (Num. 13:33).

OFF-GRID AND OFF OFF-GRID (THERE IS A DIFFERENCE)

I hope that by now you have noticed that the title of this book is a call to *OFF OFF-GRID Living*. This was not an error in typesetting. You have all heard of living Off-Grid (or "off the grid"), but most of you will have never heard of living OFF Off-Grid. It is necessary now that I define the two phrases and philosophies, and differentiate between the two.

OFF-GRID LIVING

If you said to the average person today, *"I live off-grid"*, the reply would likely be something like this... *"Oh, that's interesting, how do you get your power? From a generator? From solar power? From wind power?"* You see, off-grid living today implies being separated from the industrial power grid unto a separate or independent power grid that supplies all the same perceived benefits and "necessities", only (it is claimed) cheaper and more sustainably. So in the minds of most people, "off-grid" means that you supply your own power, or that you live with some alternative form of power. So, in effect, "off-grid living" usually and generally makes no comment or passes no moral judgment on the manner of living (the stuff powered by whatever form of power production is utilized). This form of living (living off-grid), though somewhat wiser and safer than living on the grid, never does investigate or question the principle foundations or maxims of modern life. It is basically a "supply side" option – it changes the manner or method of power generation or transmission, but does not question or deal with the manner of life supported by that power. It is a shifting of dependency. It is like deciding that, though you are completely healthy and have no physical need for a wheel chair, you will stay in a "self-powered" wheel chair rather than a motorized one (or even maybe a solar powered wheel chair, rather than one charged by the electrical grid). What this philosophy does not ask is, "If you are able to walk, why don't you?" It never really challenges the precepts and presuppositions of the consumer life. Most people, then, do not even begin to consider that the so-called "necessities" of modern living are not actually necessary at all. I talk to hundreds of people who are considering separating from the modern world and moving off-grid. Their first impulse is always to ask themselves, *"How do I do all or most of the things I do now without being attached to the power grid?"* But our philosophy ought to require that we look at every single assumption and question it. Every technology must be examined to see if, in the long run and with all things considered, this technology actually benefits us in the process of daily obedient living. Does this technology help or hurt our overall plan of being independent and separate from the world? Does this technology even deliver what it promises? Does this technology lock us into some necessary and continued adherence to the industrial system? (in other words, what does it really cost?) Is it sustainable? These things are not usually ever addressed or questioned, even by people who see the grid system for what it is and who desire to separate from it. For this reason, I have called the "off-grid" system just a *step-child* or an *offspring* of the grid system.

Some people today do indeed live "off-grid", but they do not recognize that they are just one step removed from the grid. They have, in effect, created a separate grid system which, though it admittedly makes them a single step more sustainable than the world, in the long run it is just a faint copy (a copy of a copy) of the grid system from which they have endeavored to separate. Much of the meat of this argument will be fleshed out during the remainder of the book, but it is important for our purposes here that we identify a difference between living "off-grid" and "off off-grid".

Off Off-Grid Living

By contrast, the Off Off-Grid system is the system that is the most sustainable, and it is closest to the ideal way of living as portrayed for us in the scriptures. By *"Off Off-Grid"* we mean that we have not just taken a single symbolic step away from the industrial/urban system by creating our own grid system with which to replace it. *Off Off-Grid* means that we are moving towards a purely God-reliant, separated, survival life. In the Off Off-Grid system, we have eschewed and rejected the accepted maxims of industrialism and urbanism, and we actually dare to question whether the perpetual 72 degree myth and the lie of "time saving" is beneficial to our long-term survival and happiness. We actually dare to question whether some very modern conveniences are really necessary. We actually dare to ask if we are better off and more holy and spiritual since we have determined that carnal comfort is the single most critical element of our well-being and happiness.

THE EVER-PRESENT, NEVER-CEASING, PROFOUNDLY KNEE-JERK HYPOCRISY CHARGE

I know it is common, as I mentioned in the introduction, for worldlings to have an "all or nothing" mentality. This means that in the mind of the modern worldling, if you accept any technology or so-called "advancement", it is absolutely necessary that you accept every technology and "advancement" without question. They will say, "Oh, you reject grid power? Well then if you use any technology at all (such as a screwdriver or a pie plate) then you are hypocrites!" In fact, if history holds true to form (and it usually does), after this book is published, it is likely that some genius will post a review of it; and I can prophesy to you right now what he will say... something akin to, "Ha! This guy is writing a book about getting off-grid and not using technology, and I bet he wrote it on a computer and he is having it published using technology! Hypocrisy!"

You can't fix stupid.

AGRARIANISM AND TECHNOLOGY

(This is the part of the book that the hypocrisy hunters will not have read, or that proves that they never read the book at all.)

I have written about this before in many venues and at great length, but we must emphasize again that we are not "anti-technology". There is a really sick kind of institutional (colonized) blindness that assumes (whether purposely or not is always the interesting question) that any limits put on the use of technology by those who willfully limit its use is automatically hypocritical. Let me explain this in the same illogical thought process used and followed by most people:

Step 1: *"Oh, you are an off-grid 'Agrarian'... like the Amish. That's interesting."*

Step 2: "Well why are you on the Internet (if you are), and why do you have a truck? (if you do)" (Note: if you are not on the Internet, or you do not have a truck they will say, "Why do you use store bought tools or frying pans –which are all technology?" or, "Why do you own a screwdriver?") The assumption is that anyone who dares question or reject ANY technology must reject all of it or he is automatically a hypocrite and should be ignored or dismissed.

Step 3: *"If you are going to preach that technology is evil* (which we do not preach)*, then you should get rid of all these things."* So, according to the modernist, if you reject a home phone and grid electricity because you do not find them necessary, or because you do not want to allow some ungodly company to wreck your land and destroy the view by running poles and lines on your property, then you are a hypocrite and you must also reject frying pans, steak knives, and matches. Since any simple machine or tool can be considered technology, and since the worldling wrongly assumes that you reject all technology, then you are automatically a hypocrite even if the only technology you use is a stone wheel to crush walnuts. To most modern world-lovers ALL technology must be embraced without question; Industrialism, technology, and so-called "advancements" are a complete and inviolable package; and with every toothbrush you must also warmly accept bluetooth technology. Regardless of the criteria you use, or the philosophy behind your thoughts in rejecting some so-called "advanced" time-saving gadgets (a lie if ever there was one), and accepting some others, you must realize that to the modernist-industrial-colonized mind you are a hypocrite if you do anything more than stand naked and starving in a cave until you die. There is no middle ground and no gray area. You must accept technology as morally neutral and embrace every bit of it, or you must reject every single bit of it without prejudice. Of course if anyone really believed this false dialectic it would prove every human ever born to be a hypocrite.

This is a really stupid idea, I know, but that is what the modernist thinks of any attempt at rejecting modernism. Even those who admire the simple life or who think it quaint and interesting will conclude (whether openly or privately, whether consciously or unconsciously) that the plain and simple separatist is really a quaint and simple little hypocrite. When they accuse us of hypocrisy, it is because they do not know what we believe (nor do most of them really care - they are in defense posture, so it doesn't really matter). The worldling accuses the separatist of hypocrisy because if they do not, then they are faced with examining all the lies they have believed, and all the truths that they must avoid at all costs. The principle truth that their worldview requires, is that they never, ever consider what God has to say about it:

1 John 2:15 "**Love not the world, neither the things that are in the world. If any man love the world, the love of the Father is not in him.**"

The colonized mind must defend this world and its ways because it loves the world. That is a fact. It is a sad and scary fact, but it is a fact. The world will not listen to your reasoning as to why you have rationally and reasonably come to reject their worldview. They must not listen, because if they do they will come face to face with their primary love... their love of the world. They must embrace this world and never for a minute weaken their grasp on it, because it is all they have. Never mind that:

a.   their culture is evidently crumbling around them.

b.   with all their time and labor-saving devices, they must work harder with less (in real terms) to show for it. Where a man used to be able to work to support his whole family, now, most two-earner families must utilize mountains of debt in order to maintain a worse standard of living. Families suffer, marriages are temporary, children reject God (or embrace a fake 'god' of their own mind and creation), and the worldling can't stop for a moment on the treadmill of this worldly life or they will be crushed under the weight of the cost of their lusts.

c. their religion is designed to fit neatly into their worldview. It is rubber and flexible and doesn't for a minute challenge or confront the world that it upholds so wonderfully. True Christianity was once called *Contra Mundum* (against the world), but today, in fact, modern "christianity" is merely the religious arm of the industrial world; it is a fully owned subsidiary of the world system that hates Jesus Christ (Luke 19:14, John 7:7). This is why I call modern "christianity" *Jesus Christ, Inc.*

Religion (at least modern plastic religion) is indeed the opiate of the masses, and for those who are fully and completely brainwashed and colonized by the industrial religious cult, any defection from complete and idolatrous worship of technology and the industrial Leviathan is treason of the highest order.

So just who is the hypocrite? Let's see...

Do our accusers embrace ALL technology without question? Of course they do not. Not one of them. Go to your accuser and ask them if there is any technology that they have rejected. Does your secular humanist friend have every gadget out there and does he accept all new technology without question? If not, why not? Has your modernist "christian" friend already received a *Digital Angel* personal tracking microchip? Then ask them if they will allow such a chip to be put into their right hand to be used for monetary transactions, and if they do not already have one of these, ask them, "Why not?" These tracking chips are already available and they have been for many years!

HYPOCRISY!

I saw a chef on a television show one time that used a hand whisk to beat eggs. Why would he use a hand whisk when beautiful and expensive electric egg-beaters are available to enable him to save time? The chef said that he used the hand whisk because it made the eggs lighter and fluffier and allowed him to have better control of the texture of the final product. Hmmmm... What can we determine from such thinking? Is it possible that some non-electric technology is actually better and more effective? I attended some carpentry classes where the master teacher used nothing but hand tools. He explained (and showed) that he could make beautiful hand-crafted trim and molding before the machine-using carpenter could even get his tools out and get them ready to go! And his hand-crafted work was of better quality, and would receive a higher price in the market. Is it hypocrisy for someone to actually examine each technology and decide on a case by case basis if that technology is wise and good for the situation or the job? (It is not hypocrisy. However, it is heresy. It is heresy against the One World Industrial Cult.) Would any reasonable person accept every technology just because it is technology and not examine the claims made by that technology? Would anyone really dare accuse a television chef of hypocrisy for refusing to use an electric egg-beater?

So, let's get this straight... virtually every intelligent and sentient being makes value decisions about their use of different technologies and how they fit into their particular worldview, and how those things are used in the process of work. This is a fact. If other men are free to make value decisions (according to their worldview) about the technologies they embrace and accept, why then are we attacked for doing the same thing?

I will tell you the answer...

We are NOT attacked because of the technologies we choose to reject or accept. We are attacked because the philosophy behind our choices condemns and exposes the lies of industrialism and exposes the modernist's love of the world. When some folks hear that we do not have grid electricity, in their consciences they hear:

YOU ARE BAD AND WICKED AND EVIL AND YOU LOVE THE WORLD

Now, if this were not true, they would not care and would not suffer much over it, but they know that it usually IS true, and that is what they are really defensive about. People are defensive because they feel they are being attacked, but since we have attacked no one, it must be the conscience of the modernist that is attacking him.

TECHNOLOGY AND THE MYTH OF "TIME-SAVING"

There is a second issue at play here, and I want to address it here while we are defining terms. The second reason that modernists reject the concept of Off-Grid (and especially Off Off-Grid Living) is that they have allowed their minds to be bifurcated and fragmented (more on that in the next chapter). In addition to the assumption that all technology must be good (or at the least morally neutral), the worldling is taught from a very young age that technology saves time and effort and creates wealth and leisure time, which must be good.

During a speaking trip up north several years ago I was asked some questions about Agrarianism; questions that are actually pretty common today. The natural response by the colonized mind when confronted with Agrarianism as a philosophy is to question why anyone wouldn't, just as a default, accept technology as good, beneficial and acceptable. The challenging idea that all technology may not be beneficial runs completely counter to the training present in the colonized mind. People will ask, "So, am I supposed to get rid of my cell phone and my computer?" Others will say, "God gave us a mind. If we use our minds to create time-saving technologies aren't we just doing what we're supposed to be doing?"

There are some automatic pre-suppositions that create and support these questions or positions...

The erroneous pre-suppositions are these:

1. As we have mentioned, that Agrarians are anti-technology, or reject all technology.

2. Therefore, as I have mentioned, if an Agrarian uses any technology, then he is a hypocrite.

3. Because technology is automatically good, or at the least morally neutral, then any use of technology must also be morally neutral; therefore if technology can be used for things that are automatically considered good, then... Technology is good.

4. "Saving time" is automatically good, regardless of the results or the reality of whether or not real time was "saved" or not, or if the time saved is used for eternally good purposes or not.

5. Therefore if the human mind is capable of devising it, and it can be marketed as time-saving, efficient, or necessary, then it should be accepted without question.

There is a corollary to these false assumptions – another maxim of modern society. The corollary is this: If the corporate human mind can rationalize something as good, then it is good for all individual humans without question.

You didn't think there was going to be this much math, did ya?

Here are answers to these presuppositions:

1. *As we have previously shown, Agrarians are not anti-technology,*

nor do we reject all technology. A frying pan is technology; a plow is technology; a shovel is technology. We all use technology and Agrarians do not at all universally reject technology. What we reject is the presupposition that all technology is good or at the least "morally neutral". Because we reject (or are moving away from) some technologies as harmful to ourselves, our families, our way of life and our worldview, does not make us anti-technology.

2. The use of technology by a separatist Agrarian does not constitute hypocrisy. I've examined this issue at length in the previous section.

3. Technology is not universally or inexorably good, nor is it naturally morally neutral. It cannot be considered outside of its purpose and use, and purpose and use cannot be morally neutral. Some of these presuppositions intertwine. There is an assumption made by most colonized minds that technology is fundamentally good. Some people believe that in the very worst case, technology is morally neutral. In reality, every technology exists for a purpose, or is used toward an end. Every technology must be considered and judged as to whether:

    a.)...its intended or actual use is morally positive towards our philosophy and worldview, and is conducive to our Christian survival, success, and happiness.

    b.)...the reasons and logic used to determine that a thing is "good" or not is true and biblical. We do not want to produce "false positives" by assuming that a thing is good just because it enables some result or action that is presupposed to be good.

    c.) ...the results promised are actually the results received.

4. Saving "time" is not always "good". In fact, in very real terms, there is no such thing as saving time. Time may be reallocated, but never "saved". Some technologies promise to be "time-saving" when in

reality none of us using that technology have any more time available for spiritual pursuits than we had before the use of the technology. In fact, we quite often have less time, because we have to work to pay for and support the technology. The concept of "time-saving" assumes that "work" itself is not spiritual, and is a bad use of time. A main (agrarian) character in Tolstoy's <u>War and Peace</u> said something akin to, "God gave the strength, and God gave the day. The strength and the day are sanctified by God, and labor is its own reward". Regardless of our opinion on what might be a better use of time, time passes the same for all of us whether we use technology or not. In fact, "time saving" devices do not save time at all. A device or technology may shorten the amount of time necessitated by a certain job, but they do not "save time". There is no time bank where saved time is deposited. We all just go do something else. For example, high-speed travel is considered a "time-saver", but as we have traveled faster, the world has expanded and there were suddenly more places to travel. Men and women used to walk to the garden for tomatoes and to the chicken-yard for eggs, now they drive to the store at 70 m.p.h. to get tomatoes or eggs. The question is have we really saved time? Planting and growing tomatoes and raising chickens used to be considered by Christians to be spiritual and holy acts of faith and hope in the Providence of God. By contrast, time-saving devices usually just reallocate time to some other industrial or unbiblical use. In fact, most time-saving devices actually cumulatively require more money (which takes time and labor to earn or produce), more services (such as electricity, which requires money, which requires work), or they simply shift the time requirement elsewhere. If it were true that all the "time-saving" devices invented since the advent of the industrial age actually saved time, then the average citizen in the industrial society, because of the conglomeration of all the time-saving devices and methods used throughout the last century or so, would have nothing at all but free time on his hands. Why does it take more than one income to support a family today when it used to take just one? Well, it is not because incomes have not kept pace with expenses. The fact is that the average family has dozens (even hundreds) of time-saving devices that must be purchased, maintained, and serviced (usually by debt). It takes at least two incomes to maintain all of the time-saving devices and advanced technologies! Unhappily, people in the time-saving society have less true relaxation and leisure time than those in the generations before the advent of the industrial society.

The presupposition exists that saving "time" is good for its own sake, as if just because a task took half the time (if it actually did) then somehow we are better off (presumably doubly so) for the time saved. This is rarely the case. The cult of "time-saving" has never saved anyone any time - it has instead produced mentally and spiritually crippled people who are unable to do the most basic and necessary tasks. People today are ignorant of the means of basic survival and unable to hunt, grow, build, fix or create. Yet they believe they have some mystical bank somewhere filled with "saved time" deposits.

The argument for saving time has become an end in itself. No one is willing to ask the scary question, "Save time for what?" or, "What is the cost?" Are our lives really more spiritually full and complete now that we are surrounded by "time-saving" devices that must be served by us, no matter the cost? At the root of this deception is the question, "What are we here for?" If God put me here to be perfected as I am digging post holes and planting a garden and building fences, am I really well served to be able to do all of that in ¼ of the time with machines that do the job for me, separating me from the lessons God intends for me to learn, and leaving me to serve the machines and to spend more time on spiritually and mentally debilitating pursuits? What am I really here for?

5. Just because the human mind is capable of devising it, and it can be marketed as time-saving, efficient, or necessary, does not mean it should be automatically accepted.

By rejecting the concept of "time-saving" as being intrinsically or unquestionably good, we can also come to the conclusion that many of the devices created by men for that purpose are also not good. Just because an invention promises me that it will save me time and be easy to use, does not mean that it is *good* for me to use it. Buying industrialized butter from a commercial chain store may be easy and nominally time-saving - but is it good? Would I have been eternally (and physically) better served to go through the process of making my own butter? Would it be better for me to know how to make butter? Am I more likely to survive if I already know how to make, and practice making, butter? Those are the real questions, and are the questions we are begged never to ask by the prophets of the industrial age.

Because of the high regard humans have for their own thoughts and ideas, they generally are not willing to question the character and the state of the mind that thinks the thoughts and that comes up with the ideas. By that I mean that man naturally believes his own heart to be good, and since his mind tells him something is good, it must naturally be good. Speaking of the mind of man, the Bible says that the heart (which is the mind) of man is desperately wicked, and naturally at enmity with God:

"The heart is deceitful above all things, and desperately wicked: who can know it?" (Jer. 17:9)

"For to be carnally minded is death; but to be spiritually minded is life and peace. Because the carnal mind is enmity against God: for it is not subject to the law of God, neither indeed can be" (Rom. 8:6-7)

It seems to me it would be wise to automatically question whatever the world tells us is the way to do things, especially if you believe that the wide road leads to destruction. It seems to me that questioning worldly wisdom ought to be a default for those who seek to live life by a higher wisdom. It seems to me that I ought to automatically question something when my carnal flesh is naturally inclined to it.

ADDICTION

Addiction is the state of being enslaved to a habit or practice or to something that is psychologically or physically habit-forming, as narcotics, to such an extent that its cessation causes severe trauma.

It is interesting to note that in virtually every addiction, the addict must eventually become a salesman for the addiction (or of the addictive product) so that he or she can afford to feed the addiction. The dope smoker or the crack addict must eventually sell dope or sell crack in order to make enough money to feed his addiction. Likewise those who become addicted to the world and its time-saving and leisure devices must eventually become spokespersons and defenders of the ideas that support the sale and perpetuation of the addiction. There is a scary fact here that most people are too frightened to examine too closely:

> If enough people were to pull out of the system and begin questioning all technology and rejecting most of it, then the industrial system that supports the massive sale of these addictive drugs at low cost will collapse.

"So", you may be asking, "is this guy a Luddite?" The Luddites were a sect during the Industrial Revolution who rightly saw the mechanization of life as a threat to their lives and way of living. So they violently attacked the looms and the equipment and the factories that they felt like were warring against them. No, I am not a Luddite. I'm not asking anyone to attack anything or to do violence to any person or property. I am just teaching folks to walk away. The "stuff" will destroy itself if no one buys what it is selling.

Most of the people who defend worldly living are completely and utterly supported by that system. As I have shown before, they are unsustainable as people, and they cannot live outside of that system. Therefore the thought of the destruction of that system necessarily means that they would have to separate from it or perish. Herein lies the conflict, and here is why this will be a very emotional and confrontational area of your life if you pursue separating from worldliness at any level. Revolution is warfare. This is the revolution, and welcome to it.

This leads me to the final term I want to define in this chapter, because you will need it for the next one.

REVOLUTION

A "rebellion" is... an attempt by unauthorized and unlawful means to overthrow and replace a lawful system of authority or governance.

The word "revolution" has as its root the term "revolve" or to turn over or around. As opposed to a rebellion, a revolution is the overthrow or removal of an unauthorized or unlawful form of authority or governance, or a usurper government, with an authorized and lawful one. When an illegitimate power is overthrown by those with legitimate power you have a revolution. When a people who have been brainwashed since birth, forcefully colonized, and illegitimately ruled by a colonial power, throw off the shackles of that colonial power, it is properly called a revolution.

I have told you that the majority of all people alive in the world today have "colonized minds". The decolonization process is painful and difficult, but it takes nothing short of a revolution to overthrow the illegitimate system that currently rules over the colonized mind and heart. The next chapter is about this wonderful and needful revolution.

CHAPTER 2
REVOLUTION

WHAT IS POWER?

For most of the last six millennia, the world has lived without electrical power. Cheap electrical power has only been readily available for less than 100 years and only appeared in most of rural America about 30 years before I was born. This means that likely upwards of 100 billion (a guess, I know) people were born, lived their whole lives, and died on this earth having never made use of electrical power. Yet, as we have said, if the electrical power grid were to collapse today, and if it were to remain unavailable for some great amount of time, it is likely that a majority of the people alive today would die within a year. Readily available and cheap grid electricity has resulted in a world filled with unviable slaves, and it has made man dangerously dependent on a system that has proven itself in many cases to be unreliable; a system that many people are coming to believe is contrary to their eternal best interests.

It is very interesting that we call both the electricity that supports and enables life today, and the force that keeps people under the sway and thumb of the world, by the same name...

"Power"

I can think of no more deliciously appropriate irony. Let us take a look at a few relevant definitions of the word "power" from Dictionary.com:

Power: Great or marked ability to do or act; strength; might; force.

Power: The possession of control or command over others; authority; ascendancy: *power over men's minds.*

Power: Work done or energy transferred.

Power: Energy as distinguished from hand labor.

Power: A person or thing that exercises authority or influence.

Isn't it ironic that we have come to believe that electrical power frees us and gives us comfort and leisure, when in fact it is the primary means by which we have been colonized and enslaved by the world "powers"?

ALL POWER IS COERCION!

Write that down. You'll need to remember it. Some coercion is good and legitimate, such as when we teach and train our children up in the way they should go (according to the Bible, this way would be "the old ways," and "the old paths"). Coercion can be brutal and tyrannical, or in other forms it can be benevolent, or subtle, or political. When we use means to bring about good and biblical ends, we are exercising coercion. When the world uses marketing, advertising, and trickery; when it plies the lusts, the carnal desires, or fears in order to bring about cultural or social change, it is using coercion. Never deny, even for a moment, this truth... that all power is coercion. To deny it is just to stick ones head in the sand.

As we have previously mentioned, man has chosen to use a word (power) for the force and energy that travels through cables and into machines, a force that supposedly makes life easier and more comfortable and more fulfilling; and he has chosen to use the same word to define and represent the authority that coercive energy holds over his mind and life. It is fascinating to note that the Bible teaches that Jesus came to His people, *"to open their eyes, and to turn them from darkness to light, and from the power of Satan unto God"* (Acts 26:18). Satan has (and has had) coercive power over the people and that power is used to keep them in darkness. Likewise, mankind has become totally dependent upon earthly electrical power to supply and maintain his desires. Grid electricity is only a part of the overall coercive grid "system" in the world today, but it is inarguable that grid electricity has made man dependent on it for his survival; and it has, in the past 100 years, become the basis for earthly political and social power. I guess it could be said today that POWER is POWER.

When grid power is used to coerce minds and enable the lusts and desires of man, political and social power results. One hundred years ago, much of America, indeed much of the world, lived independently from any system of grid power. Under that system, most rural people lived lives of relative freedom. It is true that forced slavery existed throughout history, and it is also true that rural people have been enslaved and colonized by others throughout history. However, it is notable that, prior to the advent of grid power, the people could only be subjugated by military power, or by the persuasive power of philosophy or religion. Historically, coercion had to come from outside the individual person, group, or society. It was readily identifiable. If the people were slaves, they were slaves to superior might. They could see their masters, and they could see their chains. They were slaves to superior might and not slaves of themselves and of their own material and carnal lusts. Contrarily, under the system of cheap and ubiquitous grid electrical power, the people became enslaved to the philosophy and religion of this world, and they submitted willfully to it, because by it they were enabled to fulfill their carnal desire for apparent comfort and security. The slave is held most securely when he is held by the chains of his own will and of his own fears, and when he is locked down by his own slavish desires for a comfortable life. For a slave mind to turn against his master and seek to return to a life of freedom, a revolution is in order.

A quick word about Revolution: In the last chapter I said that when illegitimate power is overthrown by those with legitimate power you have a revolution. I don't want people to be confused. Conflicts are often called *revolutions* that are not revolutions at all. When one tyrant is overthrown and replaced with another one that has the same ends or the same goals and the same basic philosophy, you have had a *coup de tat*, but not a revolution.

The overthrow of the Russian Czar system is called The Russian Revolution, but the results show that it was really a *coup de tat* and not a proper revolution. The book *Animal Farm* by George Orwell illustrates how the new rulers adopted the same tyrannical methods and philosophies of the old rulers. The Russian people, poor and powerless after centuries of life under the thumb of the Russian Czars, threw off the shackles of the czar only to find themselves under the thumb of the Communists. While it is true that many Russians did have hope that things would get better and that they would be afforded basic freedoms and that their conditions would improve, in reality, after the revolution, they wanted the same things they had always wanted. There was no real change. There was no revolutionary change in the philosophy of living. If the Czar had offered the peasants some fundamental freedoms, they would have been more than happy to continue under the Czar. The people had not experienced a wholesale change of heart and mind - they had just had enough. Most Russian peasants wanted one simple thing; the government to get off their backs. The average Russian countryman didn't have an overwhelming love and admiration for the Bolsheviks or the Mensheviks or for any other new political voice or party. The people just figured that any government that promised them freedom had to be better than what they had been experiencing. Freedom sounded better than the serfdom they had experienced under the Czar. This is, unhappily, the truth behind most so-called "revolutions." When the people find their current state intolerable, they go along with whoever might overthrow the latest tyrant. We will examine these motivations and their results more later on in this chapter.

THE FIRST REVOLUTION: REVOLUTION IN THE MIND AND HEART

If the people of Russia had been truly converted to a whole worldview of freedom; if they had individually and corporately experienced a conversion to a compelling and complete philosophy of freedom; if the average Russian (and the people as a whole) had been committed and irrevocably bound to a truly revolutionary idea; then the Communists would have quickly gone the way of the Czar. Once a man is wholly and truly converted to a right philosophy of freedom and life, he is never going to be satisfied with less than that. A true revolution, then, is founded on conversion in the mind and heart. When the mind is converted, the man naturally follows. Tyrants know this. Colonizers know this. Why do you think that the prophets of industrialism and consumerism spend billions and billions of dollars on converting minds? What do you think advertising is? The industrial consumer society is built wholly on consumption, and the minds of consumers must be completely and utterly colonized in order to make the people true believers. Jesus Christ knew the power of the marketing forces of the world. This is why His apostles warned, *"We brought nothing into this world, and it is certain we can carry nothing out. And having food and raiment let us be therewith content"* (1 Tim. 6:7-8). Jesus brought a revolution, and He did it by converting the minds of men. He and His messengers taught men that worldliness (the world's way of doing things) was folly, and could lead only to eternal disaster. The multiplication of needs was seen as fundamentally anti-Christian. This philosophy was revolutionary, in that those who were converted to it valued nothing (even their lives, families, etc.) more than they valued obedience to Him and His Word.

When I teach that the mind has to be decolonized, I am teaching and advocating nothing less than true revolution. This revolution must take two forms. The first revolution is internal. It is a conversion of the mind; an overthrowing of the old way of thinking, of the old lusts and desires, and of the old worldview. The second revolution is external. It shows forth the product of different wants and desires, different principles, and a different worldview. Decolonization is a revolution. Decolonization is the process of coming to different conclusions than we have come to before (or than the world expects and pushes) based on the facts in evidence. It is the process of having our minds rewired so that we think differently, so that we want different things, and it is the process of shedding the lifetime of false conclusions we have reached based on false and misleading evidence. Every element of the industrial system (which is the prevailing system of the world today), its foundations, its systems of survival, its methods and maxims, must be examined. From our youth, when our carnal minds were first encouraged to abandon the old paths and constantly seek whatever new and modern wisdom was being preached by the prophets of "success" and "comfort," we have been undergoing training and indoctrination into the global industrial system. The system calls us "consumers" because that is what we are. The world system needs eaters and buyers, so it creates and trains them. Colonizing and training minds is the ultimate purpose behind public education. In an industrial/consumer society, the mind must be colonized and that colonization must begin at an early age so that real production forever remains in the hands of the elite, and so that no one ever dares examine or question if the emperor is actually wearing any clothes. Only if you have followed the world's system of colonization, and only if you have succeeded in showing yourself an apt and able proselyte of the consumer religion, will you ever be accepted (or even tolerated) by the world system.

As I mentioned in the last chapter, words have been redefined, reality has been obscured, and old truths have been convoluted and twisted until people actually believe that they are the philosophical offspring of their forefathers, even as they reject everything that they believed. Every American child is told, "If you work hard and excel and do what the world expects from you, why you could grow up to be the President!" Hereby the child is trained to believe that freedom exists in the possibility that right behavior (meaning behavior consistent with the desires of the colonizer or of the system) can ultimately lead to political power and the authority to coerce others. These children are not told that most of their ancestors came here because they had had enough of government coercion (and of the coercion of government churches, by the way), and that they wanted nothing more than to be left alone so that they could farm the land and be free. We have been taught what to want, and we have been taught that wanting the right things is what makes us good and valuable to the system. Our first revolution, then, must be in the mind and heart. In a sense that parallels the Christian experience, we must be converted. Our desires must change, and we must be convinced – not just in our minds and in our hearts – but we must be *spiritually* convinced of the dangers and death that accompanies the world's way of doing things. Only when it is given to us to see the world as it is, will we be made willing to engage in revolution.

THE SECOND REVOLUTION: OVERTHROWING THE SYSTEM

The second revolution is external. When the colonizer finds out that revolution is afoot, he becomes very, very angry. When the slave-holder comes to learn that his slaves have been turned against him, he will become distressed and fearful. When the proselytes of the industrial/consumer religion see that you have become a renegade to their cause, they become avowed enemies.

The first step in the Second Revolution is the recognition that *something must be done*. Decolonization starts as an internal process, but at some point it must break outwards into the world in which we live. If the mind and heart are converted, the body will inevitably begin to obey its new "operating system" (much like computers obey their programming). Once we learn and believe that our system has produced death, destruction, cultural and social decay, slavish dependence, rampant immorality and an unviable life, it is natural that we will want to begin to exit that system and free ourselves from its influence.

Ultimately, this book is about this second revolution; however, in order to extricate ourselves from our dependence on the world and its consumer system, we must first recognize that we are slaves to it. That is the purpose of the first few chapters of this book. If we do not recognize our slavery, we will never move towards freedom.

A Pair of Tests

Here are a couple simple tests that you can use to judge your dependency level, and whether or not you are a slave to the current system. In order for these tests to provide useful information for you, you must be totally and brutally honest with yourself. The tests are shockingly simple, but it is also remarkably easy to cheat on them. Remember, the carnal mind is capable of rationalizing any behavior and any lie. So, if you cheat or lie to yourself, you will only be harming yourself.

The Dependency Test

Ok, here is the first test. We'll call this first test the "Dependency Test". Answer each question honestly. I recommend that you get a pen and paper and that you write down each answer fully and thoughtfully:

1. Would you call the world we live in today morally and culturally *good*, or morally and culturally *corrupt*? Are you and your generation more wholesome, holy, and righteous; or do you believe that society and the culture has degraded through time?

2. If you know anything about your own history or your own ancestry, would you say that you are more or less dependent on the world "system" than your ancestors were?

3. Can you feed and clothe yourself? Can you provide heat, light, shelter, etc. for yourself and your family? If the world grid system (electricity, "just in time" food, water, etc.) was to collapse, and no outside help was forthcoming, would you be likely to perish? Be honest here, because here is where the mind is able to fantasize and create unrealistic "solutions." If today or tomorrow, starting at noon, your electrical power was cut off, and you had no access to the JIT food and water delivery system, would you survive? If so, for how long?

4. If you were able to survive for a time (maybe you are a survivalist, or a "prepper," or maybe you have access to survival material sources, or stored food, and maybe you live next to a clean water source), is your survival temporary or is it sustainable? Is it based on "pulling through" or bare survival; for example, making it until the grid system comes back or until help arrives from outside?

5. If you are "prepared" or if you have provided alternative means of providing a life and living, do you actually live that way, or are you counting on "switching over" when things get bad? History shows that most preparedness plans and survival techniques fail if they are not inculcated into actual and continuous practice. Are you counting on things or practices that you don't currently use?

Now, depending on how honestly you have answered each of these questions, you ought to have some kind of indication of how viable you are in your current situation and how dependent you are on the world system for your well-being and survival. Many, many people are as deceived about their physical condition as they are about their spiritual condition. I hear it all the time, people will say, "I have 3 months (or 1 year or 7 years) supply of dehydrated food," or "I live where there are a lot of deer and other game animals," or "I took some survival courses," or my all time favorite, "I will just go into the woods or the wilderness and survive off the land." Right. Anyway, as we mentioned in the last chapter, the concept that "survival" is just a way to temporarily bridge the gap during a crisis situation until things return to "normal" is a failed survival philosophy. It insists that the anomaly of grid living experienced during the last century is "normal" and it presupposes that the industrial/consumer grid system is "good" and it absolutely rests on the ridiculous notion that the industrial/consumer Ponzi scheme can continue indefinitely without collapsing.

THE SLAVERY TEST

The first test was the *Dependency Test*, and it was designed to make you consider how dependent you are on the system. This next test can be a little more painful. I call it the "Slavery Test", and I am hopeful that it will cause you to think very carefully about how enslaved you are to the current system. This test necessarily rests upon what we have learned in the previous test.

Ok, here we go:

1. If you were to determine through prayerful consideration that the current industrial grid system is dangerous for you and your family and harmful to your physical and spiritual condition, could you walk away? Immediately?

2. Write down what conditions hinder you from walking away. Are you broke? Are you deep in debt? Are you locked into a long-term mortgage or some "obligation" from which you feel you cannot walk away?

3. If you became convinced that moving to an off-grid or off off-grid lifestyle was the thing to do, would you be hindered from doing so by your family? By your friends? Would you be threatened with the loss of the ties of family and friends if you rejected their lifestyle and moved away from it? Would the persecution you would suffer from renouncing the world's way of doing things keep you from obeying your conscience?

4. Are you hindered by your ignorance? Do you feel like you don't have the skills, the strength, the know-how, or the courage to leave the grid system?

5. Are you hindered by your circumstances? Are you physically or mentally unable to make a change in your lifestyle? Are you suffering from the consequences brought about by your poor or unbiblical decision making? Are you hindered by an unbelieving spouse, or some other situation that is regrettable, but of your own making?

6. Are you paralyzed by fear? Does the thought of leaving your comfort zone keep you from ever challenging the things you have believed all of your life?

Answering these questions can be very painful or irritating. Chains are often painful and irritating... especially those we may not have admitted we have.

We have now arrived at the precise spot where the rubber meets the road. I hope you have been honest in taking these two tests, and I hope you have written down your answers. Slavery is often identified by the use of chains. Chains represent the restriction of movement, and their use represents the submission of the slave to the one who has put him in chains. Chains can be physical, mental, or spiritual. There are multiple types and kinds of *chains* used by the world to keep folks under the impression that they are helpless or powerless to change their condition, and it would serve us well to do a quick study on these methods (or chains).

BLIND MICE AND A CARVING KNIFE

Secular government intelligence agencies learned decades ago that there are basically four factors that motivate individuals to join or support certain causes or movements. Agents or sources can be recruited or manipulated by using these four principle motivations. These motivating factors (or chains) are used by intelligence agencies, politicians, individuals, corporations, families, and nations to motivate individuals and groups towards certain actions. In the espionage business, these four motivations are known by the acronym M.I.C.E. Knowing what M.I.C.E. means, and being able to recognize what motivates people (and ourselves) will go a long way in helping us to identify and quantify the chains that bind us:

M – Money (includes Debt, Comfort, Leisure, "Stuff", etc.)

I – Ideology (Patriotism, Religion, Philosophy)

C - Coercion (Compromise, Fear, Force, Hostility, Grudges, Disaffection)

E - Ego (Excitement, Position, Status, Importance)

Understanding M.I.C.E. helps us get a grasp on what motivates people, and a thorough study of it can help us identify what chains are being used to attempt to hold us or manipulate us. Go back through your answers on the Slavery Test and next to your answers try to identify and write down which motivational chain is being used to keep you enslaved. Every spy or "asset" in history was recruited according to a motivational propensity or predilection and one or more of these motivational categories were used in the recruiting. Satan uses all of the tools in these categories to motivate worldlings to operate according to his power. Every world religion and cult except True Christianity uses one or more of these categories (and the elements within those categories) to motivate to action or bring about loyalty.

True Christianity is the only religion that concedes in its doctrines that these motivations are inadequate for the production of true, spiritual loyalty and love. True Christianity teaches that a love of money is the root of all evil, and that the desire to operate according to the principles of mammon is a sign of the damned and not of the elect. Jesus Christ taught that feigned or human loyalty would crumble under pressure and stress. True Christianity teaches that there is a new and spiritual Kingdom, not of this world, and that the desire for the things of this world (money, position, power, status, etc.) will be one of the first things slain in the heart of the regenerate. Jesus Christ and His Apostles taught that we could not obey or love Him without His gifts of Grace and Mercy, and that we must receive a new heart and a new mind from Him in order to see and hear clearly and to obey Him. The Bible teaches that coercion or servile fear (like that used by modernist "christianity" to motivate or "save" people) is insufficient to move people to godliness and obedience, and that we must have the gift of new operative principles divinely imputed and imparted to us in order for us to operate truly as Christians. Jesus Christ taught that the low and humble would be made high, and that the meek would inherit the earth. He taught that those who would be rich will be made eternally poor, and that the poor in spirit would be the rich in His Kingdom. He taught that we are of a different country, and that we are ambassadors of a different and spiritual nation. In light of this wisdom, it can be a very valuable for us to re-examine our motivations and see how we are shackled by our own sinful principles.

Let's do some exercises. Here are some other things I hear or read almost every day when I am contacted by people who read the things that I write. Pay attention to what people are saying, and see if you can identify the motivation. Then, maybe write down some things you yourself have said, or some things that others have said to you, that expose and uncover our true motivations. Here are a few examples:

> *"I was raised on a farm, and I would never want to go back to that life! I love the conveniences of modern society and don't want to change anything."*

From this we can determine that this person is motivated by category "M", specifically leisure, comfort, and money.

Let's do a quick rundown of many of the other excuses. The motivational chains will be listed in parenthesis:

> *"I have a family to support and debt to pay off." - (Money, Fear, Philosophy, Coercion)*

> *"I have a job and things are tough out there. How would I survive?" - (Money, Fear, Philosophy, Position)*

> *"My family (friends/church) would disown me. My children will think I'm crazy. My wife will leave me." - (Fear, Position, Status, Philosophy, False Religion, Ideology, Ego, Compromise)*

"I don't have any skills. I would be lost. I'm old/young/single and unable to do what I would like." – (Fear, Compromise)

"I was always taught that this (the way of the world) is the way to live. If it was good enough for my parents, then it is good enough for me." – (Ideology, Philosophy, Status)

There are no lies as dangerous as those we tell ourselves about ourselves. Most slaves and most colonized people are not willing to rise up and overthrow their oppressors for a few basic reasons:

First, they do not believe that they are slaves, or they think that their condition of bondage is acceptable, or that slavery is better than freedom. In some cases, the mind is so thoroughly colonized or the slave has been so thoroughly brainwashed that he actually comes to have the same mind as the slave-holder or the colonizer. There is a term in psychology called *The Stockholm Syndrome.* The term "Stockholm Syndrome" was coined to identify a psychological reaction often seen in abducted hostages. Quite often, when a person is captured, enslaved, or abducted against his or her will, after a time they will come to identify and show loyalty to their captor or hostage-taker. Although the psychological response has been around forever, the term was first used after a bank robbery in Stockholm, Sweden in 1973. In that case, bank robbers held the employees of the bank hostage for six days; and during that time, many of the hostages became loyal and emotionally attached to their captors. Some of the hostages even fought to defend their captors after they were freed.

I believe that most of the people who defend this current world, who love it and become emotional or defensive when it is disparaged, or who advertise for it and who are loyal to it, suffer from a mental condition that is identical to Stockholm Syndrome.

Second, they have been taught from a very young age that conformity and syncretism are good and right and that they will lose everything and be poor, hungry, and miserable if they do not conform to the world's way of doing things.

Third, their consciences are seared. To admit that they are slaves (especially to their own lusts), or that they are helpless to improve their condition, or that the philosophy and ideology on which they have based their worldview and lived their lives is wicked, would be a final burden on a conscience already seared by a lifetime of compromise.

Examining our motivations helps us to understand just who has the rule over us, and exposes what lies we have believed. Many revolutions have begun when the people, brutalized by tyranny, weighed down by burdens they cannot carry, and hoodwinked by lies and deceptions, suddenly come to an understanding that things do not have to be the way that they are. A revolution ought to start with a good and accurate sense of our current condition.

Revolutions are bloody things, and they can never be done half-way. A revolution will (and ought to) cost us everything. Jesus said, *"Think not that I am come to send peace on earth: I came not to send peace, but a sword. For I am come to set a man at variance against his father, and the daughter against her mother, and the daughter in law against her mother in law. And a man's foes shall be they of his own household. He that loveth father or mother more than me is not worthy of me: and he that loveth son or daughter more than me is not worthy of me. And he that taketh not his cross, and followeth after me, is not worthy of me. He that findeth his life shall lose it: and he that loseth his life for my sake shall find it."* (Matt. 10:34-39).

I said towards the beginning of this chapter that the Second Revolution begins when we admit that *something must be done.* That is the topic of our next chapter.

CHAPTER 3
SOMETHING MUST BE DONE

"SOMETHING MUST BE DONE"

Let's examine these words a little closer:

Something – Not just any thing, or nothing, but some particular thing. Some new course of action must be adopted, engaged, and followed. You hear a lot of talk about "change" today, especially in politics. People shout "change" as a mantra, as if change in-and-of itself is valuable and intelligent. When most of the people who shout "change" as a political platform are questioned as to the specifics and the target of the change, they are usually unable to provide any details. When radicals or rebels demand change, they usually get it, and history proves that they are rarely happy with what they receive. They say, "We need change," but are not willing to say what that change is or what it will be. Change is only good and intelligent if it is specific, objective, achievable, and moral. When we say, "Something Must Be Done," we do advocate change -but it is necessary that we also identify our destination, and that we understand the means and methods used to bring about that change, and that we intelligently pursue the specific change we advocate. "Something" is a particular thing, some correction or right action that will bring about positive change.

Must – The word "must" means "to be obliged or bound to by an imperative requirement." *Must* means "to live or to be under a requirement," "to be compelled" to some particular action. When we find ourselves in an untenable situation, if we are intelligent, engaged, and responsible, we come under a compulsion to move. We are bound by our responsibilities to our duty, to ourselves, to our families, to others to whom we owe service or protection, and most particularly to God, to engage in some change of course that we pray will bring about substantive and positive change.

Be Done – Be attempted and hopefully, and prayerfully accomplished. Our methods must have an end. Our endeavors need to have a direction, a goal or destination in mind. Understand that, when we are obedient and dutiful, results are not under our power. Obedience is ours, results belong to God. We are responsible to act properly, to move and act deliberately and according to moral and intelligent means, but this does not mean that ends or purposes become an idol. Obedience is our intent, but it is an intention that works towards a specified end. When we say we plan and hope for substantive change, we ought to be declaring that we have a specific change in mind, and that that change is our focus.

Something Must Be Done

Now let us put this understanding into a real world context. If we have set off on a course for Dallas with the intention of arriving at that destination, and if we learn that our course was erroneous, or that situations have caused that course to be no longer maintainable as a means to achieving our destination, then we must intelligently and deliberately re-chart our course. Course changes are often necessary, good, and right. Sometimes we do not learn about our mistakes and errors in planning until after a disaster or calamity has occurred. Other times we may not see things rightly for months or years, and God may let us continue in error for long periods of time. Oftentimes we only see our failures through the window of regret and sorrow. This is the purpose and the cause of repentance when it is given to us. Sometimes we do not know how we have failed until it is brought to our attention through other means. Even then, so long as we are alive, and so long as we have survived our ignorance and failure, we are invited to repentance and ought to be exhorted to use our failures as effective tools for change. Just because we have been wrong all along does not mean that we should give up or quit. That we still live means that we still have duties and obligations, and that we still are responsible creatures.

A TRUE STORY

For thousands of years (or for as long as you think the world has been), in every civilized society, the elderly have been permitted to die in their homes – in the bosom of the family that loved them and that they loved. People figured that it was the least they could do for the generation that raised them and gave them care and comfort and life and hope.

It has been a relatively short time since Western society embarked on the great industrial experiment - shorter than you probably imagine. I would like to tell you a story of how our philosophy and how the things that we think and believe, ultimately affect us and our destinations.

When my grandmother was a young girl, her life was not much different than that of little girls 300 years before her (or 500 years for that matter). She was born in 1909, 100 years before this book was started. Motorized air flight had become a reality six years before her birth, but the thought of flying was still science fiction for most people (almost everyone). In most of the world, most of the people had never even met a person who had seen the earth from the atmosphere. Most of you have heard or read about space flight, but it is almost certain that you have never been on a rocket ship. In 1909, there were motorcars, but most people, except those in large Eastern cities, had never even seen a car, and that was the year Alice Ramsey, a 22-year-old woman from New Jersey, drove a motorcar across the whole United States. It took her two months. Only a handful of people had ever made such a journey in a car. By contrast, almost all travel in 1909 in rural Texas where my grandmother was born was by way of horse power, just as it had been around the world for most of the preceding millennia. Alice Ramsey, the intrepid motor car record holder, was the anomaly and the exception in 1909, whereas my grandmother was the rule.

Most of my grandmother's food was grown by her family, and it was cooked in woodstoves and later in gas stoves (but not until after 1922, when gas appliances became more common) using fire for heat. She did not have running water, or indoor plumbing. In fact, historically speaking, it would not be improper to say that, compared to the lives of many little girls in Rome in the 4th Century, my grandmother lived a pretty basic, uncomplicated, and simple life. She would have been considered a rustic, backwards, and unsophisticated, by the Romans. Life in the early 20th Century (for most people) was not remarkably different than life in the 15th century or even in the 12th Century (although things were about to change, and very, very rapidly!) Rural folks lived lives of relative freedom in America in the first couple of decades of the 20th Century. Until World War I and America's participation in it in 1914 (when my grandmother was 5), most American men had never traveled outside of their county. They didn't know much of debt and mortgages and tricky financial instruments. Most people owned their own land, or they worked as tenant farmers for a land-owner. Whatever a family needed that they didn't provide for themselves, they purchased, traded, or bartered for from folks who had what was required. If you'll remember the earlier quote about the Greeks, rural America still primarily operated by the "household economy", and in the villages and towns, by the "urban economy". The people were not yet enslaved to the tyranny of large urban markets nor manipulated by the whims of the consumer economy. Sadly, my grandmother and her family did not even know how free they really were, because they had not yet had a glimpse of the slavery that modernism would bring, nor were they aware of all that the new industrialism (new at the time) would cost them. The Industrial Revolution had been going on for more than 100 years in 1909, but in real terms, without electrification or motor vehicles, the Industrial Revolution really just meant that there were some handier and cheaper gadgets available at the store for the back woods people of the early 1900's. The change was on its way, but it hadn't yet arrived. The most important elements of life and living had not changed for hundreds and hundreds of years – there were still no cars, no huge factories, no telephones, and no planes crisscrossing the skies.

MANUFACTURING NEEDS

In order for industrialism to take root, and for it to have its intended impact on the lives of rural Americans, an intensive period of colonization and brainwashing was necessary. Remember, by 1909 the rise of "super cities" was well on its way. The island of Manhattan had a population of over 2 million in 1909; more than it has today. Eastern population centers were bursting at the seams with workers who needed jobs because they no longer provided for themselves. There was capital and there was labor... what was needed was consumers.

Have you ever thought of the word "needy"? Jesus said that man only *needed* sustenance (food, water) and clothing – we might even stretch that to mean shelter – but "needy"? It was the urban masses, the bankers, and the industrial elite who were "needy". They needed suckers (consumers) to buy things that they didn't yet know they needed. After all, what is it to be "poor"? Isn't it to not have things you think you need? How then, do you make people want things they don't need? If the American "peasant" only bought what he needed (food and raiment), what would happen to the millions who were piled on top of one another in the cities? How do you sell people who have all that they "need" a new lifestyle of consumption?

It's actually quite easy. You tell them that they are "poor" and that they are missing out on *the good life* that they deserve.

Why be poor when you can have *the good life*? Advertising agencies would be enlisted to vividly portray the ease and comfort of *the good life,* and of course, anything short of *the good life* = poverty.

My grandmother's generation was even then being taught that they were poor and "backwards" and bereft of all of the "good things in life", and that the only solution to their newly understood condition was to fully embrace the onrushing of a new and Great Society – the home of *the good life*. A couple of generations before her people had lived much the same way that she did; but none of her ancestors would likely have considered themselves to be poor. My mother and aunts and uncles told me that they had no idea they were poor... until they were exposed to the rest of the "world" though the burgeoning media, radio, magazines, and travel.

In the Bible, the "poor" were widows, orphans, and those who because of some infirmity or affliction were forced to beg for food. In other words, *if you were not begging bread, you were not poor!* No one working the land and with food and raiment considered themselves to be poor. The concept of someone being considered poor just because they did not have all of the most modern conveniences would have been strange. The word "poor" didn't come into its modern usage until the Industrial Revolution - by way of advertising, marketing, merchandising, and consumerism. It was a marketing ploy, a rhetorical button. It was all about engendering rampant covetousness and the burgeoning consumerist mentality. In the early 20th Century, everyone who lived without electricity and without the newest modern time-saving conveniences (which is to say everyone who lived exactly like their parents and ancestors had lived) was to be convinced by the advertisers and the marketers of the new order and by the public educators and prophets of the Industrial religion that they were the pitiful poor. According to the new thinking, everyone was poor except the very rich, and everyone was inundated with mass advertising and with cultural and social pressure that they should want more than anything else not to be considered poor. Upward mobility was the new hallmark of success, and financial condition was measured solely by how assimilated a person or family had become with the new consumer world, and within that society or mindset there was no other more objective way to measure ones spiritual or physical condition. Either you had electricity, or you did not; either you had running water, or you did not; either you had an automobile and a refrigerator, or you did not. It was unthinkable that someone would not embrace and rush out to purchase these things... unless they were (gasp!) poor. The poor were to be pitied and not admired. No one would choose to deny their flesh such "necessary" toys, that is, nobody except someone who is crazy. It was understandable if you did not have the latest gadgets, but it did mean that you were poor. The only possible excuses for simple living was either poverty or insanity. If you did not choose to be without gadgets, you were poor. If you chose to be without them, you were crazy (backwards). This became the new thinking, and it does not take long for "new thinking" to become common, and for common thinking to become gospel. Your parents think the way they do because their parents were made to think that way. It all rolls downhill.

Whenever the new thinking, however weak and anemic, becomes the common thinking, the mind becomes quick to lock out the old thinking as "impossible" or "not practical or desirable." An equivalent comparison today can be made by looking at modern air-conditioning. I am young enough to remember when air-conditioning was considered an option - either in the house or in the car. Most houses did not have air-conditioning and it was absolutely not considered "standard" to have air-conditioning in the car. Today, air-conditioning is not even considered an option for most people (especially in Texas). The new thinking has prevailed, and thousands of years of experience have been thrown into the dustbin. The single comment I receive the most by people who first come upon my philosophy is this one: "I don't think I can live without air-conditioning. I just wouldn't make it," which is to say, "I'm more unviable and weaker than 99.9% of the 100 billion souls who lived on this planet before modern air-conditioning was invented!" It is a sad commentary on the barbarism of their society, but the ancient Greeks and Romans "exposed" their children if they were weak or if they thought they would not strengthen the family and the state. To "expose" a child, was to leave it to die without food or water. That was one sinful extreme – but it emphasized that those civilizations understood that their society required strength and hardiness, because they were constantly beset with war and physical challenges. In the modern West today, people actually openly claim that they "cannot live without air-conditioning". This is the other sinful extreme. They actually believe that to be weak and unviable makes them superior! Once the mind is colonized and trained, decolonizing it is a monumental task.

My grandmother's generation was told that all the new things and ideas that were coming would be good for them, and would free them from hard labor to a comfortable life devoid of stress and turmoil.

> *An aside... to flash forward and to risk giving away a bit of the ending, it must be considered here that if these young people early in the 20th century had been told how things would end for them; that they were, most of them, going to die penniless and alone in a sterile and cold nursing home (a waiting room for those waiting to drop off of the earth), crying out for a modicum of familial love and the simple warmth and care of home, I believe many of these people might have rejected the new way of thinking. Salesmen, however, and the prophets of modernism are not likely to mention the unhappy reality of death when they are trying to sell consumption and corruption. It is bad salesmanship.*

No, the salesmen of modernism focused on the middle future and on the happy corporate dreams created by well-educated advertising executives. "No," they would say, "do not ponder such dark and trivial things as death and eternity. The push-button society is going to free man to pursue intellectual and spiritual endeavors, and will eradicate poverty, inequality, and need!" If you have become convinced you are poor, why would you not sign on to a philosophy that had as one of its main tenets the abolition of poverty? Why not grasp and hold a worldview that enthrones the idols of leisure time and endless entertainment? I'm not saying we blame the people who fell for this. They didn't know any better, although a thorough study of the Bible and of history might have taught them differently.

By the middle of that same century, modern society, high on the cliffs of the new industrial/consumerism, and flushed with paper money, was the envy of the entire world. This was the precipice (a high and lofty place) from which a people would be thrown into an abyss of mental and physical slavery. A couple of World Wars and a concocted Great Depression had weaned the people from any concept of self-sufficiency and had enthroned paternalist government. Loyalties were transferred from land, family, and tribe, to government, corporations, and the nebulous promised land of "upward mobility". By the 1950's, it seemed as if the promise was within reach. Everyone was rich, and only the willfully ignorant (the simple, or the un-clever) or lazy were poor. The massive carnage and destruction, culturally and financially, that would one day come of the consumer society had not yet shown itself. In the 1950's families were still relatively intact, and although the culture and morality were headed into serious decline, things still looked pretty good.

The elements of the so-called "good life" that had the most dramatic impact on lives (electrification, cheap and easy mass communication, and automobiles) all happened during my grandmother's lifetime, and were as contemporary to her time as the home computer revolution is to my own. On the day she was born, her father would have never imagined the changes that would happen in the span of her lifetime. He had seen the advent of the motorcar and of the aeroplane, and remembered when those things were just dreams. Together they saw the arrival of readily available and cheap grid electricity, and the arrival of the farming tractor and the subsequent death of the horse-powered farm. International manipulations, cultural imperialism, and the continuous reality of foreign wars and entanglements had created legions of newly colonized foreigners eager for American goods (here we see the exportation of the consumer society). But the harsh results in real terms would not be evident for many decades. In four generations, our family, like most families in America, went from a family with the skills to provide almost all of the staples and necessities of life, to one that relied on the world and its corrupt system to provide everything for them. In four generations, our family went from a family of producers and freemen, to a family of consumers and slaves. In four generations, we went from being a nation of large, strong, patriarchal, nuclear families, to a nation of fractured, broken, and unnatural families of disconnected individuals with no historical understanding or memory. The change has happened so quickly it is stunning; and the worst thing is that most people don't even know that it has happened, and most of them do not want to know. I am reminded of the words of a Robert Earl Keen song:

"I wanna know...

Did your father own an automobile or a two horse carriage with wood spoke wheels?

I hear you used to walk to school seven miles a day

Did you ever ride a railroad train?

And the very first time you saw a plane did you think the world had gone insane?

Tell me what you've got to say

I want to know.

(Robert Earl Keen, "I Wanna Know")

The failure of the industrial experiment is one of the most evident but unspoken and unrecognized truths in the culture. It seems to be a contradiction that some fact can be "evident" but "unrecognized." That is the reality of colonization. It causes us to be blind to obvious realities, and to deny facts in favor of our conditioning. The truth is right in front of anyone who cares to look (therefore it is evident), but the brain that controls the eyes, and the thoughts that process the information from the eyes, is a tool that has been programmed by the colonizers (therefore it is unrecognized). When I think about a once vibrant, stable and strong culture now trapped on the industrial treadmill, drowning in the consumer mentality, enslaved by the insatiable needs of "time-saving" devices, mobilized only in the desire for any new entertainment, any employment, or any mental excitement or wonderment that will anesthetize the mind just long enough to keep it from recognizing its miserable existence - and its eventual end - I cringe, and I am saddened.

Back to our story... My grandmother died blind and lonely in a nursing home. I'm sure you didn't see that coming.

Her last year was a sad exit from a world that had sold her all of these lies. This is a story that no one would like to talk about, and that people would love to deny, but it is one that is repeated millions of times a year. It is likely a story that is true even in your own family. It is the third rail of family history; you just don't touch it or talk about it, because it is the most prevalent truth in the story of growing old in western society today, and of death and dying in the Industrial world.

One of my clearest memories of my grandmother's final year was of random and frightened phone calls from her in the middle of the night, or throughout the day. My parents had purchased her a phone for her bedside in the nursing home. The phone had extra-large buttons so that hopefully, despite her blindness, she could count through and figure out what buttons to push if she needed to talk to us. However, whenever she became frightened, or lonely, or when she panicked, she would grab the phone and vainly, frantically, and randomly press buttons until somebody would answer. Since most of our numbers had been programmed into the speed dial, you never knew when she would call. And she wasn't calling me, she was calling *anybody*. Actually she was calling a concept of family and of comfort and love that she had once known, but that the Industrial society had killed; but she couldn't have known that that was what she was doing. Usually she was frightened and mumbling to herself, praying that someone, *anyone*, would come get her and talk to her and maybe take her out of that place. Her mind was mostly gone, sure; but somehow I know she knew what was happening to her.

Don't get me wrong. Her children loved her and wanted only the best for her - *at least the best of what they knew.* They only acted according to the training they had received from the society that had colonized them. Her children were trapped in the modern system and were exhausting themselves on the treadmill of achievement, debt, comfort, and status. They didn't have the time or the ability to care for an old, blind, helpless woman – and keep their own sustenance system afloat. The desire for stability, advancement, comfort, and purpose-driven progress made it all but impossible for them to be able to care for her at the very end. You could see it on their faces. They wanted to do more, but they couldn't. They just couldn't. Their worldview, philosophy, and the reality of the modern world did not allow for it. When the entire concept of survival is based on "going to work" and earning more money, and when the lusts for stuff and for comfort have caused you to live a life that requires every adult to "go to work," then... every person *must* go to work. It seems like the only way, and since no one will ever question the premise, then, in reality, *it is the only way.* Happily for them, the industrial world had conceived of a solution: the nursing home - or the "adult care facility" or the "senior care home" or whatever you want to call it. Specialization is king! Aren't there people out there who can specialize in this sort of thing? So the consumer society responds... "Let us take care of your parents so you don't have to." Just think of how many people now have full-time jobs, getting paid to take care of other people's old parents. These are very real high-paying jobs. Nurses who care for the old can then spend their money in stores and on services so you and the children of the aged can have jobs! It's the circle of life! It just works! Specialization has an answer for everything.

Now, to be fair, my family did make the effort. My grandmother lived with my aunt for most of her final years, and I am grateful for that. And most of her living children pitched in for her care, until the point where her body grew too weak and her mind started to go and she just could no longer care for herself while my aunt was away at work at the hospital. A few of my cousins and I tried to keep her out of the nursing home by rotating and staying with her on the nights that my aunt worked, but we were all in college and trying to get a toe-hold in the Great Society for ourselves. We had been trained by the Industrial society as well, and we had the hope that one day we could claim *the good life* for ourselves (and the cycle repeats... one generation is shuffled off, while the next pursues the dream). All of my grandmother's living children worked jobs in the modern system. The "system" made it easy to hand her off to the nursing home. The marketing arm of the Great Society kicked in and offered the right solutions to the problem of "transitioning" old people out of this world. The family told themselves that it was nice, and that it was clean, and that she would be cared for. Everything she owned of value, including her home, would need to be sold off to pay the nursing home fees. I guess it is wrong to call such a place a "nursing home". Some nursing goes on, but it is certainly not a "home." It is a weigh station and a waiting room for the unwanted and unneeded as they await their time to drop off of the planet. It is where you take old and worn out *human units* so you can get them out of the way while you continue your own journey there. It is the island of unwanted toys, only for people who have outlived their usefulness.

We all visited her, and then we all went home. She cried, and her mind went. Sometimes she was lucid and talkative, other times she was lost in her own mind, having no idea to whom she was even talking. Sometimes she cried and begged to be saved from that place, and all along I still had the feeling that she knew what was going on.

She had given birth to seven children, and had provided for the six of them that lived into adulthood. Her husband died several decades before she did, so she spent her last several decades without a spouse. She had been married as a teenager because that was the common practice in the rural area where she grew up. She did what she was told; she raised her family, worshipped her God, and ultimately she believed the lies of a culture that didn't care one whit about her except for what service she could perform for the benefit of the Great Society. She went from being a living and breathing freeborn human to being a consumer cog in the industrial system.

At one time my grandmother could have been called an Agrarian. She raised a garden, cooked on a woodburning stove, shelled peas and snapped beans in the summertime, and knitted and sewed in the winter. She was a country girl who had been dragged into the Great Society by the overwhelming flood of modernism and necessity. She was a product of her time. The world believed that people should leave the farms and the land (so that the land could be turned over to the industrial farmers who would raise all of the food by the miracles of modern chemistry and machinery) and go to the city. At the very least, it was believed, rural Agrarian people should adopt all of the new industrial methods and gadgets that the city would be producing. If you can't or won't come to the city, the city will come to you. You must be either a customer or a consumer – there is no third way. Trying to live in both worlds was a hope that soon became an impossible dream. The Great Society was littered with hidden traps and costs, and, soon enough, country people found out that "making it" in the country was very nearly impossible, especially when there were all these new bills to pay, and when it took two working parents to make ends meet. Most farm folk embraced this new reality. They stopped growing food and started buying it at the store where it was cheaper, easier, and more abundant. As people embraced the Great Society, the more reality conspired to make a fuller embrace inevitable. So her husband left the farm and got a job at an industrial dairy in West Texas. There seemed to be no other choice, and the world taught them that this was the right thing to do. She eventually went to nursing school and helped bring thousands of babies into the new industrial world order.

They have a plaque honoring her on the wall of the "birthing center" in the hospital where she gave her time and her heart for a couple of dozen years. She was a fixture there for several decades, but no one there now remembers her. She's just a name on a plaque.

They Taught Her That She Used To Be Poor

They taught her that she used to be poor so she bought a car, even though she went to church and to the grocery store right down the street from her urban house. She had no more real need for a car than a poodle has for a parachute, but she went and got herself a car because only the poor didn't have cars. I bought that car from her almost 20 years later, and she had only put 25,000 original miles on it.

They taught her she used to be poor so she got electricity, even though she had lived her whole life up until that time happily without it.

They taught her that she used to be poor so the candles and oil lamps on her shelves and tables became antique ornamentation, while electric light (all sold cheaply by the watt) flooded her rooms.

They taught her that she used to be poor so she moved on up in the world. She got air-conditioning and an electric iron and a refrigerator and all of the other gadgets that the world told her she should have just to prove she wasn't poor anymore.

She raised her children, saw them educated and married off, and played with her grandchildren.

My grandmother's children are all nice folks, and those that are living are the salt of the earth. They are not criminals; they try to do right and they work hard. They have played by the rules and they have reaped the temporal rewards. Now they all feed the same machine and they can't see their way out of it, nor would they want to, because, after all, they all used to be poor, and who would want to go back to that? All of their lives they have been taught that the worst thing in the world is to be poor, so they each sell their lives as cheap fuel for the industrial machine because "Momma used to be poor." Some of them will get plaques on the wall where they used to work, but most won't, and as their families continue to fragment and scatter, most of their stories will be forgotten as well. It's the nature of a fragmented society. People aren't stories they are cogs in a machine. They are Dixie Cups. When their usefulness is done they get thrown away. Some of them have played the game well enough and they have made enough money to die at home with a home health care nurse to care for them. It is a strange marker for success, but you'd hate to inconvenience the next generation of consumers and besides, who wants to watch their parents die?

"I WANT MY CHILDREN TO HAVE MORE THAN I HAVE HAD!"

It is the mantra of the modern age, and like all modern mantras, it is a lie. That is what we tell ourselves, but it is just a rationalization for covetousness, greed, and consumerism. Some of my grandmother's children got educated, and all of them said that it was because they wanted their children to *"have more than we had"*. Such a phrase is a powerful anesthetic. It makes one feel better when he says he did all of this for the next generation, especially if he doesn't actually have to study and see what is happening to each subsequent generation. Each generation is taught that the previous generation was poor and miserable, and each generation watches the next generation grow more selfish, more miserable, and more arrogant, with ever increasing moral weakness. Each generation seeks its own success and comfort, and each claims to be doing it for their children and the grandchildren. The grandchildren have more all right: more debt, more stress, more diseases, more pharmaceuticals, more divorces (it becomes impossible to even count them all), more step-relatives, more wickedness, more modernism, and, well... they just have more. They have less of God and true religion, less character, less freedom, less practical intelligence, less integrity, less moral uprightness, and even less probability of surviving the slightest of disasters. Less is more, and more is less. Somehow, if we ponder on it long enough, and if God gives us enough light, and if we are humble enough to believe the truth, we can see the most apparent irony... people who had less, had more... and those who now have more, have less....

For whosoever hath, to him shall be given, and he shall have more abundance: but whosoever hath not, from him shall be taken away even that he hath. Therefore speak I to them in parables: because they seeing see not; and hearing they hear not, neither do they understand. And in them is fulfilled the prophecy of Esaias, which saith, By hearing ye shall hear, and shall not understand; and seeing ye shall see, and shall not perceive: For this people's heart is waxed gross, and their ears are dull of hearing, and their eyes they have closed; lest at any time they should see with their eyes, and hear with their ears, and should understand with their heart, and should be converted, and I should heal them" (Matt. 13:12-15)

And they told her *she* used to be poor...

Today, our most ancient and successful ways of living have become by-words and pithy catchwords for *poverty* and *backwardness* (remember Rome). If someone wants to exalt their now lofty position, they contrast it with humble and sorrowful beginnings. They say, *"When I was a boy, we didn't have running water or electricity! In fact, we had to use an... (gasp!) OUTHOUSE!"* Or if they want to emphasize how far they have come, they say, *"When I was young, we didn't have a television, and we had to walk to school."* None of this is new. Rome is being revisited, and we are too stupid and historically ignorant to know it.

> *If there were no wind we might, we think, hear the earth grind on its axis, or history drip in darkness like a leaking pipe in the cellar. (Robert Penn Warren – "Evening Hawk")*

One of the sad truths about moral and cultural blindness is that the morally and culturally blind do not have the eyes, or the ability, to see their blindness. As each generation slips further away from the ideal (whether we are considering true religion, morality, or the ability to provide the basics of survival), they move further away from the old historical landmarks. They are more prone to lose their way and less likely to even accidentally end up where they ought to be. Each generation becomes the default leaders and teachers of the next generation, and the blind lead the blind ever deeper into the ditch.

A PARABLE

When an aircraft suffers a mechanical failure, there remains hope so long as the structure survives intact and so long as the instruments remain trustworthy. If, however, the structure *and* the instruments are destroyed, it ought to be assumed that a crash is imminent. Miracles can always happen, but by definition they usually do not. When we say, "Something Must Be Done," it is in this context. Catastrophes and disasters do not usually strike without any warning whatsoever. There is generally some period of time between the moment when we are made aware that something is terribly wrong, and the moment when the catastrophe finally hits, or when the full impact is registered. This period of time, however short or long, is when decisions are made. Now, it is during this interim when our true character and the things that we have truly believed become known. It ought to be a time of action, because it is the time when something must be done.

Survival (like revival) requires an unbending and inflexible demand for the truth. We must require facts, and we must see those facts as they are, and not as we might want them to be. Deception is the enemy of survival. Self-deception is the most heinous enemy because it is the equivalent of smashing our own instruments when they are needed the most. When our internal compass is inoperative, survival becomes a wish and a dream but not a real likelihood.

The modern world, with its society and culture, is an aircraft that (at a very high altitude) has proven to have inoperative instruments while it has simultaneously suffered a massive systemic and structural failure. Things do not look good. But there are a couple of options:

One option is to do nothing. We are perfectly free to continue to live on in delusion and denial. One thing about most modern aircraft is that they have comfy blankets and a nice pillow for your head. Humans are perfectly equipped to deny all of the available intelligence and to remain blind and deaf to reality, but we must say here that the end will not change merely because you might wish it to. If you become determined to do nothing and to remain in denial, you are going to be extremely irritated with anyone around you who doesn't choose to share in your deceptions (In fact, if this is your inclination, you are probably already pretty angry with me). Those who will deny reality and who will deny facts cannot suffer someone who has decided differently. It is extremely uncomfortable and irritating to have your conscience seared with a hot iron as your plane is crashing. So if someone is determined to deceive themselves, then they have to do something about the guy who is trying to ruin their perfectly good delusion. Towards this end, they usually have a handy trick left in their bag. If they can dismiss you as a pessimist (or as a kook), then they can alleviate the stress and the pressure; they can salve their own conscience, and they can feel better about themselves and their lives. Better, they say, to be ignorant and distracted so they can remain in relative comfort as they rocket towards the ground.

Here is something for you to write down and remember: facing reality is never pessimistic. Believing the truth, no matter how difficult that may be, is the ultimate act of optimism because it opens up the panorama of options that will free us from further deception. *Taking off a blindfold is never an act of pessimism.* Getting angry at the truth (or at the messenger who delivers the truth) is a self-deceptive act of narcissistic theater, and it is a colossal waste of time.

All of the data is out there for anyone who cares to spend the time to study it and analyze it. Modern society is peopled with folks who are suffering from group dementia and a paralyzing allergy to the truth and to facts. The Industrial system has succeeded in providing cooked books, powerful and deceptive narcotics, smoke and mirrors and sleight of hand by way of billions of dollars in marketing and advertising, in order to sustain the illusion of safety and security. Those who wish to stay on the plane, believing it will arrive safely at its destination despite all the available facts to the contrary, are free to do so. I was asked if it would be possible to just write this book without mentioning the condition of the world, or "scaring people" with tales of doom and gloom. Yes, it would be possible. It just wouldn't be honest. I am not predicting some worldwide calamity, although many calamities are very, very likely. The devastation I warn you of is cultural, and social, and spiritual. It is already here. Our society, like Greece and Rome and like Sodom before us, is already wicked and evil to the core. Destruction is inevitable, but that is not the point of this book. The destruction of Rome by Alaric and the Gothic Barbarians was just the period at the end of a very long sentence. Western Society is crumbling, but it is being destroyed on the inside first.

I don't think that anyone ought to be motivated primarily by fear. Some fear is good, and it is given to us by God for our preservation and for our safety. If you are standing in the middle of a highway with cars coming at you, the fear that you feel is a good thing, and it ought to motivate you to right action. I think, however, that people ought to be primarily motivated by morality, by intelligence, duty, obedience, and courage. Maybe you shouldn't have been on that highway to begin with? One of the ingredients that will eradicate fear is faith, and another is a love of the truth.

Before anyone gets too angry at me, let me say that no one is going to rob you of the freedom that you have to destroy yourself and your progeny. You are free to choose to do nothing. You are free to dismiss me as a kook and an alarmist. That is your right. If you are honestly convinced that nothing is wrong with our society, and that there are no real dangers, and that the realities I mention to you are not systemic or not that important, then by all means go in peace. You may still gain something from the things taught in this book, so I will encourage you to read on, but if you do believe that even some of the problems I mention are serious; if you do see danger signs; or if you question the stability or morality of the system, then it would be wrong to submit to the inevitability of it without considering that there might be another option. It would be wrong to squander the gift of sight by doing nothing. Most people, when they are confronted with the true facts, will not have the eyes to see their condition. They will deny the truth at all costs. Most are already blinded by their own lusts and their own corruption, and they are not able to see. If, however, it is given unto you to see your peril, I believe it would be wrong to yield to some pessimistic view of "fate" without intelligently and carefully considering your duty to survive. Remember, true survivalists are the real optimists.

The second option is to admit that "something must be done." If there is to be any true survival, let us start by admitting that we have to do something. We cannot just wish our errors and troubles away.

Let's quickly list a couple of options under the category of proactive action (remember our plane is going down):

We can attempt to fix the plane in flight, to repair the instruments, and to cobble together some repairs to the structure in order to attempt to maintain airworthiness.

Or maybe it would be wiser to make use of parachutes if some are available – which means to agree in ourselves to abandon the doomed aircraft altogether. This, to me, is the ultimate act of optimism, because it is a declaration that I am not a part of this broken craft, I am free from it, and that there is still hope. Once we have accepted the true facts as they are, and once we have determined based on those facts that the plane is going to crash, we can choose to jump out of it. The thought might seem frightening, but it also ought to seem exhilarating. Now, there is no guarantee that our plans are going to succeed. Maybe the chute will not open. Maybe we land on a power line (oh, how ironic would that be?) But there is an absolute guarantee that if we do not do something that we are going to go down with the plane – and we can know that that option is positively not survivable.

We have options, and this book is about making those options known. It is about hope and optimism. It is a parachute. Something must be done, and that is a fact in my life. I have accepted it. I hope you will too.

CHAPTER 4
DEBT SLAVERY

"The rich ruleth over the poor, and the borrower is servant to the lender" (Proverbs 22:7).

In Chapter 2 we took what I call "The Slavery Test". I had hoped that taking that test might expose some realities we might not have previously been willing to face. I have spoken and counseled with hundreds of people over the years about moving towards a more separate and sustainable lifestyle, and I can tell you that the single excuse (or reason) I hear the most from people concerning why they cannot get out of the system, is that they are in too much debt, or that their current expenses make a move out of the system seem too difficult. Many people say they want to get off-grid, but they cannot see a way out of their current condition.

I know it is not fun to talk about, but the topic of debt slavery can be interesting and illustrative if you will apply yourself to it and pay close attention. The story of debt slavery ought to be of great concern to those who are interested in history, mysteries, and conspiracies. There are several different ways that people are likely to respond to this topic:

1. You aren't in debt, so you say, "Hey, I'm on the same page. Debt is bad... Got it. Let's move on." To those of you who have no debt, I want to congratulate you and encourage you to stay steadfast and strong in that position. But I still encourage you to read and study this chapter, because there is some fascinating information here that may very well help you in the future, and that may also help you help others

2. You aren't very deep in debt, so you say, "I don't have much debt. My debt is manageable. Certainly I'm not a slave to it. I'm not sure

this information applies to me." Again, I would encourage you *first* to get totally out of debt. This does not mean that, like the use of other intermediate means, some types of debt might not be legitimate and manageable. In some cases, the purchase of land in our current system is virtually impossible without some use of debt, even if it is only short-term. I still would encourage all of you who read this to consider debt a mortal enemy and a danger to yourself and your livelihood. If you must use debt at all, make sure you make use of it in as short a term as possible. This is a proper attitude towards debt, and it will keep you right-minded as you make decisions in the future.

3. You are in debt pretty deeply. This category includes those who may not have a great amount of debt per se, but who have managed their lives in a way that they have accumulated a large amount of monthly payments, so that the necessary cumulative monthly expenditure limits ones freedom or makes one susceptible to disaster. You may know that debt is bad, and you may grieve over your mistakes, but now you are in it and therefore you believe there is no hope or answer to your problem. Or, maybe you can see your way out, but you are disheartened by the challenge. Although I think everyone will benefit from the information and philosophy in this chapter; it is primarily written to you – and I think the bulk of my readers will fall into this category if they honestly examine their circumstances. If your monthly necessary expenditure is more than a few hundred dollars (the amount that can be earned with a few hard day's work) – then, whether you like it or not, you are in some level of debt slavery.

I know that many of you do not want to hear about how bad debt actually is. You think you have all the information, and that there is nothing more you can learn about debt that will help you. Maybe you are right, but I ask you to read on through this chapter anyway. Perhaps you will glean some new insight or tidbit that can help you on your way out of the system. Also, I do not pretend that this chapter is a complete (or even adequate) discussion on debt, slavery, credit, or any other topic. It would take many books to cover these topics in any kind of depth. What I do hope is that my admittedly cursory review of the issues, *from a different worldview*, will give you some new insight, and that it might spur you to further study the issues yourself.

As I have said before; in order for us to make a change in our circumstances, we have to know what we *do* want, and how we *do* want to live. Then we have to be convinced that a good and right change is possible, and that it is certainly possible for us to move towards a more free and sustainable way of living. We have to look past the giants in the land and trust in God and His promises. *The single biggest link in the chains of our slavery is debt.* But debt is something you can control, IF you really want to. The major part of coming to a right view of our condition is being able to see it properly, historically, and through eyes that are not shaded or clouded by the colonized mind and the lies of the slave-master. It is also important that we realize a salient fact: every slaveholder has a vested interest in keeping his slaves ignorant, indebted, and pacified.

THE HIGH PRICE OF FREE CORN

I'd like to illustrate a critical point by telling you a story that was sent to me several years ago by a friend who knew I'd appreciate it. This is a legend (or a parable) that has been around awhile (maybe you've seen it?), but it is so appropriate to our subject that I thought I needed to include it here. I cannot say for certain who wrote this story, but whenever I have found it, on the Internet or elsewhere, it has usually been attributed to *"Steve Washam, based on a telling by George Gordon"*. I hope that that will suffice for attribution. Anyway, here is the story:

THE WILD AND FREE PIGS OF THE OKEFENOKEE SWAMP

Some years ago, about 1900, an old trapper from North Dakota hitched up some horses to his Studebaker wagon, packed a few possessions -- especially his traps -- and drove south. Several weeks later he stopped in a small town just north of the Okefenokee Swamp in Georgia. It was a Saturday morning -- a lazy day -- when he walked into the General Store. Sitting around the pot-bellied stove were seven or eight of the town's local citizens.

The traveler spoke. "Gentlemen, could you direct me to the Okefenokee Swamp?" Some of the oldtimers looked at him like he was crazy. "You must be a stranger in these parts," they said. "I am. I'm from North Dakota," said the stranger. "In the Okefenokee Swamp are thousands of wild hogs." one old man explained. "A man who goes into the swamp by himself asks to die!" He lifted up his leg. "I lost half my leg here, to the pigs of the swamp." Another old fellow said, "Look at the cuts on me; look at my arm bit off! Those pigs have been free since the Revolution, eating snakes and rooting out roots and fending for themselves for over a hundred years. They're wild and they're dangerous. You can't trap them. No man dare go into the swamp by himself." Every man nodded his head in agreement.

The old trapper said, "Thank you so much for the warning. Now could you direct me to the swamp?" They said, "Well, yeah, it's due south -- straight down the road." But they begged the stranger not to go, because they knew that he'd meet a terrible fate. He said, "Sell me ten sacks of corn, and help me load it in the wagon." And they did. Then the old trapper bid them farewell and drove on down the road. The townsfolk thought they'd never see him again. Two weeks later the man came back. He pulled up to the general store, got down off the wagon, walked in and bought ten more sacks of corn. After loading it up he went back down the road toward the swamp.

Two weeks later he returned and again bought ten sacks of corn.

This went on for a month. And then two months, and then three.

Every week or two the old trapper would come into town on a Saturday morning, load up ten sacks of corn, and drive off south into the swamp. The stranger soon became a legend in the little village and the subject of much speculation. People wondered what kind of devil had possessed this man that he could go into the Okefenokee by himself and not be consumed by the wild and free hogs.

One morning the man came into town as usual. Everyone thought he wanted more corn. He got off the wagon and went into the store where the usual group of men was gathered around the stove. He took off his gloves. "Gentlemen," he said, "I need to hire about ten or fifteen wagons. I need twenty or thirty men. I have six thousand hogs out in the swamp, penned up, and they're all hungry. I've got to get them to market right away." "You've WHAT in the swamp?" asked the storekeeper, incredulously. "I have six thousand hogs penned up. They haven't eaten for two or three days, and they'll starve if I don't get back there to feed and take care of them."

One of the oldtimers said, "You mean you've captured the wild hogs of the Okefenokee?"

That's right."

"How did you do that? What did you do?" the men urged, breathlessly. One of them exclaimed, "But I lost my arm!" "I lost my brother!" cried another. "I lost my leg to those wild boars!" chimed a third.

The trapper said, "Well, the first week I went in there they were wild all right. They hid in the undergrowth and wouldn't come out. I dared not get off the wagon. So I spread corn along behind the wagon. Every day I'd spread a sack of corn."

"The old pigs would have nothing to do with it. But the younger pigs decided that it was easier to eat free corn than it was to root out roots and catch snakes. So the very young began to eat the corn first. I did this every day. Pretty soon, even the old pigs decided that it was easier to eat free corn. After all, they were all free; they were not penned up. They could run off in any direction they wanted at any time."

"The next thing was to get them used to eating in the same place all the time. So I selected a clearing, and I started putting the corn in the clearing. At first they wouldn't come to the clearing. It was too far. It was too open. It was a nuisance to them. But the very young decided that it was easier to take the corn in the clearing than it was to root out roots and catch their own snakes. And not long thereafter, the older pigs also decided that it was easier to come to the clearing every day."

"And so the pigs learned to come to the clearing every day to get their free corn. They could still subsidize their diet with roots and snakes and whatever else they wanted. After all, they were all free. They could run in any direction at any time. There were no bounds upon them."

"The next step was to get them used to fence posts. So I put fence posts all the way around the clearing. I put them in the underbrush so that they wouldn't get suspicious or upset. After all, they were just sticks sticking up out of the ground, like the trees and the brush. The corn was there every day. It was easy to walk in between the posts, get the corn, and walk back out."

"This went on for a week or two. Shortly they became very used to walking into the clearing, getting the free corn, and walking back out through the fence posts. The next step was to put one rail down at the bottom. I also left a few openings, so that the older, fatter pigs could walk through the openings and the younger pigs could easily jump over just one rail. After all, it was no real threat to their freedom or independence. They could always jump over the rail

95

and flee in any direction at any time."

"Now I decided that I wouldn't feed them every day. I began to feed them every other day. On the days I didn't feed them the pigs still gathered in the clearing. They squealed, and they grunted, and they begged and pleaded with me to feed them. But I only fed them every other day. And I put a second rail around the posts." "Now the pigs became more and more desperate for food, because now they were no longer used to going out and digging their own roots and finding their own food. They now needed me. They needed my corn every other day. So I trained them that I would feed them every day if they came in through a gate. And I put up a third rail around the fence. But it was still no great threat to their freedom because there were several gates and they could run in and out at will."

"Finally I put up the fourth rail. Then I closed all the gates but one, and I fed them very, very well. Yesterday I closed the last gate. And today I need you to help me take these pigs to market."

End of story

This story was originally written to emphasize the absurdity of the modern financial system and the idea of so-called "free money," however it perfectly illustrates how the modern industrial society has created slaves of a once free people. Free money has a very high price, and the concept of credit (debt) is originally sold to us as easy or free money. In the end, we see that this society has created a whole herd of Debt Slaves, and that most of those slaves do not really see how they have actually enslaved themselves. The entire consumer society is designed around the idea that if you make things seem easier for people; if you coddle them so that they have no real skills and so that they become unviable outside of the system; if you control every aspect of their lives, and pander to their every lust and desire; you can control their behavior and make them do your bidding. It makes it easier when, like the man with the pigs, what you want for the victim to do is CONSUME. In ancient societies, slaves were needed to do hard physical labor – like building cities, pyramids, obelisks, or temples. Today, slaves are needed to eat, drink, purchase, and consume.

THE SLAVERY CONSPIRACY

We only recently (somewhere around the year 2007) passed the 200 year mark since the transatlantic slave trade came to an end, and less than 150 years have passed since the 13th Amendment to the U.S. Constitution outlawed slavery throughout America. Although the enslaving of a conquered people was biblical, **there is no doubt that slavery** *based solely on race* **and man-stealing was an unbiblical precept and a monumental evil** (Ex. 21:16; 1 Tim. 1:10). But it was an evil shared and participated in by every people and race and nation and tribe; including indigenous "Indians" in the Americas, blacks in Africa, by northern slave-traders and businessmen, as well as by southern plantation owners. The enslavement of stolen men brought the judgment of God down upon peoples and nations all around the world, and rightly so. While some forms of slavery were evidently permitted or tolerated in the scriptures (such as the enslavement of nations who were losers in war; or who are otherwise sent into slavery by God as punishment; or of criminals; or the enslavement of those who sell themselves into bondage), nowhere do we find license or permission for slavery based on skin color alone; nor do we find any sanction at all for man-stealing, which would be considered a crime against God and man. In fact, the book of Exodus prescribes the death penalty for man stealing: *"And he that stealeth a man, and selleth him, or if he be found in his hand, he shall surely be put to death"* (Exodus 21:16). It is important to note that this form of slavery was considered unnecessary and immoral in the nations and places where Biblical Agrarianism predominated as an economic and cultural philosophy. Nor would slavery have been needful or profitable under a pure Agrarian model. The unjust forms of slavery flourished only when urbanism predominated, and when pure Agrarianism gave way to specialization.

When urbanism and the mercantile system of commerce made such slavery profitable, it became necessary. It is critical for our understanding that we solidly link in our minds the institution of slavery with the rise of specialization and of modern commerce, the ascendance of the cash crop and Mercantile Agrarianism, and the beginnings of Industrialism. Of ancient Greece it is said that slavery triumphed in the cities, but in the countryside, where a family need only produce what it could eat, slavery was considered superfluous. Country men wanted sons, not slaves.

When trade ceased to be local and personal, unbiblical slavery was the inevitable result. This type of slavery was a stop-gap, or, an intermediate measure, filling the need for massive amounts of physical labor until the industrial system could invent and produce the machines that could keep up with the newly created wants (actually "lusts") of the people. Aristotle taught that slavery would exist everywhere until all menial labor could be done by self-operating machines. He was half right.

The industrial world always knew that race based slavery would never be profitable in the new industrial economy, but forced or conscripted labor seemed necessary so long as the culture demanded more comfort and leisure in a time when the technology had not yet advanced enough to allow for the mechanization of low skill tasks. Slavery had always existed, but wholesale man-stealing didn't become profitable until the urban, mercantile, and industrial age. The prophets of greed and progress believed that forced slavery was necessary during the transition from a Mercantile Agrarianism to a more industrialized economy. We cannot know if the early slave traders knew whether or not it would last, but we do know that forced slavery could not continue for long; neither would the industrialists want it to last. This fact creates one of the most interesting ironies. Forced slavery became necessary because society had abandoned pure Agrarianism and was moving inexorably from Mercantile Agrarianism towards Industrialism. Yet the advocates of Industrialism claim that Industrialism was the engine or motive behind the abolition and death of race-based slavery. But were the industrialists really acting philanthropically when they became abolitionists? Was the rabid abolitionism of the northern industrialists truly based on a hatred of the concept of slavery – when, in fact their fathers were the ones who imported it?

The Industrialists knew that slaves (under the old system of slavery) didn't have any money to buy products, and the chains and whips of the slaveholder are never big or thick enough to cause men to work harder when they can conceive of no possible personal reward or benefit. Industrialism needs an ever growing number of consumers, and traditional slavery does not produce consumers. In fact, with the advent of affordable harvesting and processing machinery in the early 19th Century, this form of slavery was already on its deathbed, even in the South. The Greek country dweller didn't want slaves because slaves ate. The northern industrialist didn't want slaves because they didn't eat enough.

In the middle of the 19th Century, northern bankers and other industrial and trade interests knew that Industrialism was dead unless the South could be soon brought under its umbrella. The north was running out of raw materials, which were plentiful in the south. The north was running out of markets and mouths for their products, which they also thought were plentiful in the south. The problem was that southern agrarians didn't want or need northern goods. Agrarianism in the south could never be allowed to stand. A nation of people providing for themselves most of the necessities of life is not a market for commercial bankers and industrialists. Even though the South had already succumbed, in some measure, to the slow poison of Mercantile Agrarianism and the deception of the "specialized cash crop" (which enabled and encouraged slavery), the movement towards commercial industrialism in the south was too slow to save struggling northern business interests. Therefore northern banking and religious interests came up with a two-pronged approach for the destruction of southern Agrarianism:

First, any attempts by the south to rid themselves of the burden of slavery would have to be thwarted. These attempts have been well documented and are readily available to the diligent student of history. But the north knew that if the south was free to divest themselves of slavery, it seemed obvious that they would immediately return to their more historic and idyllic Agrarianism. This would never do. Free men make horrible debt slaves. In fact, to the industrialists, the slavery problem in the south had to be amplified. To the banker, war heals all wounds. Thus numerous attempts by southern legislatures to mitigate and ameliorate the slavery problem were stopped cold by northern meddling, by the activism of northern agitators pretending to be southerners, by court cases, and by mandates from the federal government. This is not to say that there were not rabid slavery supporters in the south, because there were, just as there had been rabid slavery supporters in the north so long as slavery was profitable in the North. Let us not forget that sin has no borders. We have to keep in mind that the so-called "Civil War" was not primarily about slavery, at least not in the way we have all been taught in school. Slavery was certainly an issue, but it was an ancillary issue. The war was another in a long line of wars of conquest, the ultimate purpose of which was the destruction of any way of life contrary to the interests of the prophets and kings of this world. War in the 19th century was no different than war in the 5th century before Christ; it was about expanding markets and government power, destroying competition, grasping natural resources, and increasing consumption.

Next, the northern states passed laws which would amplify the slavery problem for the south. Alexis de Toqueville in his book _Democracy in America_ stated that northern states chose a very interesting form of emancipation for themselves (remember, slavery was still legal in the north). By a system of "gradual emancipation", slaveholders in the north were forbidden by law to sell their slaves within their own state (note that they were not forbidden to sell slaves, nor were they forbidden to profit from the selling of slaves), and since northern slaveholders knew that, due to the new laws, there would be no market for their slaves in other bordering northern states, they took their slaves south where there might still be a free market. The new laws ensured that slaves could not be sold profitably unless they were taken south. Thus, by clever legal intervention, northern states were able to accomplish several key goals:

First, they rid themselves of what they considered a "burden", and they did so without suffering monetary loss, something later (at the prodding of the northern banking interests) they would absolutely require of the south. When former northern slaveholders later became avid abolitionists, they demanded that southern slaves be freed and not sold, and they hypocritically made this demand on moral grounds; quite a handy demand since they had already divested themselves of their own slaves at a profit. Southern slave owners were forbidden by law to export their slaves north, or to repatriate them back to Africa.

Second, northern racists were able to make certain that millions of northern slaves would not be moving into their own communities. They had driven their fears to the south, thus shifting the "burden" onto other shoulders. Knowing that southerners at the time believed much like they did themselves, they required that the south free the slaves in the south (and keep them in the south), and northern states even enacted laws forbidding southerners from driving their slaves up north to free them there. *It was the official policy of the northern army at the advent of the War of Southern Secession to capture "escaped" (often freed) slaves and forcibly return them to the South.* Later, northern military minds determined that "freed" slaves would make better soldiers than neighbors. Poor northern military leadership left their armies constantly in need of more cannon fodder, so they offered emancipated slaves (who were generally uneducated, broke, and had no real hope of gaining employment or earning a living in the north) pay and other promises (primarily land and political power in the "new" south) if they would sign on to fight in the northern army.

*For those interested in an in-depth concurrent study on this slavery scam, please read R.L. Dabney's book – *A Defense of Virginia and the South.*

Northern banking and industrial interests recognized that they needed a south that was under their thumb, and they would use the southern states as an example of how empire building and colonization could create consumers and customers for northern industrial products. If you want to know why America is at war in Afghanistan and Iraq, look to the business interests who profit from it. When backwards desert and cave dwellers get a taste of Burger King and McDonald's, a whole new generation of consumers will be born. It is not surprising that no country with a McDonald's restaurant has ever made war with America.

So you see, the South's covetousness and greed first caused them to fall for selling out their pure Agrarianism for specialization and Mercantile Agrarianism. Under Mercantile Agrarianism, many farms that were once primarily a means of providing food and material to support families became very specialized commercial businesses, providing cash crops for the massive and growing populations of northern cities. We confess that there have always been cash crops in any purely Agrarian system, but cash crops were usually what the farming family grew above and beyond that which was needed for the supply and maintenance of the farmer's household.

Later, greed and the lust for comfort and riches caused southern farmers and plantation owners to institutionalize the trade and enslavement of stolen humans in order to maintain that cash crop system. Finally, the hungry and insatiable behemoth to the north used military might to put an end to the Agrarian system in the South; thereby creating of the several united states one industrial/consumer entity: A Babylonian beast that would rival Rome and the Greek empire during their heydays. The unbiblical enslavement of one race of people was to be replaced with the slavery of everyone but the very elite. The system of debt slavery was to be color-blind if not class blind. It did focus its energies on the poorer classes of people.

THE CREDIT CONSPIRACY

The next step in the scam was to make sure that all the new "consumers" who were created by anti-agrarian machinations, by wars, and by conquests, would be able to purchase industrial/commercial goods.

Under pure Agrarianism, "credit" was in no way the debt-based credit system we know of today. Basically, if a free man had two dozen eggs, he could take those eggs to a local merchant who would give him some amount of "credit" for those eggs. Credit was not a debit in accounting terms it was a "credit". It meant that the merchant owed YOU. As his profit, the merchant would keep a few of the eggs for himself and for the profit of his store. Some par value would be established, and then the store "credits" could be used to purchase other items from the store. Credit, then, was merely a way to make sure that barter was encouraged and expedited. Under this system, no debt was incurred. When pure Agrarianism gave way to Mercantile Agrarianism (where farmers began to focus on specialization and "cash crops", instead of merely trading or bartering their excess), a more stringent and debt-based credit system evolved. For example, store owners would give a farmer large amounts of bulk seed with the promise of a portion of the crop when (and if) it came in. Now, credit became a debt. As Mercantile Agrarianism disappeared into the maw of commercial industrialism, the merchant or the banker now required some form of collateral for such "loans". Generally, land and property were the preferred forms of collateral. It did not take long for most people to become mere tenants on the land once owned by their fathers; lands which were now actually owned by bankers and commercial interests.

It is necessary that we take just a moment here to speak about property taxes, and their role in creating debt slaves. Prior to the 19th century (the first century fully owned and operated by the Industrialists), most land, if it was taxed at all, was taxed on a flat per acre basis. Many people believed this to be a method of taxation that unfairly benefited the rich, since it did not account for the relative value of the land. For example, a wealthy landowner who owned prime real estate (such as a port, or land that had access to roads or rivers) would be taxed at the same rate as a poor farmer who had no such access. The poor landowner paid a much larger percentage of his net worth in property taxes. Pioneers, many who never considered that the whole concept of taxation on property was immoral and unjust, desired to eradicate the inequality of flat rate taxes on land by pushing for "Universality" laws, which were laws that would set the tax rate based on "value" (*ad valorem*) rather than on the number of acres owned. To the pioneers and settlers, this made sense because the property tax rates would be set by elected officials, which meant (in a fair and representative system) that they would have some power and control over their eventual tax rate. Little did they know that the Universality laws could backfire on them if ever the political system became corrupted. Pushed by the industrialists and the banking powers, from 1818 to 1896, around half of the states in the Union adopted Universality laws as it applied to property taxation. Most of the remaining states would eventually follow suit. With the advent of these *ad valorem* property taxes, in a very short amount of time, virtually 100% of the land became, in truth, owned by banks, commercial interests, or by the government. You could say you owned your own land and property, but so long as you had to make a monthly or yearly payment in order to maintain the right to make such a claim, the claim was just a fantasy that everyone agreed to accept as reality. The imposition of *ad valorem* property taxes was only one move in a very long chess game designed to make the people slaves on the land once conquered by free men. Ad Valorem taxes had another destructive consequence. Rich men were now able to buy huge tracts of uninhabited land for a pittance. So long as they left this land unimproved, the land would appreciate in value, but the taxes would remain negligible. In other words, the rich were able to buy up all the land without fear of being bankrupted by the property taxes on it. The poor, who could barely afford land, if they could afford any at all, were now forced to buy the land from the rich, who had every incentive to sit on the land and not sell it (they were making money on the appreciation of the land). Today, the reason you cannot buy land cheaply in America is because most of the available farming land is owned by rich individuals or corporate conglomerates who have no incentive to sell it, or even improve it. With ad valorem taxes, if the poor man builds a cabin, a shed, a barn, or any other fixed structure, his taxes go up significantly. On all of the surrounding land, where nothing whatever is done to improve the land or make it productive, the taxes remain low. The rich have a disincentive to build, while the poor have a disincentive to improve their properties so that they can take care of themselves. Under a flat property tax, especially one that exempted (or maintained low rates) small-holders, who use their land to provide for themselves and their families, the large landholders would soon find it untenable to hold on to huge sections of land, and millions of acres of very productive farm land would be available at low cost to those who want to provide for themselves. As you can see, the scam of "Universality laws" fit perfectly into the overall credit scam. Regular folks were pushed off of the land by high taxes and numerous other government implemented disincentives, all while they were being told that they could make a good life in the cities and the suburbs – and all on credit. Production would remain in the hands of the industrialists and the corporations. Consumption, spurred on by credit, was the job of everyone else.

In some form or other, credit had existed for thousands of years, but up until the Catholic Crusades, crop credit (and other early forms of credit) was generally only extended personally (meaning between individuals, friends, or family members who knew one another). Although out-and-out usury was illegal in most nominal "Christian" countries, new forms of credit would soon be devised by the "church" in order to maximize church power and authority throughout most of Europe. During the Crusades and other Roman wars of conquest, the Roman Catholic Knights Templar (the fore-runners of the Jesuits) created a system of credit accounts whereby individuals, groups, guilds, or any other "body" could entrust valuable goods or monies to the Knights Templar in exchange for the protection and profitable distribution of those goods. From this early protection racket evolved the system of credit that would eventually become modern consumer credit (usury masquerading as expediting and easing trade).

All of this may seem complicated and confusing, but here is the important part for you to remember... These two issues (debt and slavery) are not unconnected. The Apostasy from true religion (which once righteously regulated human transactions), meant an apostasy from God's plan for man and the creation. The wealthy of this world had a plan, and that plan involved making long-term slaves of almost every man in every nation.

God knows what is in the heart of man. The Bible provided for laws and regulations that allowed for true community to exist and thrive without the manipulations and machinations of evil men. Justice and righteousness were originally found in the decrees and commandments of God, and with the revelation of Jesus Christ they were to be found written on the hearts of regenerate men. Life in a Biblical society was governed by an over-arching law of Sabbath cycles. There were the Sabbath days, Sabbath years, Land Sabbaths, and eventually the Jubilee year. The idea that God's creatures needed rest, and that true, vibrant, and just community required the hope of freedom, was inculcated in men from a young age. Every seven days, everyone (even slaves and animals) rested; they were freed from their burdens; this happened for thousands of years as a prophetic lesson. On the Sabbath year (every seven years on the seventh year), all debts were cancelled and anyone who was enslaved or indentured because of debt was freed. This concept brought about a constant renewing of harmony, equality, and community life. During the Jubilee year (the year following seven Sabbath years - or 49 years), on the 50th year, all debts were forgiven, and any land or property was to be returned to its original owner (except, interestingly, for the property of city-dwellers residing within city walls). While most Christian nations determined that the very stringent land regulations stipulated in the law applied only to the Hebrews and to the land given to the several tribes, the idea that debt forgiveness was required during the Sabbath and Jubilee years was almost universally accepted in all Christian nations, including in America. In order, then, for the great conspiracy to move forward, it was necessary that these accepted laws and traditions be overthrown via religious apostasy, which, not coincidentally, accompanied the war against Agrarianism. While the War against the South was the crowning blow in the battle against Agrarianism, the battle was actually lost much earlier in many lesser known skirmishes, not the least of which was when the Unitarians captured Harvard in 1805. Up through the mid 1800's we would see more and more denominations and "churches" abandoning God's commandments and laws in favor of more syncretistic and worldly doctrines. As time passed, the pulpits no longer rang with condemnations of sin and encouragements to keep the commandments of God. The new "modern" pulpits were more likely to ring with exhortations to civic advancement, political activism, national pride, and the golden calf of upward mobility.

Apostasy from right religion in the north was a necessary precursor to the Trojan Horse of northern aggression and abolitionism that led to debt slavery for most of the world's inhabitants. Like I said, it is a bigger topic than can possibly be tackled in a short chapter such as this one. Do some research, it is worth the effort.

DEBT BONDAGE

Technically, *Debt Bondage* is:

> *"An involuntary arrangement whereby a person is forced to pay off a loan with direct labor in place of currency, over an agreed upon or obscure period of time. When the debtor is then tricked or trapped into working for very little or no pay, or when the value of their work is significantly greater than the original sum of money borrowed, some consider the arrangement to be a form of unfree labor or **debt slavery**. It is similar to peonage, or indenture"* *(Via Wikipedia).*

Through myriad interlaced arrangements, modern debt can appear to be free of the accusation of being "involuntary" or of being "debt bondage," though in reality it is probably the most perfect form of it. The lender can say, "Modern debt vehicles are not involuntary", but a close examination of the realities of this world would prove this statement to be only technically true. The society does encourage debt (and from an early age), and often requires some history of debt and debt management in the disposition of some benefits (some jobs, for example). Also, the system itself is so intimately intertwined with the debt culture, that most people are never educated about the alternatives to the use of debt. In fact, back in 1985 on my first day at a State University, as I registered for classes, I was handed a sack full of credit applications. What was I to conclude but that the state, the University, and the society desired for me to be a part of the debt culture? And how was I to get started, and pay for all the "stuff" they told me I needed, if I didn't use credit cards?

The lender can also say, "We accept currency and not labor, therefore we cannot be guilty of engendering debt bondage," when in reality, again, these lenders are so inextricably intertwined (through government incorporation, debt, and other financial machinations) to the corporations (state creations) that employ almost 100% of the people, that the difference is purely illusory. You have to work at some corporate job to make "currency" to pay the debt you owe to corporations. In fact, both the state and the corporations created by that state profit from the debt bondage encouraged by lenders, and reciprocate by creating and legitimizing laws that reward predatory and unbiblical lending practices (why do you think the American government just recently gave almost a trillion dollars to the bankers for making bad loans?) Almost any fair, honest, and in-depth examination of the modern debt system in the Western world would have to conclude that the system of debt that is prevalent today actually constitutes *debt slavery* for most participants.

I hope I have not made this confusing, and I have to tell you that trying to cover such a huge and complex conspiracy in just a few words is a very difficult and daunting task. I will endeavor to simplify it...

An industrial/consumer society requires one thing in order to maintain itself, and that one thing is GROWTH; meaning that there must always be more industries, more services, and more products and most especially an ever-growing customer base. This is the inviolable law of the industrial/consumer society. This is true whether we are talking about ancient Rome or modern America. In a growth-based consumer economy, debt is no problem (in fact it is encouraged) so long as there is never-ending growth and regular "cost of living" increases for consumers. So long as growth can be created, enforced, or conjured, the system will continue to *seem* alright. But when growth slows and eventually stops; when resources, be they human, natural, social, cultural, or philosophical, are weakened, drained, or otherwise become scarce, the collapse of that system is inevitable. The result is the collapse and disaster I have described for you in the first few chapters of this book. This collapse is imminent.

DEBT AND YOU

So far we have discussed the debt conspiracy as it has unfolded in time, but what about YOUR debt? There are some things you ought to know. Regardless of its origin, consumer debt is the product of covetousness and greed; both on the part of the lender, and on the part of the borrower. For the borrower, it is the result of convincing himself that he needs things he really doesn't need, or that he needs something *now* that he cannot afford. It is necessary that you take personal responsibility for the sinful attitudes and actions that have put you in slavery. Debt is a result of the colonization of the mind, but we must be willing to confess that our colonization has been willful, because the right answers have always been made available to us. Often unrighteous debt is the result of thinking only "inside the box" that the colonizers have built for us, and it is always the result of not thinking within the boundaries of wisdom and guidance given to us by God. Debt is a problem of ignorance, and it is a beautiful but scary fact that eliminating debt requires eliminating ignorance. It is always possible that the miraculous (or in some cases maybe it is a curse) may occur that will free us from our debt without hard work, but for most of us, becoming free from debt is going to require that we work hard and follow a few important rules:

RULE #1 – SELL EVERYTHING!

Sell everything, because that is the first step in eradicating debt. Consumption and the acquisition of unneeded "stuff" is almost always the primary cause of debt slavery, so reducing consumption and liquidating unnecessary property is going to be a tool of our deliverance.

Here is a neat way to look at this. As in all things, I always try to picture important principles, and I try to do so using history.

In the beginning, "money" was basically these things (and this is by no means an exhaustive list): land, cattle, food (seed, grains, fruit, etc.), spices (those with preservative value), pure water, and a category we will call "other" (meaning items that don't fit neatly into one of these categories, but that had natural and intrinsic value, such as weapons, tools, etc.) You will notice that money was something with a universally accepted store of value. It was something that was worth something in and of itself. It had value because of its utility and because it increased the probability of survival, not necessarily because it could be easily carried or traded for other things of value. For the most part, "money" was something that benefited and advanced the opportunity for survival and the perpetuation of life.

In the next phase, "precious" metals were added as a form of "money." Such metals had value primarily because they were rare, were easily formed or shaped, and because they became widely accepted as a store of value. Initially "precious" metals were traded as bulk metals which were weighed and graded to determine their value; only during the Babylonian era did metal coinage begin to reign.

From there, precious metal coinage became paper, and paper has now become a physical representation of digital debt. Debt is then quantified in the lives of most people by the accumulation and consumption of mountains of historically and eternally useless "stuff".

If you want to see a roadmap showing you how to get back to a place of freedom, you must merely walk backwards through this historical "money" trail. Do your best to divest yourself of historically and eternally useless "stuff". The end goal, of course, is to end up with those things which were considered wealth in the earliest ages. This is the key to surviving off off-grid, and therefore it is the key to our freedom.

As you get rid of your "stuff", try to use every dollar gained by selling "stuff" towards eliminating the future need of more dollars. In other words, try not to spend the money you get from selling personal items except in ways that will eliminate the need for future spending. For example, if you were to sell your furniture and buy bees (or cows, or sheep, or chickens) with it, you will have intelligently utilized the dollars you have gained by the sale of the furniture. With every such exchange you are increasing survivability and viability outside of the system. Remember that every dollar you eliminate in monthly debt (or payment) load is a link off of your chains. When you do spend money, like I said before, try to make sure it goes towards something that will provide more for you in the future.

RULE #2 – SIMPLIFY, SIMPLIFY, SIMPLIFY!

Do not keep things for sentimental value that will have zero real value in your Off-Grid life. In helping people move Off-Grid, I have noticed a few things that might help you as you get started. Many of the people who I have worked with who are moving Off-Grid have started (very wisely) by moving into a much smaller space. For example, if they were going to move into a camper or a small cabin, they would soon find that about 80% or more (probably much more) of the "stuff" they have accumulated will not fit into their new living space. Many of these folks (me included) started out by renting a mini-storage unit because they didn't know what things they might need someday. Well, lo-and-behold, after a year or so of living off-grid, they determined that they never needed that stuff anyway! Almost all of the "stuff" we owned in our previous life became worthless to us in our off-grid life, especially almost anything with a cord attached to it. My advice is to make a very minimal and simplified list of the "stuff" you absolutely will need, and then sell all the rest. It is not a good idea to keep things (and to pay for their storage) just because you might need them some day. Constantly remind yourself to simplify.

It would be an interesting exercise (and illustrative to my point) to sell absolutely everything in order to turn it into some form of money. Take this net value and subtract from it your remaining debt. The amount that is left (for most people this would be a negative number) is your net worth, meaning it is the cumulative value of all the "time saving" and "life enhancing" industrial products and services you have ever purchased. If you are left with a negative number, now divide into it the amount of hours you will have to work to pay for all of those time and labor saving devices the world told you that you needed. Like I said, I'm just making a point. The converse position, however, does not mitigate the point. If after engaging in this fun little exercise you are one of the few who ends up with a positive balance, do not think that your time and labor saving lifestyle has purchased you any time or ease, because it has not. Again, if there were a cataclysmic disaster or economic collapse in the near future, it won't really matter how many "time credits" you think you have accumulated. Rich folks are usually the ones who are the most harshly affected by systemic collapse... something for us all to remember. As the song goes, *"Somebody told me Wall Street fell, but we were so poor we couldn't tell."*

Back to reality. Once you have sold virtually everything; once you have eliminated all the debt that you can eliminate; and once you have simplified your life very radically, then you can get a better picture of your situation. If you still find yourself in debt slavery, it is time to take more drastic action, which leads to Rule #3...

RULE #3 – EDUCATE YOURSELF

"No servant can serve two masters: for either he will hate the one, and love the other; or else he will hold to the one, and despise the other. Ye cannot serve God and mammon" (Luke 16:13).

It is very important at this point that I encourage you to educate yourself on the true nature of "debt" and what God has to say about it. A starting point would be to learn, study, and pray about what *legitimate* debt is, and what *illegitimate* debt is. Study contracts so that you know your rights. Every element of a contract, even if you have entered the contract ignorantly and through blindness, can be used legitimately and righteously for the benefit of those who are parties to the contract. Read the "either... or", or, "if... then" clauses of the contract. There are legitimate, legal, and honorable "outs" for people who have entered into many of these scam contracts. If you are in over your head in a contract for the purchase of a house or a vehicle, consider returning the house or the vehicle to the bank or lender. In many cases this is a viable alternative, and in some cases (provided you still want the house or the vehicle), in our current economy, the lender will be willing to work with you to help retire the debt at a much lower cost, especially if they become aware that they are going to absorb a bigger loss if they are not willing to work with you.

There is much, much more I can say on this topic, but again, it would take an entire book to just lightly handle the subject. I encourage everyone to do your homework and to endeavor with all your abilities to free yourself from the slavery of debt.

In the next chapter, we will discuss "the grid", and the adventure involved with getting untangled from it.

CHAPTER 5
THE GRID

A TRIP THROUGH TIME

In the next chapter we will begin our discussion about actual ways to live without electricity, but first we have to learn a little something about the history of electricity and electrification. We just learned about the evils of the debt culture, and how debt has enslaved people to their own lusts. In the last chapter I told you that debt was one of the biggest links in that chain of slavery - but it is only one link. Our dependence on grid utilities is another link in that slavery chain. The problem I face as a writer is that most people today are profoundly ignorant of history. History is an "off-grid" lamp by which we may guide our feet, and only knowledge and wisdom will set us free from our chains so that we can rightly use the lamp.

To begin our discussion on the electrical grid, I want to take you on a bit of a journey through time to the year 1752, the year that Benjamin Franklin was reputed to have flown a kite with a metal key on it in a dark and stormy Philadelphia sky.

Contrary to how life was still lived in the Old World of Europe, there had developed in the colonies a very broad and thriving middle-class in America. There was a very wide and stark chasm between the very rich and the very poor in the Georgian era in Europe, but in America the large middle-class was considered well-off, landed, and substantially independent and self-sufficient. Travelers through the colonies in the middle of the 18th Century reported that there were few great estates to be seen, and that the bulk of the people lived well and comfortably, even on the smallest land holdings.

Although there were a few very rich people in the colonies in the

1750's, the great mass of the people existed in the comfortable expanse of the middle-class. Yet throughout that middle-class (even in its lowest environs) most farmers considered themselves to be pretty well-off. They answered to no human Lord or royalty. They were masters of all they surveyed. They were able to produce more than their family and their household could consume, and there were no government agents snooping around trying to micro-manage their lives. In short, prior to the Industrial Revolution, *the middle-class free land-holder in the American colonies did not live by fear.*

In Europe, if you were not of the rich, landed, and titled class, you were expected to live your life in the service and fear of rich men with power. It is said that when poor men would see a man on the road wearing a wig, they would flee as if for their lives, because they knew that a wig was a representation of arbitrary political and economic power. In the colonies, very few people (except slaves) knew anything of such fear. In South Carolina, it was virtually impossible to find anyone who was willing to serve in the government, even with the promise of political power, because most men had land and comfort and were responsible to their God and to themselves. They had no desire to exercise power over other men's consciences or lives. In Europe, joining the military was not always voluntary, but it was considered a way to escape the desperation and squalor of abject poverty. In Georgia, the Carolinas, and Virginia, it became difficult to get men to commit to the military defense of the colonies at the behest of the distant King, because even the lower classes considered themselves free gentlemen and they lived good and comfortable lives. Landed freemen had no desire to get mixed up in the King's intrigues when there were negligible benefits and everything to lose. In the northern colonies employers complained that they were forced to pay extraordinary high wages, *even to low-skilled workers*, to keep them at their work, even going so far as bringing employees to their homes to eat at their own tables, because any good man who was a hard worker could easily and inexpensively purchase his own land and begin his own estate as a gentleman farmer (this was before the advent of *ad valorem* taxes). While there were some spectacularly rich and powerful estate and plantation owners who owned thousands, or tens of thousands of acres, 90% of male citizen farmers owned estates of less than 200 acres; in fact, most colonial farms were around 40-50 acres, which was considered the maximum amount of land that a family could work without servants or slaves.

In 1752 in Virginia, virtually every farmer grew at least some tobacco for sale, usually just enough to provide for the next year's cash needs, and almost every farmer had milk and beef cows, pigs, corn, vegetables, and a comfortable house. Yet, we are told by modern educators in public schools and by many historians today that electricity was the great "equalizer" of men, and that all men, except the very rich, were poor, miserable, and downtrodden prior to the electrification of the country. This lie is the product of government paid educators, history revisionists, and henchmen of the industrial elite. **GO DO YOUR OWN RESEARCH!**

This is the point I really want to drive home with this chapter, because in the next chapter we will be discussing alternatives to the way we do things today. The fact is that for 300 years in America there were people living healthy, happy, and productive lives without an electrical grid. And the massive middle class in 1750 was made up of individuals that by every standard of comparison would be considered very, very rich today. Words can be twisted, and can change meaning; educators on the public dole can make anything sound good or true, even lies – but facts are facts. Unhappily for these liars, there were people who wrote things down in **BOOKS** back then, and those books are available for you to go read. Never listen to what some government lackey writing history books for a State University says. Go read the books that were written at the time. On the other hand, since the powers that be know that most people will never go check things for themselves, the lie will continue to be repeated in every public school in America. The Corporate/Government gospel is that you are better off now that you have cheap and readily available electricity, than any generation before electrification. It is heresy to say otherwise. But...

Let's compare... Let's take a modern "middle class" family, maybe yours. Do YOU own 50-200 acres outright? Or do you either rent or owe money on a quarter-acre plot next to people you hardly know? Did you produce a large crop for sale last year without debt? Or were you paid wages to go to work to pay for stuff you don't need? Do you own milk and beef cows, pigs, gardens, fields, pastures and a comfortable house... *all without debt*? Or do you get all your "stuff" from the corporate store, using government scrip backed by debt? Are you indebted to no man, such that you can reject employment offers, offers from the government for positions of power, or for high military office? Are you even solvent? It is a ridiculous assertion for anyone to claim that electrification has made people better off. That cannot be substantiated by any fair investigation. We are fatter. We are more carnally, even criminally, comfortable for a time. We do have more gadgets and entertainment. But we have lost so much more than we have gained.

I think this is the thing that is the hardest for people to grasp, because modernists have been so brainwashed, corrupted, and colonized by less than 100 years of electrification.

As I began to study these things, I was shocked by many of the things that I learned. But, I guess had I been paying attention, I should have been asking questions of my teachers back when I was in school. Like, for example, why do you see so many pictures of southern gentleman and southern ladies dressed up in heavy clothes and coats, even in the summer? Isn't it unmanageably blazing hot in the South in the summer? Without air-conditioning and electricity, wouldn't they all be wearing shorts and t-shirts, standing under some magnolia tree in the shade, cursing the day they were born? Is it possible that those southern plantation houses were actually designed to remain cool in the hot summer? And what's the deal with the lemonade? Didn't those southern rascals know that without refrigeration there could be no ice? And without ice lemonade is just... icky? And how did those Europeans have so many fine soirees, balls and dances after dark? Is it possible that people who never knew anything about electricity found brilliant ways to live good and comfortable lives without it? We've been taught that people were just sitting around, poor and miserable in the dark for thousands of years until some precious industrial savior like Thomas Edison came along and flipped on the light. I found out in my studies that nothing could be farther from the truth.

Do this... I promise you will not be disappointed, and you will learn more than you can imagine. Go get some historical novels: Get Tolstoy's *War and Peace* or *Anna Karenina* (tons of high living, parties, soirees, balls, dancing, etc.); get Thomas Mann's *Buddenbrooks*, or *Magic Mountain*; get Turgenev's *Fathers and Sons*, or *Torrents of Spring*; read Thomas Hardy, Dostoyevsky, or even Mark Twain. (Although I wouldn't do it, you could read Jane Austen, just to make the point) Or, better yet, just go read *Gone With The Wind*. Just pick an era and read novels written during that era. That's what I do - and when you read the books, think about how those people lived and how they did things. Ask yourselves, were these people ignorant cavemen?

Electrification was not, as is often advertised, the end of the dark ages of backwardness and discomfort, when millions of ignorant rubes climbed out from under the rocks of ignorance into the glorious light of Industrial genius and bliss. Electrification was actually the beginning of a new spiritual dark age - It was the enthronement of an old triumvirate: The unholy trinity made up of the lusts of the flesh, the lusts of the eyes, and the pride of life.

Electrification, for most of the world, happened towards the end of what is called the "Second Industrial Revolution." It was the crowning achievement of the whole Industrial Revolution, and brought to fruition the hopes and dreams of the industrialists, the bankers, and the prophets of the new consumer religion.

It is necessary, now, that we go through a quick overview of the Industrial Revolution.

THE FIRST INDUSTRIAL REVOLUTION

The Industrial Revolution, although it was really only one long undivided industrialization process, is often bifurcated into two parts by historians (the First and Second Revolutions). The first revolution began in the 18th Century (roughly between 1760 and the 1780's) with the advent of the factory, the invention of the Spinning Jenny for the mass production of yarn, the improvement of the steam engine, and the development of advanced methods of working iron and other metals. This part of the "Revolution" saw the very beginnings of the factory system. Smokestacks began to sprout from every city skyline like weeds, and masses of people abandoned the farms in large numbers and went to live near the factories. The main historical product of the First Industrial Revolution was that it moved masses of people off of the land and into an urban life. The revolution engendered specialization, so that even those who stayed on the land no longer provided most of the products and services they needed to survive. People, even planters and farmers, became *specialists.* Before the Industrial Revolution, a man might say "I am a farmer", and it was understood to mean that he produced most of the things he and his family needed from the earth. It meant that he had cows, pigs, horses, chickens, gardens, crops, etc. After the Industrial Revolution, a man would say "I am a tobacco farmer", or "I am a cotton farmer". His land was given over to specialization, and he took the money he earned from his cash crop to the "store" to buy the things he needed to survive.

I cannot stress the importance of this understanding enough. If you want to know how to live without electrical handcuffs and chains, you have to have a vision of what life was like when men and women were free. Just as in ancient Rome, people moved in massive numbers from the farms to the cities, and as people became specialized cogs in the urban machine they almost instantly began to lose their survival skills and sense. The wisdom of thousands of years of off-grid living began to atrophy almost immediately. Remember, only a few generations are required to remove valuable skills and knowledge from the collective memory. Once specialization and urbanization began to take hold, the ground was paved for the rapid and radical advances of the Second Industrial Revolution.

THE SECOND INDUSTRIAL REVOLUTION

The Second Industrial Revolution, also called the "Technical Revolution", began in the middle of the 19th century as advancements in rail travel and transport accelerated, and as new shipping technologies (primarily advances in the manufacture of steam ships) multiplied opportunities in trade and commerce. The old adage that "all roads lead to Rome" surpassed even its old literal meaning during this stage. With the advent of mass transportation, urbanization accelerated at a frightening rate. From here we see the rise of the mega-cities, and more and more people would begin to leave home looking for the fabled and mythological "good life" and riches in the city. The New Rome rose up on the banks of the Thames and the Volga, the Hudson, the Rhine and the Seine. Any city with a port had the opportunity of becoming the new Rome, and most of them did. Chicago, on the banks of Lake Michigan, went from a small village of 200 people in 1833, to a city of 3.3 million people only 100 years later in 1933! Almost 2 million of those people arrived in Chicago after the city "went electric" around the turn of the 20th Century.

The Second Industrial Revolution saw major advances in chemistry (such as the refinement of petroleum products), which preceded and laid the groundwork for the oil-centered economy; the invention of the means of mass communication and advertising (telephone, telegraph, radio, etc.); and the invention and mass production of the means of rapid transit (cars, airplanes, etc.). As the population became more mobile, the world shrank noticeably, and just as men and women started to consider the rumors that life might be better near the cities, mass advertising and broadcasting arrived to reinforce that idea. However, the prophets of industrialism knew that everyone wouldn't move to the cities, and they didn't necessarily want them to. The new spiritual Rome is bigger than the walls of any city. If you weren't willing to go to the city, all of the new technologies would soon bring the city to you. *Buy more Ovaltine.* The Second Industrial Revolution saw the mass production of consumer items that would allow the lower and middle-classes the time to pursue other consumptive activities. The advertisers would tell you what to buy, and the magazines and newspapers would show you what areas of "the good life" you were missing. Towards the end of the Second Industrial Revolution came the wide-scale use of machines replacing workers in those industries that were still considered somewhat "agrarian", and, of course, just in time, we would begin to see the electrification of even the most rural areas.

AN INCONVENIENT TRUTH, AND THE RISE OF STATISM

Electrification, marketed by the world's prophets as the "great equalizer" of men and the magic solution to all of man's problems, by any measure (especially in America) has had the opposite of its advertised effect. It has made slaves of virtually all men equally. Between the late 1700's and the 1930's, America (and the whole world) stratified into very clearly delineated social and economic classes. The rich had become richer, and the poor had become poorer. More people had become landless, unskilled laborers, lost in the vast ghettos of the big cities. Left-Wing, Socialist, Marxist, and other statist organizations were formed to protest the inequalities of the system that had promised them equal access to wealth and comfort. Labor unions rose up everywhere, supposedly to protect these landless laborers from exploitation by the prophets and kings of Industrialism; the same prophets and kings who had promised them equality through electrification. Right-Wing statists (akin to our modern neo-con movement) rose up to defend the Industrialists and the Bankers and to bring them under the sway of the more reactionary arms of the government. Thus we have the modern political dialectic, where Leftists and Rightists (statists all) fight one another for the right to plunder the poor and the middle class.

Even today the lie that the Industrial Revolution "created" or expanded the middle-class and broke the power of the landed and the elite is still considered to be unquestionable gospel. Wikipedia, on its Industrial Revolution page, under the category of "Social Effects" says this:

> *"In terms of social structure, the Industrial Revolution witnessed the triumph of a middle-class of industrialists and businessmen over a landed class of nobility and gentry."*

That statement is so absurd that I really cannot believe that anyone would seriously believe it. This myth is **THE BIG LIE** still repeated in classrooms all over the world every day. While it is true that the Industrial Revolution witnessed the triumph of the industrialists and businessmen over the landed class, it is not true that the industrialists and businessmen were "middle-class" while those in the landed class were the "nobility and gentry" (except in Europe). The industrialists and businessmen were the very European bankers and secret-society aristocrats who had so enslaved all of the Old World. According to virtually every honest history I have ever read of the middle 18th Century (which just preceded the Industrial Revolution), the vast middle-class of Americans prior to the Industrial Revolution were "landed". If Industrialization and Electrification was the victory of the "middle-class", where did they end up and where did all their land go? Who were these millions of poor factory workers swarming into the bulging cities of the Industrial world, and where did they come from? The Industrial Revolution destroyed the landed middle-class, shifted millions of people from the country to the cities, and made mind-numbed consumers out of all of them - all the while making billionaires of the already wealthy bankers, businessmen, and industrialists. The fact that the bankers, businessmen, and industrialists were financed and supported by the old monied classes of Europe is established fact. Even the land went to the industrial farmers, who were (and are) just corporate country businessmen, fully owned and operated by the banks and the food merchants and conglomerates.

The Industrial Revolution and Rural Electrification in America brought about the largest transfer of real wealth *from* the lower and middle classes *to* the wealthy elite in the upper class in the history of the world. Communists won't tell you that, and Fascists won't tell you that. No political power will ever tell you that, because none of these statist groups want you to know that REAL wealth lies in the private and individual ownership of land, cattle, and the means and ability to raise crops for sustenance.

URBANIZATION AND CORRUPTION

After the War against Southern Agrarianism, the northern cities, which had once virtually locked their doors against freed slaves or poor whites, threw open their doors to anyone willing to work long hours for very low wages. In the same northern cities and states where blacks had once been unceremoniously thrown into trains and wagons and driven south to advance the purposes of radical abolitionists, freed blacks and poor, disenfranchised whites were now welcomed back by the millions. The cities themselves, and the industrialists who built them, needed two things in order to survive: They needed consumers, and they needed low-skilled (and thus lowly paid) workers. The grid was beginning to take form, and you could get just a glimpse of its outline if you looked closely at the tenements and apartments growing up towards the sky in the ghettos and slums of American cities, or the telegraph poles running alongside the railroad tracks that steamed the commercial goods and products out of the city, out into the world.

In order for the mind to be satisfied in de-humanizing labor, it must first be fragmented and colonized. It must be broken. Workers were given very menial, repetitive tasks, and they were told (rightly so) that there were a thousand people lining up to take their jobs from them. The carrot and the stick were ever-present. There were always billboards and stores that displayed wondrous new products that you might be able to afford someday if only you could manage to work harder and move up in the world; and at the same time there was always the threat that if you slowed down for a minute, even to survey whether you were making any progress, you would lose everything and become a pauper or a vagrant.

Upton Sinclair exposed the inhumanity of this Industrial reality in his book *The Jungle* which displayed the horrible reality of life in the industrial packinghouses of Chicago:

> *"Here is a population, low-class and mostly foreign, hanging always on the verge of starvation and dependent for its opportunities of life upon the whim of men every bit as brutal and unscrupulous as the old-time slave drivers; under such circumstances, immorality is exactly as inevitable, and as prevalent, as it is under the system of chattel slavery." (Upton Sinclair, The Jungle)*

> *"To be tracked by bloodhounds and torn to pieces is most certainly a merciful fate compared to that which falls to thousands every year in Packingtown--to be hunted for life by bitter poverty, to be ill-clothed and badly housed, to be weakened by starvation, cold and exposure, to be laid low by sickness or accident--and then to lie and watch, while the gaunt wolf of hunger creeps in upon you and gnaws out the heart of you, and tears up the bodies and souls of your wife and babies." (Upton Sinclair, The Jungle)*

Of course, the response to the horrible working conditions of the 19th and early 20th Century was not, as we might have hoped, a widespread return to the land. Instead, new power centers (statists in the trade unions and others who claimed to stand for the worker), and political power blocks rose up, and along with power, as we can expect, came corruption.

If you'll remember, when America was still agrarian, wages were very high (disconcertingly so for many employers) because every worker could afford to walk off of his job and go start his own farm. But now, especially with ad valorem property taxes, the land was being bought up by speculators, by the railroads, and by commercial farming interests, so land prices were very high; not to mention that these urban workers had already abandoned that old life, putting all their eggs in one industrial basket. There was no "home" to which they might return.

Most of the things being produced by the new industrial society were things that, only 30 years earlier, nobody knew they needed. But the new world system would absolutely require that these unknown needs be made known; and not just these, but a million more needs would have to be created. This "manufacture of needs" would multiply rapidly with the advent of electrification and the arrival of the oil-based economy.

In 1752, no one could have imagined the need for a cable that would bring electrical current into every house, farm, or business in America. That spring, when Benjamin Franklin supposedly tied a key to that kite string and sent it up into that stormy Pennsylvania sky, he could not have imagined what would come down the line along with the electricity. Safe, cheap, and readily available electricity would be the springboard for the "manufacture of needs". And it started so simply...

SELLING THE AMERICAN DREAM (NIGHTMARE)

Think of it. Electricity was easy to sell, and the American dream hinged on it. It was probably one of the easiest sales jobs ever. With electricity in your house and barn you won't have to produce, make, store, or buy candles, fat, or kerosene. Imagine just walking up and pulling on a chain and having your room *flooded* with light! Think of getting up at night to go to the restroom, and not having to light a candle or a lantern. Then, think of all the things you can do now that it won't be dark all night. Your day can start earlier and end later! Think of all the time you will save! (*ching, ching!* goes the time bank) And, if you already have power coming to your house to provide electric light, why not think of what a refrigerator will do for you... and a freezer... and a washer and dryer, and an iron, and an electric stove. I mean, you already have electricity, why would you deny yourself *the good things in life?* All of these can be added for a nominal fee, and each (on its own) is relatively cheap to operate. And if you cannot afford them all right now, you can get credit at the store or from the manufacturer. You can pay it off by the month in easy payments. Of course, you'll have to work harder and longer hours, but that should be easy with all that electric light right at your fingertips. If it gets to the point where your farm will not support all the new payments you've accrued, you can always get a job in town... but you'll need a car... and insurance... and your taxes will go up so you can have a nice road to drive on... but, then, your wife can get a job too.

Electrification was supposed to make everyone equal, but it precipitated the largest transfer of real wealth in all of history. Electrification was supposed to save everyone time and money, but it caused people to work harder and longer hours, and eventually necessitated that both parents go to work in order to finance the costs of all those newly manufactured needful things. Electrification was supposed to broaden horizons and educate and free the masses from ignorance and superstition, but instead it shrunk the world and, through specialization, created generations of ignorant, unviable, colonized, debt-burdened slaves. Electrification destroyed the concept of local community, and replaced it with a faceless global metropolis operating by a soulless global morality.

The most important victim of electrification and the industrial revolution was the Biblical concept of family. In 1752, most Americans would live their entire lives and rarely travel more than a county away from their homes. Most children, when they were in need of care, instruction, or wisdom, had both parents around them all of the time. If they needed older wisdom, or some historical perspective, they could usually walk less than a mile and talk to aunts, uncles, grandma or grandpa, and usually great-grandma or great-grandpa (who probably remembered what life was like in the "old world"). If they needed a doctor, he would come to your house, and he'd probably take milk, eggs, or butter as payment.

By 1852, the destruction of this distinct way of life was on its way, but it was only then on the horizon. The war against Agrarianism and the old paths was still on the drawing board in 1852, but it was as inevitable as the sunrise. The winds of war were already blowing through the boardrooms of Yankee corporations, and the sanctuaries of the corporate churches. The prophets of syncretism were already stirring the pot of greed and covetousness. The factories were already belching black smoke into the skies over hundreds of cities and the power elite were growing ever richer as the trickle of country folk moving into the cities became a flood.

At the turn of the 20th Century, the march towards global slavery was just becoming a full gallop. In ten short years, mankind would leap farther forward technologically than he had in the previous 3000 years put together. By 1910, the world had seen the invention, or the widespread adoption of electricity, air-conditioning, commercial refrigeration of meats and foods, the telephone, the radio, the automobile, and the airplane.

By 1952, 200 years after Ben Franklin flew his kite, the transformation was mostly complete. A couple of world wars had put an end to what was left of America's once dominant farming heritage, and most Americans had lost any cultural memory of the old Agrarian world that had given birth to so much freedom and wealth. Many people claim that the last Confederate war veteran died that year, and only a few years later, in 1956, the last Union veteran died. With them died any memory of what America had been like before the bankers and corporate interests had induced them to fight over it.

In the 200 years covered in this chapter, America went from a land peopled with strong, intelligent, and virtuous farmers; a people who had benevolently conquered the land and the elements, and who had lived lives of relative peace and freedom; to a land of consumer slaves and thoughtless eaters; a nation of people who allowed the land and their most sacred cultural traditions to be raped and destroyed for the benefit of the very rich and powerful.

Historically a "bastard" is someone who doesn't know his own father, or who is of questionable heritage. Today, when I speak to people about living without electricity, the eyes of most of them glaze over and I can see that they have no concept of their own history. They are intellectual, cultural, and economic bastards, orphaned in the land of their fathers. "How can anyone live without electric light?" they say, "Without air-conditioning? Without refrigeration? And, who would want to? Impossible! Only a fool or a sadist would even entertain such a thought." By such ignorant statements, we have become a nation of slanderers, defaming our own ancestors; a nation of wasters who squander the intellectual, moral, and social resources of a people who were far greater than we are.

In the next chapter, we are going to begin to learn how to live successfully without being attached to the "grid". Specifically, we will talk about light and heat.

CHAPTER 6
LIGHT AND HEAT

When the excitement of rural electrification began sweeping the country in the 1920's and 1930's it would have been hard to imagine that one day, turning off a light might be a revolutionary act. In 1925, less than half of the 6.3 million American farms were receiving centralized electric services. By the late 30's a large majority of the remaining farms had electricity; and by the early 1970's, fully 98% of American farms and homesteads were "on-grid".

As you can see, moving away from grid electricity, or from any electricity at all, is certainly a move against an enormous tide. As a philosophy, de-electrification is *Contra Mundum* (against the world). When rural electrification programs multiplied during the early and middle decades of the 20th Century, very few people ever even stopped to ask themselves whether or not it was a good idea. The world said it was good; the government said it was good, the flesh said it was good, so it must be good. *Electricity = Good* became an unquestionable and unassailable maxim in the minds of the developed world, and as the generations passed, this presupposition became "hard wired" into new young brains being raised completely on-grid. The brain works very similarly to the wiring in a house. In an on-grid house, so long as there is not some devastating disaster, some horrible accident, an electrical short, or some purposeful re-wiring, the electricity tends to always make the same route through the house. It doesn't just decide to re-route itself through the studs or the through the sheetrock. If no change is made or nothing radical happens, it always does what it always has done. Therefore each successive generation is raised in a world where electrification is automatically considered good by default (or it isn't even considered, because it is always there and never in question). Where electricity is ubiquitous, somewhat affordable, and necessary to maintain the world's preferred lifestyle, the juice just keeps running down the line, and nobody ever questions if there might be another way... or considers that someday, the juice may stop.

DECOLONIZATION IS RE-WIRING

Generally, in order for some change to be made in the way things have always been done, something radical, subversive, or revolutionary has to happen. Some event has to cause the entire system to be questioned. When remodeling is done on a house, or if there is some short or wiring problem that demands that the wiring be examined or re-considered, only then does the whole system fall under scrutiny. There are many such "shorts" and wiring problems going on in the world today. There is a lot of remodeling going on too. The world seems like an old house whose wiring has become frayed and dangerous. Perennial warfare, terrorism, statism, pervasive government spying on the people, the destruction of the nutritive value of the food supply, the slow death of the petroleum based economy, recession, depression, globalism, etc., are causing many people to go through a wholesale reassessment of modern life and living. The whole system is being re-examined, and a lot of people are coming to the conclusion that something is horribly wrong, and that the accepted ways of the past may not be sustainable or even desirable.

The problem is that when *electrification as gospel* has been so hard-wired into the system (and into the brain) for so long, the concept of just pulling out the wires altogether to save the house does not usually ever occur to most people. So, the default response is: "If grid power is the problem, or is unreliable, then I *might* consider going 'off-grid'", but by that they usually mean, "I will consider having my own alternative power". There is usually not a question as to the manner or foundation of living; the question is usually only about what source is to be used to maintain the current way of living. Therefore, alternative power becomes the next unchallenged gospel.

ALTERNATIVE POWER IS NOT THE SOLUTION. IT IS AN ALTERNATIVE PROBLEM

When most people begin thinking about living off-grid, they automatically think about electricity, and how in the world anyone could possibly live without it. This is not at all to say that electricity (or a dependence on it) is our greatest weakness as a people, or that the electrical grid is the system that is solely responsible for our mental colonization and slavery. In fact, many different but complementary systems (such as the petroleum products system, or the JIT philosophy of provisioning) are just as potentially dangerous and could possibly be even more addictive. I have started our discussion with electricity in order to exemplify the nature and tendencies of "the grid" as a whole, because electricity is the most illustrative and the easiest to understand portion of the varied systems that make up the larger industrial and consumer driven grid. However, it would be an error to think that the electrical grid is the only (or even always the primary) system that makes up the grid. The grid is the whole chain of enslavement – dependence on electricity and the "time saving" promises it makes is just a link in the chain.

The electrical grid is not the whole grid, but, it is often the most ubiquitous of the varied grid components so we interact with it more completely and become dependent on it at a younger age than we do with the other parts. My explanations of the differences between Off-Grid and Off Off-Grid living in the first chapter go a long way towards explaining how these smaller but sometimes more pervasive and addictive systems can become just as dangerous and poisonous to our well-being as the mainstream electrical grid system. For example, if in "going off-grid" someone were to just replace all electricity and all electrical grid components with a substitute grid system made of non-electric machines running entirely on petroleum based fuels (say... propane, gasoline, or diesel), has the problem really been solved? During a widespread disruption or disaster, or even in the very likely situation where the price of oil, and the products made from it, skyrockets again, anyone dependent petroleum based fuels would quickly (or eventually) find themselves in an unviable and unsustainable situation. They would eventually be in precisely the same situation as those who choose to remain on the mainstream electrical grid. Our dependence and addiction to petroleum based fuels is just as debilitating as our dependence on cheap and readily available grid electricity, but when the mind of modern man wrestles with what it considers to be the impossibility (or difficulty) of living life off of the grid, it focuses initially on the benefits and the "necessity" of electricity (or "power"), and only secondarily, if ever, does it consider adopting a life without the machines that use that power.

It is automatically assumed by some people that by having an alternative power system, or redundant "backup" systems, we are immune to, or protected from, disruptions or the loss of critical systems. But, this is only true in the short run. Let me give you some examples:

EXAMPLE #1: ON-GRID WITH ALTERNATIVE POWER BACKUP

A man I know lives his life using regular grid power, but he has prepared his whole house to also run on alternative power in an emergency. In this case he has gas generators for lights, refrigeration, cooling, etc., and he has a large reserve propane system for heating and cooking. His assumption is that by having redundant systems, if the electrical power grid fails he will still be able to maintain most of his "critical" systems using the alternative grid he has developed; this is true, at some level. He will be able to operate for longer than those who are solely dependent on the grid, but, if the disruption lasts long enough, or is serious enough, his private grid will also eventually fail. His plan is better than no plan at all, but in the long run it is also unsustainable. Alternative power systems are also quite expensive. So, we have to ask, "How much did the alternative power back-up system in this example cost?" Well, in this case it was probably somewhere in the $5000-$7000 range, and that was many years ago. How much time did it buy? Without a pretty serious storage system for gasoline, even with rationing, the generators will likely only be useful for a couple of months. This means that all of the systems that currently require electricity will be unusable after the gas runs out. In this case that means that, since this is the primary means of food preservation and storage, the food and water supply will be questionable after only a few months of service disruption. The propane storage system will provide a bigger cushion. If all things remain equal (meaning there are no system failures, no accidents, leaks, or disasters, and no added needs that cause the propane to be used at a faster rate) this man would have a few years of heating and cooking utility, *If* his propane tanks are full when the failure or emergency happens. This plan, though better than a purely on-grid lifestyle, is quite expensive for what it actually delivers, and in the event of an extended emergency this system will likely be a failure. My analysis does not take into account that a long-term emergency is likely to be preceded by huge and rapid increases in the price of fuels and parts, which are likely to weaken the overall survival plan. This philosophy relies too much on services and materials that are unsustainable and unreliable.

EXAMPLE #2: ALTERNATIVE POWER WITH PREPAREDNESS BACKUP

In this example, a man and his family actually do go "off-grid". They build a rural cabin and power their off-grid life using solar (*photovoltaic*) panels and wind generators. They have a gasoline generator for back-up power or for support when there are long periods without sun or adequate wind, but the generator is not considered "mission critical", so the system will function without it. The family has electric lights with kerosene lamps as backup, and also uses their off-grid electricity to power a freezer and a refrigerator. Now, this family has also done some research, and they have stored up supplies in case they lose the utility of their off-grid electrical system. They have a woodburning stove in storage, and have stocked up on canning supplies, candles, dehydrated foods, and other emergency essentials. How good is this plan? Well, it is much better than the situation in the first example, but again, this is a very, very expensive plan and it has many weaknesses. Altogether, in this situation, you would likely be looking at an initial "getting off-grid" cost of well over $20,000 (not counting structure construction) *and probably much more than that.* And the lifestyle is still dependent on a system that is susceptible to breakdowns, interruptions, and scarcity of parts and supplies.

Most people who are not already living an off-grid life, but who are considering one, believe that solar or wind power is some miracle way to receive "free" electricity. This is hardly the case, as we have mentioned before. These systems require batteries, and even if one is able to afford large, long-life, high-capacity batteries, they are susceptible to problems and failures. These batteries do have to be replaced eventually, and they are capable of failing long before their usual expected life span. On my off-grid solar power system, I had two of the twenty original batteries fail within months of initiating the system, and my story is not unique. Quite often, when you are new at utilizing an alternative power system, user error can cause failures in batteries and other components. It is an unhappy fact that when you have one of these batteries fail, if it is not identified and replaced immediately, it will usually cause a cascading problem of failures in the other batteries in the system. One or two weak or ineffective batteries will usually ruin the rest of the batteries in the system in short order. I know people who have had to replace their entire battery bank after this type of cascading battery failure. So, what if their failure happened after some game-changing disaster or crisis?

While it is true that the family in our example #2 has made emergency plans for living off of their alternative power grid, if they are not regularly practicing how to use and do these things effectively then they could end up in real trouble trying to do so in an emergency situation. We have learned from our experiences that everything we do takes trial and error, practice, practice, and more practice. If people do not learn by real, hands-on experience what works and what does not work, then all the survival equipment and supplies in the world may not account for much in the long run. It is much harder to go completely off off-grid by necessity, immediately, in a crisis, than it is to do so deliberately and methodically before the crisis. And, if a drastic situation catches the family unawares, it is likely that they will have invested a lot of money and resources in a questionable system that they may lose the use of in a long emergency.

Could those resources have been better spent? Would it be better if this family had spent even a portion of that money going completely off of the grid to begin with? Would it have been wiser to start living that life almost immediately; to follow a deliberate and methodical plan so that their lives would not be so radically altered after a major disruption? Almost no one ever considers the fact that massively changing a lifestyle and manner of living *while under stress* and while in possible danger is always an endeavor fraught with peril. Would you ever say, "I'll learn to swim when I fall out of the boat?"

Here is a shocking fact: Starting and living a life without these alternative power systems is much cheaper, and, in the long-term, much safer than any of the alternatives. I would say that one of the comments I hear the most from people who contact me for counsel or advice is this: *"I want to move off-grid and live a simpler, plainer, and more deliberate way of life... but I cannot afford to do it now."* It seems ridiculous to have to say, but it is easier and cheaper to not have electricity at all, than it is to purchase and operate an alternative energy system and then have to abandon it or bypass it when it becomes unusable or unsustainable. Most people are only looking at the problem as an "A" or "B" choice:

a. Remain on the grid, which is expensive but means no expensive start-up costs; or,

b. Move into an "off-grid" (and by this they mean "alternative power") lifestyle which can be very expensive at start-up.

It is NOT an "A" or "B" Choice!

This will take some explaining and illustration, but our solution (Option "C", or, "None of the Above") could very well be the right choice.

Unhappily, many folks from every conceivable location on the spectrum of political and social opinion have focused on the wrong things when it comes to going Off-Grid. Many environmentally conscious liberals have focused their energies on alternative electricity applications as a solution to global and individual concerns. They tout electric cars and focus on maintaining a "smaller carbon footprint", as if reducing our dependence on petroleum products and shifting that dependence onto electrical power (which is generally, but not always, somewhere along the line, produced with petroleum products) will fix every problem. Even if we say we have created our electricity with solar power or wind power it is very likely that the components of our alternative power systems are all made using grid electricity and petroleum products, and many of those components themselves are manufactured in a way that, in the long term, is unviable or destructive. Let's look at a prime example.

Lithium Batteries

Whenever off-grid living is mentioned in conversation, or in magazines, or on most internet sites, virtually every bit of the conversation revolves around alternative energy sources. In fact, I do not think it would be unfair to say that for most people, the phrase "off-grid" merely means "alternative energy". The accepted "off-grid" wisdom is that if you find a newer and better source of power (to do all of the same things you already do), then you are on your way to viability, sustainability, and off-grid bliss. Because this has been the accepted wisdom, much time and energy is now focused on alternative ways of capturing and storing electricity for off-grid use. Of late, a lot of that energy and focus has been on the recent advancements in battery technology, particularly *Lithium* batteries.

Lithium has been promoted by many environmentalists and by corporations as the miracle element that is going to save the planet. Most modern hybrid and electric vehicles utilize Lithium batteries for the storage of electricity. In fact, many off-grid homes and businesses use Lithium batteries for storing the electricity captured via solar panels or wind generators. Lithium is supposed to be the miracle solution to our unhealthy and destructive dependence on a dwindling supply of oil in the world. When you see a Hollywood star driving around in a hybrid vehicle and pontificating about how they are "minimizing their carbon footprint", and how they are saving the planet by using "alternative energy", you have found someone who has been brainwashed by the new Lithium cult. Here is another little tidbit for you to consider when you are looking into these things. ***When someone is selling you something, always question their statistics.*** Remember, there are "lies, damned lies, and statistics", which is to say that salesmen are very good at making the numbers say whatever they like. The truth is that Lithium is maybe a worse bet than is oil for the future, and it has many of the same problems as petroleum... only, there is less of it.

As an element, Lithium is relatively rare – which ought to surprise you if you listen to the mainstream Off-Grid and alternative energy people. Most of the world's Lithium is unusable because it exists in rocks and in ocean water at very, very low parts per million (ppm); and most of that Lithium is of very low grade. Fully half of the world's usable reserves of Lithium are in the Salar de Uyuni area of Bolivia - historically an unstable country with a long history of revolutions and civil wars. The next largest reserves of Lithium are found in Chile and China. Lithium is not only a comparatively rare element, but access to most of it could be cut off at any time. In every respect, Lithium is a rarer and more unstable element of energy storage system than is oil. Lithium just doesn't get as much bad press because it doesn't have a tailpipe with black smoke coming out of it.

Just as I was writing this chapter General Motors announced that it will soon begin selling its Chevy Volt hybrid vehicle and the announcement perfectly illustrates my point. The car manufacturer shocked the world when it announced that the Volt was preliminarily rated at *230 miles per gallon!* (Subsequent to this it was learned that the real mileage was closer to 40 mpg) I have watched with interest as the press feeding frenzy ensued. But is the Volt a solution to the problems it is meant to address? I don't think so. The car will reportedly cost close to $40,000, which means that almost every customer who buys one will be accepting as much as twice the amount of debt than that which they would have otherwise adopted if they had purchased a conventional vehicle of the same size and class. Think about that. That means that people will have to work even harder, and it will take many more years of payments to service that debt in order to afford the car. Every one of these "invisible" elements is not considered when the salesmen and their statisticians compute energy consumption, by the way. These cars have to be plugged into an outlet every night, meaning that they will be drawing electricity from the power grid, which will increase both the burden on an already over-burdened power grid, and the amount of money that these consumers will have to pay on their power bills each month. The statisticians say, "Yes, but this is cheaper and more plentiful "off-peak" power," but that is only true if the cars don't catch on with the public. In other words, it is only true if the Volt fails. When the salesman or statistician makes that claim, he is acting like he assumes he will fail, because clearly if their sales scheme succeeds, then *everyone* will be plugging their car in at night... right? All of this means even more work and more debt for the customer, and in some cases, more fuel consumption by the power companies, many of which use coal and petroleum products to create power.

AND WHAT ABOUT THE LITHIUM-ION BATTERY?

In a recent interview, one of the Vice-Presidents of General Motors claimed that the battery would be expected to last "10 years", but when he was subsequently asked what it would cost to replace the battery, he refused to say. One reason he might be reticent to give a price is because the Volt uses Lithium-Ion batteries, and it is hard to say whether anyone will be able to acquire or afford a replacement Lithium -Ion battery in ten years. And these are only the beginnings of the possible problems with this shell-game. In an interview with the Seattle Times, then Vice-Chairman Bob Lutz admitted that the first-generation Volt was *not expected to generate a profit for GM*. GM, due to the recent bailout mess, is primarily owned by the United States government, meaning that it is likely that more taxpayer money will be required to keep this company in business... so that they can sell more unprofitable cars to more people who don't want them, engaging them in more debt, engendering more consumption, which will put more strain on the grid system, which will raise the prices of grid electricity! If you are a taxpayer and you use grid power, you are now paying for a new Chevy Volt, even if you don't ever get to drive one!

My point here, of course, is to illustrate how our problem is not one little element of the system (like petroleum or grid electricity) that we need to work around. Those who think that electricity is the solution to our oil dependency have not really seen the scope of the problem. Here is a clue... when you admit that we (or you particularly) have a dependence on something; whether it be oil, electricity, or donuts for that matter, the next step is to admit that the problem is *dependency*, not oil, electricity, or donuts.

THE PROBLEM IS DEPENDENCY

This is going to sound shocking, so you might have to take a moment to let it soak in... *Dependence* is *the opposite* of *Independence*. Seriously. Think about it.

But the problem does not just run one way. Just as there are those who have declared war on oil and so-called "fossil fuels", and have insisted that alternatively derived electricity is the answer, there are a whole lot of people who have gone precisely in the other direction. Many survivalists, "preppers", and Off-Grid folks have eschewed the electrical grid system only to replace that system with petroleum consuming generators and other non-electric energy hogs that are just as likely to ensnare them in their own comforts and lusts, and are just as likely to leave us dependent on things and systems that are undependable. You see, our answer is not going to be found by focusing on the power source. The solution is not in finding new or better ways to feed some really bad and destructive habits. The solution is not in finding safer and more sustainable ways to keep our families and communities addicted to consumption and entertainment. The solution will be found by focusing on how the decisions we make really and truly affect us and our loved ones and our progeny. We have become slaves, not to products or to energy sources, but to our dependence on those energy sources to power our destructive lifestyles. Dependency and slavery are not new things.

OPTION "C" - NONE OF THE ABOVE.

For centuries, indeed for millennia, mankind lived and thrived without any kind of power grid. Just as the wild pigs of the swamp once lived freely without fences or bags of corn, man once lived freely by the sweat of his brow and by his intelligence and God's grace. Electrical dependency is a relatively new phenomenon, and it is only the historical ignorance, covetousness, and slavish colonized mind of the worldling that has convinced him that it will be difficult or impossible to leave the system. It would be fascinating and illustrative if we could hear one of today's sad, anemic, industrially raised, commercial pigs tell one of the wild and free pigs of the Okefenokee Swamp that it is impossible to live free; or that somehow his slavish life is better than the life of freedom.

Sometimes a semblance of the truth even escapes through the modern media. George Clooney's character in the movie *Oh, Brother Where art Thou?* - which takes place in the 1930's - had this to say about the soon to come electrical grid:

> *"Everything's gonna be put on electricity and run on a payin' basis. Out with the old spiritual mumbo jumbo, the superstitions, and the backward ways (**author's note: "spiritual mumbo-jumbo" and***

140

"superstitions" means Christianity, and "backwards ways" means Agrarianism... just so you know). *We're gonna see a brave new world where they run everybody a wire and hook us all up to a grid. Yes, sir, a veritable age of reason. Like the one they had in France. Not a moment too soon if you ask me."*

Of course those of us who know history know what the Age of Reason in France produced... a little thing called *The Reign of Terror* that claimed 40,000 victims (almost half by guillotine) in about a year. You see, it was a slippery slide, as human sin always is. Men who insist on living contrarily to the commands of God always see regression as progress, and always believe that the next, newest, "age" will solve all of their problems. During the Dark Ages, it was believed that all knowledge could be apprehended via the Pope and the "church" alone. Next to come was the Age of Reason which held that all knowledge could be gained via *reason* alone, which proved to be a grievous error since reason is always limited by finite knowledge and by the natural depravity of man. Next came the Age of Enlightenment, which held that all knowledge could be gained by the use of reason subjected to the five senses, which led to some nice music and art but a lot of scientific quackery and junk philosophy. Next came the Age of Rebellion, which held that reason and the senses were useless unless they existed at the right end of a gun. Next came the Age of Industry, which said that reason and knowledge were only useful in the pursuit of gain and growth... of riches, esteem, property, "leisure time", etc. Next came the Age of Information, which holds that all of the benefits of all the previous ages can be had at 1/2 price and with little or no work if everyone will just log on and sign in, shop at the same stores, wear the same clothes, watch the same shows, and bow to the same false "gods"; uniformity in desires will bring uniform prosperity. Coming next, of course, will be the Age of Judgment, where all of these ideas and all those who have succumbed to them will stand before a righteous God who gave men freedom, intelligence, and abundant resources, and commanded them to live benevolently and lightly on the earth, and to be good stewards of His gifts.

Abandoning the grid is possible, and, in fact, our survival may depend on it. Again, the immediate tendency of those who do have the desire to move off-grid, is to find a way to keep doing all of the same things, only without being attached to the public utility grid. I must continue to protest that, although going off-grid in this way can be a meaningful intermediate step, in the long run it only moves us one step further from danger and from the overall problem of dependency; and it leaves us susceptible to long term outages, and exposes us to disaster if (more likely, when) the resources and materials necessary to maintain our own off-grid "grid" disappear or become impossible to get. Neither is moving off-grid in the traditional way inexpensive or easily manageable by most people.

If we are going to free ourselves, we must be willing to look further than our first instincts. We must study alternate methods of doing everyday tasks, and understand that sometimes we may only reach a good and final solution by means of trial and error, as well as by the use of intermediate means. Realize that you are on an adventure, and that "off-grid" is not a destination, it is just part of the journey.

STEPPING OUT

Your journey can start like ours did. We were ignorant of what to do and there wasn't a whole lot of information available when we first got started. In the very beginning, we simply decided to turn off the lights and use them as little as possible. Subsequently we bought oil lanterns and began to use them when it would grow dark. Sitting in the flickering light of our oil lanterns actually helped us to better imagine ourselves moving closer to a simpler, more traditional, and more deliberate way of life. Utilizing oil lanterns, especially when the oil is petroleum based oil can only properly be seen as an intermediate step, so here would be a good place for me to review the philosophy of "intermediate means". Hopefully this is a helpful digression:

Any solution that requires that you continue *indefinitely* to buy something that you cannot make or produce on your own is only a

temporary or stop-gap solution. We refer to it as an "intermediate means" or an "intermediate step." Ask yourself what would happen if some type of long-term disaster or world changing event were to occur. How long would you be able to keep doing some of the things you are doing now if the world was never again going to revert back to what you now consider normal? If Alaric invaded America today and destroyed the civilization and sent everyone who survived into a new Dark Age, what would that mean to you? "Intermediate means" are those things we may use for a short time, recognizing that they cannot be our final and lasting solution.

An intermediate step could be anything from, say, selling your house and furniture and moving into an inexpensive apartment or camper, to getting a part time job that allows you more time to work on developing your homestead. Intermediate steps can be anything from a propane freezer on your way to an icehouse, a refrigerator on your way to a root cellar, or a propane heater on your way to a wood burner. It is often both inevitable and necessary that we make use of intermediate means towards our ultimate goal. This is why my blog is entitled *The Process Driven Life*, since we confess that obedience to God and our work for Him here on earth, is a *process* not a *destination*. We, as Christians, are to be process driven and not purpose driven. Ultimate purposes and results belong to God, but obedience is ours.

Moving from grid electricity to some intermediate means (like propane, kerosene lamps, generators, solar power, etc.) is not only acceptable, it is a fine intermediate step, and sometimes it may be necessary. It would always be preferable, of course, in a perfect world, for us to intelligently and deliberately move directly to a life with no reliance on unsustainable means. But we must confess that this is not usually possible for most people. Intermediate means are often necessary, and, so long as we recognize the inherent weaknesses in being dependent on intermediate means, and, so long as we take steps to mitigate that dependence and the ultimate damage that could occur when (and if) our ability to use these means is lost, then we may use them to help us separate from the world system. An example: There is nothing inherently wrong with my using a battery operated drill so long as I recognize the inherent weaknesses in the dependence on battery power, and so long as I recognize that this battery powered drill may not always be available to me. If I make plans for being able to continue my work if battery powered drills become useless or unavailable to me, *and* if I practice and become sufficiently skilled in using non-electric means, then I am in a better, more survivable situation, and I am not operating from a position of weakness. This same philosophy, then, should be applied to everything we do.

With all that said, let me issue you a warning: **There is a very real and great danger to our well-being and our eventual freedom from the grid system to rely inordinately on, or to trust in, intermediate means.**

It may be hard to get your mind around what I am saying, because I am not condemning intermediate means. I am not even saying that you *absolutely must* move past them to some perfect, idyllic, pre-industrial/agrarian life and that the use of any of them after that is heresy. Some of us will likely always be using some intermediate means. I am saying a right survival mindset requires that you be able to see things rightly, and to recognize your natural proclivity to *not* do things all the way, and your likelihood to rely inordinately on intermediate means.

The basic point is that we must employ our *reason* during the process of going off-grid. Let's don't get too focused on not paying an electric bill and forget the real reasons we want to be independent from the system. Besides, if you pay $20,000 to $30,000 or more to go off of the electrical grid, and eventually end up in precisely the same place or situation as those who stayed on the grid, haven't you just pre-paid your electric bill, only at a much higher price?

WHAT WOULD GREAT-GREAT-GRANDAD DO?

It is not a permanent or final solution to replace electric lights with kerosene lanterns for lighting *unless* you can make, or have an endless supply of, kerosene. Unless you can produce kerosene or some other type of burnable, safe, lighting oil - like maybe olive oil - then lanterns may not be your solution. Sure, you can store kerosene, but you can't store enough, and eventually, if the emergency lasts long enough, you will run out. This is doubly important to realize when you know what is going on with our petroleum supplies in this world. You cannot depend on having ANY petroleum product in the future. Period. So kerosene lanterns are not a permanent survival solution. They can be considered an intermediate step as you disconnect from the power grid, but they ought not to be considered a permanent or long-term solution.

So how do we come up with good answers? Remember, I told you this is more of a "why to" than a "how to" book. We might even say it is a "how to think" book, instead of a "how to" book. So... how do we think about these things?

A good way to find solutions to these types of questions is to ask yourself what your forefathers did. How did our ancestors solve this problem 100 or 200 years ago? Do some research and keep going backwards until you find a solution that worked in the past, because those solutions will usually still work today.

Every aspect of your life has to be looked at from this point of view. It is good to be off-grid and to be able to live separate from the system using intermediate means, like propane, diesel, kerosene, solar power, etc. But in the long run we can become enslaved to those things just as easily as we were enslaved to the grid, and, if our lifestyle doesn't change; if we don't become more obedient and different from the world, then we will have merely delayed the inevitable.

Start the process now by thinking about water, heat, light, cooling, and food production, preservation, and storage; and do so using the same methodology I have described in this chapter. Research the past and ask yourself, "How did my ancestors do this?" Think of all of these things and come up with a system (a road map) that will get you where you need to be. Ask for help. Ask questions. Listen. Learn.

WHAT DO WE DO WITH ELECTRICITY ANYWAY?

When people first consider going completely off the electrical grid, a few categories of perceived needs come to mind (I say "perceived", because we are going to rethink these all quite a bit):

1. Lighting
2. Heat
3. Air-conditioning
4. Refrigeration/Food Preservation (Ice!)
5. Tools and Appliances

In the remainder of this chapter, we will discuss the first two categories: Light and Heat. In the next chapter, we will discuss the remaining three categories.

LIGHTING

How did your ancestors handle the lighting issue? I am going to give you the most obvious, yet shocking answer right up front...

When it got dark, most of our forefathers (and foremothers) went to bed.

That's an intriguing thought, and one that most people will never consider. Although there were folks in previous generations who wrote, studied, laughed, loved, and lived by candlelight or lanterns, for most of history, when darkness fell, the regular folk just went to bed. Not everyone could afford to buy, or had the materials to make, an endless supply of candles. There is something to be said for the natural tides of night and day, light and darkness. God created these contrasting periods for a reason. In the Bible, we are exhorted to work while it is day, for the *"night cometh, when no man can work"*, which seems me to hint that maybe our work should be done during the day. I suspect that there are many unrealized benefits to regulating our lives by God's natural seasons of light and darkness.

Candles are an option, *if* you can make them and *if* you can continue to produce the "stuff" from which they are made. Natural candles (such as beeswax candles) could also be a very good solution for those people who, for some reason or other, are not willing to utilize animal by-products for lighting. If you don't want to raise cows or pigs, maybe raising bees can be a workable solution for you.

On our ranch we raise pure Texas Longhorn cattle and we raise pigs, so we can make tallow and fat candles. Candles made from animal fat are a great, renewable solution, but we also need to realize that, in a long-term crisis, they will be precious and we will not want to burn them all up every night. When it is dark, going to bed is a good option, and it was the option used most often by the working-class people who tilled the land.

For lighting, in my family, we are currently still straddling the passage between intermediate means, and being totally off off-grid. As I am writing this, we use a mixture of solar power, kerosene lanterns, and homemade fat lamps or candles. As you can see, we have moved from a completely unsustainable source (grid electricity), to an unsustainable, but better, off-grid intermediate step (solar power and kerosene lanterns), and we are currently experimenting with a more sustainable, inexpensive, and readily available source (animal fat). Several of the families here in our off-grid community will be making a more substantial foray into using fat lamps and candles this year, on our way to going totally off off-grid as soon as we are able. It is also our goal to begin raising bees and making candles from the beeswax, both for personal use and perhaps for sale as well.

As I have said often in this chapter, solar power can be a very good intermediate solution, but it is not a permanent one. In order for solar power to be good for powering lights at night there must be some form of battery storage, and, as we have already discussed, batteries are an iffy proposition. In the future, they may be virtually impossible to get. As I mentioned in the discussion on Lithium, the promise and sustainability of long-term battery storage is a very deceptive con and ought not to be trusted. If you have solar power now, or if you anticipate getting solar power, do like I do and think of it as a 1-5 year head start on making yourself candle rich.

Currently, I do use small AA or AAA rechargeable batteries, and I use several different methods to recharge them. This allows me to do most of my work without having to go back and forth to town. In a crisis, the things I use batteries for are not mission critical, so I will not be at a loss to live without them. Small batteries are a good intermediate solution and they help us to do a lot of things we need to do right now as we are on our journey out of the system. I have several very low power LED lamps, as well as a few reading lights and flashlights. Usually, I try to buy items that take AA batteries, but some of the items use AAA. I buy NiMH rechargeable batteries in bulk and I recharge them using several different methods. I own a couple of small solar rechargers that recharge the batteries directly from the sun. I also have some regular AC (plug in) rechargers that I can plug into my power system which is currently maintained by solar power. This way, I always have batteries that are ready to go. We use AA batteries to power our radios and communication devices as well. There are literally dozens of new lighting ideas and sources out there that are inexpensive and that require very low wattage to power them. Shop around and begin to store up and make use of these things. Remember, especially in the fall, winter, and spring - kerosene lighting is a good intermediate solution as well. As long as this type of energy source is available and affordable we can use them as we come out of the industrial system. Our journey always involves a two-step thinking process. We ask ourselves "where do we want to end up, and what means will be valuable in getting us there?" These questions constantly remind us that our final solution must be sustainable and viable, but it also doesn't overly bias us against the use of appropriate, valuable, intermediate means.

I have found several very good small flashlights that use LED bulbs and produce a very strong beam. When I first started off-grid, I bought the very expensive flashlights that require "D" batteries or 3V Lithium batteries, but it turned out that these are very, very expensive solutions because the batteries are pricey and need to be replaced often. The small flashlight that I use the most today uses three AAA rechargeable batteries and has turned out to be a better and more affordable solution than the bigger, more expensive to operate flashlights. We also have several 18V rechargeable flashlights that came with some power tool sets we have purchased throughout the years. I will talk about the tools more in the next chapter, but the flashlights that come with these sets are rechargeable, are very handy, and are quite bright. We use these flashlights when we are milking the cow in the dark early mornings.

Consider buying several (many, if possible) of the flashlights that are available now which (they say) don't require batteries. Now, truth be told, all of these flashlights actually *do* require batteries, but they usually are more of a permanent, built-in rechargeable battery, so they are still advertised as if they do not require batteries. The point is that the customer charges the battery through some behavior, rather than having to constantly open up the flashlight to replace the batteries. The first of these flashlights that we bought were the ones that have a large magnet that moves up and down the shaft of the battery grip, through a wire coil. A current is created that charges a small built-in battery. We call these "shake lights" since you have to shake them to charge them up, but there are hand crank flashlights available as well. These "self-powered" lights are an irritant if you need immediate (and/or silent) light, but they work fine after about 30-60 seconds of shaking or cranking. In the outhouse we have a kerosene lantern, but we have also used lights that are powered by rechargeable AA batteries. Harbor Freight and Home Depot sell solar powered night lights that charge during the day and stay on all night. We use these in the root cellar, but you could use these just about anywhere there is light needed at night.

I have a couple of reading lights I purchased at the Harbor Freight store in Abilene, Texas. I have one mounted over my bed for night reading. Harbor Freight also sells dozens of different low power or hand powered lighting items including hand crank spotlights, solar powered lights, floodlights, flashlights, lanterns, LED lights, etc.

OIL LAMPS AND BETTY LAMPS

Now we get to off off-grid solutions. Lehman's sells parts for olive oil lamps, or you can make them yourselves using wire and any wicking material (we use rope from actual rope mops, which are inexpensive). These are "do-it-yourself" lamps and candles you can make that burn olive or other vegetable oils. Basically, they are pieces of twisted wire that hold cotton wicks. You can drop these handmade wicks down into any jar or largemouth bottle to create an oil or fat lamp. We use canning jars and other glass jars we find cheap at garage sales or flea markets for this purpose. Do some reading and checking around. There are many DIY (Do-It-Yourself) type lamps available that burn olive oil or any other type of bulk cooking oil. Olive oil works great, but you most likely will not have an endless supply of it and it isn't cheap. Be careful that whatever method you use won't easily start a fire. Olive oil is very safe, doesn't stink, and will not start a fire. Usually, other oils and greases are fairly safe because the temperature does not get hot enough for the oil to burst into flame; but you should always be very careful. It would be good to have a large supply of these inexpensive or homemade parts (wicks and wick holders) for emergencies. I also keep a large supply of thin, flexible, wire around in case we need to make a lot of these lamps. It generally requires less than ten inches of wire to make the wick holder for a single lamp. Once you learn the principle of the oil lamp, any and all of the parts can be made simply using alternative and more sustainable methods. Wick material can be made from old cloth, wool from our sheep, cordage, flax, and many other materials. In the past, just about any manner of container has been used to make oil lamps including: coconut shells, clay pottery, dishes, tin cans, or just about anything that is fireproof and will hold oil.

From colonial times up through electrification in the early 20ᵗʰ Century, one of the primary sources of lighting was the "Betty Lamp", which was a fat burning lamp. Fat lamps were what people used before coal oil (kerosene) and petroleum-based fuel lamps. The old "genie" lamps - those fancy lamps that are always being shown in the old movies or cartoons that are rubbed to supposedly get a genie to come out of them - were usually Arabian fat lamps. Betty Lamps often used whale blubber, rendered tallow from cows, or lard from pigs for fuel, a perfect solution for whale, cattle, or pig farmers. Fat lamps also do not require other store bought materials. Wicks can be made from cloth, wool, flax, or almost any other fibrous material.

One of our more interesting experiences while experimenting with fat lamps was the "bacon fat lamp". We raise pigs, so we often have large amounts of pig fat available. My wife likes to trim the excess fat off of any particularly fatty bacon before cooking it, and she renders this bacon fat down, just as you would render regular pig fat. From our reading, we learned that when the pioneers used bacon fat in their fat lamps, the burning fat would make the whole house smell like bacon. Now, that may be something you might like, but as much as I like the smell of freshly cooked bacon, I was not looking forward to smelling bacon all winter long, every night. The solution? When burning the bacon fat in the fat lamps I put in just two or three drops of cinnamon oil. We were shocked and pleasantly surprised upon burning the lamps that the resulting smell was all cinnamon and no bacon. Who would have guessed?

We try not to use kerosene lanterns for most of the year, except when it is cold outside, because they produce a lot of heat, which is a great by-product when it is cold, but not so great when it is not. One or two kerosene lanterns burning all night will keep the chilly edge off in a small cabin or camper, but they can really heat up a room or building during the spring or summer. *Always, always, always* make sure your sleeping quarters are vented if you have any type of flame burning overnight. **You will die if you do not.** Also, as you move forward in this new life, since you will likely have all manner of fires and flames going on inside your off-grid home from time-to-time, please always stay safety minded. With greater freedom comes greater responsibility. House fires happened all the time in Agrarian life. Procure several fire-extinguishers and learn what to do in case of different kinds of fires. Our society has had a half-century without most of the indoor fire hazards that were so prevalent in earlier generations. We need to be more diligent and take the time to learn how to live safely off-grid. Learning to live without power, means learning to live deliberately and responsibly again.

**An interesting side-note. I am writing this chapter in a hotel room in a thunderstorm. The power has gone out! So I have written a good bit of this chapter in the dark! I am always prepared, but it is interesting to type this particular chapter while in a darkened hotel room, in a city, with the power out. I also try to store up large quantities of irony... just for emergencies.

HEATING AND COOKING

Depending on where you live in the country, heating can be one of the most important issues you will face, or it may not be very important to you at all. Where your homestead is will often dictate the hierarchy of needs for you and your family. We live in an area more renowned for summer heat than for winter cold, so heat for comfort, while important, is not on our minds for most of the year... unless it is winter! If, however, you live in a place that is in the deep freeze for seven or eight months a year, it would probably be a good idea to focus on this topic.

Most people, because they have read books, or because they watched The Walton's when they were children, or because they have seen any number of old Westerns, will generally have a very loose idea of how our ancestors cooked and kept warm. It should be remembered that creating heat uses more energy and resources than anything else you can do. You cannot afford to create heat using alternate electricity, and even if you could, it would heavily tax your power storage system to produce heat in this way. The smallest electric space heaters can use 1500 watts or more just to heat a very small space. It is an unworkable situation to have to produce this much power through off-grid electrical generation to heat any good sized area. On my alternative power system, I can run two (and maybe three) freezers and a refrigerator with the same number of watts that it takes to run a hair dryer. Heat is expensive.

Utilizing propane or other fuels to produce heat is not a very good long-term solution either. While propane can be a good intermediate method, and small but very powerful propane space-heaters can be affordable and easy to install and use, in the long run we still run into the problem of scarcity. There is no promise that there will be a constant and readily available supply of propane in the future.

For many millennia, heat for dwellings has been provided almost exclusively by fire. For the most part, this heat was provided by burning wood from felled trees, or by burning other dried organic materials that could be harvested or gathered from the land. Different types of coal have been in use for heating and cooking for thousands of years, and as early as 1748 there was a working coal mine near Richmond, Virginia. Early American colonists, however, were standing on the shoreline of a continent virtually carpeted with trees, and many of those trees would have to be removed to make way for farms and villages. Wood in colonial America was often considered a waste product, so it was the primary means of heating until the Industrial Revolution, particularly the revolution in transportation, thrust coal into the spotlight as the primary means of creating heat and energy.

In the prairies where trees were scarce, pioneers often burned dried cow or buffalo "chips", or they made "hay ties", which were cleverly twisted strands of hay that would often burn for up to four hours. Before long, as the forces of the Industrial Revolution steamed across the continent, trainloads of coal made it much simpler to populate the vast treeless prairies. *Note: *I have used our abundant supply of "cow* *chips" in my woodburning stove and they burn fine with no offensive odor.*

For most of our ancestors, heat came from the burning of wood; perhaps in a fireplace, an earthen oven, a wood burning stove, or some other type of cook stove. Early colonists in the American colonies often had open fires in their structures that would be vented through holes in or near the roof. This, of course, often led to structure fires, since most of the earliest roofs were made of grass or straw. Once the colonists had achieved a level of survivability, and had acquired the basic means to sustain life somewhat more comfortably, they would have the time and resources to begin building substantial stone or brick fireplaces and chimneys. Later, with industrial advancements in metalworking, wood burning stoves and cook stoves became the prevalent means of utilizing biomass energy for heating dwellings and cooking food.

Today, advances in heating technology allow the wise homesteader to choose from several different options in home heating. For some people, the simple boxwood stove, or an old railroad style stove may be sufficient. Others, because of ready access to corn or other high-energy crops, may choose to go with a specialized corn (or other biomass) burning unit.

Most homesteaders, especially those with small and simple home structures, and those who have ready access to renewable sources of firewood (such as a woodlot or forest), opt for a combination heating/ cooking stove that allows them to make dual use of the wood resources they have. Wood cook stoves can range from the simple and affordable, to the expensive and very ornate heirloom pieces like those used prior to rural electrification in many homes in America. I looked at wood stoves for many years, and I was very disappointed at how expensive a new "antique syle" cook stove would cost. We really wanted one of these old-style cook stoves but I could not rationalize spending $3500 for a stove, no matter how nice and traditional it looked. So, I started to look at flea-markets and antique stories for the actual used antique stoves of yesteryear, but found that they were often even more expensive, because upwardly mobile "yuppies" were buying them up for display in their cracker box, look-alike, McMansions and show-houses in suburbia.

I knew there had to be a good solution for people like me; people who don't have a lot of money, but who need a plain but sufficient cook stove for real world use. After a lot of research I was able to purchase a new, affordable, and utilitarian cook stove imported from Serbia. This was the plain style of stove still used today throughout Eastern Europe, where a wood burning stove is still an absolutely necessary tool. This was not eye-candy adopted for display by suburban frauds but a real appliance for daily survival. After finding the importer who shipped the stoves out of Cleveland, Ohio (Sopka, Inc.), I learned that he also sold imperfect or slightly banged-up units on Ebay for a substantial discount. I was able to purchase the perfect stove for us at an affordable price, and we have been very pleased with it, and with the amount of heat it provides for our cabin.

We live in an area of Texas that is completely covered with very fast growing Mesquite trees, along with stands of oaks and cedars. Mesquite is an invasive hardwood not indigenous to our area, but it has become ubiquitous on most Central Texas ranches and homesteads so it is a perfect solution for an energy source. Mesquite will also grow back quite quickly when it has been cut to the ground, making it a renewable source of energy. Based on all of these factors, the wood burning cook stove has been a good solution for us. You will have to do some research in your own area to find out what the local ordinances are for wood or other biomass burning, and what options are available to you for off-grid heating.

When you are studying your homestead heating options, also consider what alternative building methods or structural add-ons might now be available to you. For example: underground structures or partially underground or "banked earth" structures can be built. Although they can be considered cool and damp, these buildings were often used by pioneers and homesteaders precisely because they were usually temperature stable. This means that, depending on the structure and how much of it is buried, a stable temperature in the fifties or sixties (degrees Fahrenheit) can often be maintained year-round, without any burning or consumption of energy at all. Some "low-impact" homesteaders are focusing on this type of building philosophy, sometimes augmented with passive solar heating to solve their heating concerns. The point is that we need to spend some time researching what is available out there, and how it will apply to us in our area.

For those of you who are just getting started, it is quite a bit cheaper to build your structure with your heating and cooling needs in mind than it is to retrofit an existing structure to fix or address issues later.

The basic premise that we will use throughout this book, is that which I have really focused on from the beginning. We need to have a new philosophy of survival. We need to always think about simplicity, survivability, and sustainability as we make our moves off of the world's grid system.

In the next chapter, we are going to talk about the big stumbling blocks in the minds of people who begin to consider Off Off-Grid homesteading: Air-Conditioning and Refrigeration; and we will also briefly discuss tools and other appliances.

CHAPTER 7
COOL STUFF

A GIFT IN THE DESERT

In the summer of 1192, in the stifling desert heat of Palestine, Richard the Lionheart, King of England, was at his headquarters as head of the Crusading armies in Jaffa. While he had won many victories, now he had a sense of foreboding. He saw no way to take Jerusalem from the Muslims. The task was just too daunting, and the Lionheart was, above all, a realist. He was in the midst of negotiations with the Saracen (Muslim) King Saladin over just who would rule in the Holy Land. Circumstances had conspired to bring him to the negotiation table. And things were not well with him. He, the mighty crusader, lay sick in his bed in the sweltering heat, worried about the war, worried about his health, and worried about the evil machinations of his brother John who was, even at that moment, conniving to place himself on the throne as the King of England. Richard needed to return to Europe to defend his title and his claims there but he did not know if his health would hold out; the infernal desert heat might just kill him first. Just as he pondered these things, and as the sweat continuously rolled off of his body in streams, emissaries from Saladin arrived. The messengers carried gifts and the concerns and best wishes of the Saracen King – his enemy. Saladin had heard reports of Richard's poor health, and he had sent pears, peaches... *and ice*, to sooth and comfort the invading King.

Ice! These desert barbarians had ice?

I think there were two messages sent by Saladin that day. The first was that he was a chivalrous King, and that he respected and honored his enemy. History has recorded it that way. The second, more subtle message was that (and we should take note) an industrious people - a people who can have iced drinks in the desert without power or machines, hundreds of miles from any mountains (the nearest source of ice), are not a people who will be easily defeated or enslaved.

If I had to pick just two statements that I hear the most often when people are telling me why they cannot or will not even consider going off-grid, it would be these:

1. I don't think I could live without air-conditioning.

2. I don't think I could live without ice.

It is absolutely certain that people can, and have, lived without air-conditioning and ice, even in the hottest climates in the world, for thousands of years. Most of those millions of people did so having never once heard of air-conditioning... or even ice. It is not the lack of air-conditioning or ice that will be the downfall of many people in this modern consumer society (if those mainstays of "civilization" are lost), it is the unhealthy dependence on those things, and the utter ignorance of how to live without them, or to provide for them in alternate ways.

Again, when we study history, we find that the colonized mind has atrophied and become weakened and corrupted. The distilled genius and skills of thousands of years was virtually lost when, within about 100 years, machines and corporations began doing the work of feeding the people and providing for the needs and wants of society. The colonized mind of the society as a whole and not just of the individual, has lost the knowledge and wisdom gained by the hard work and *industry* of previous generations.

Is the word "industry" a bad word? Unhappily, depending on your point of view, it has become one. In any case, it doesn't mean what it used to mean. The industrial revolution has fixed the word "industry" with a new definition. The common, modern definition of industry is: "a business using machines and human capital to mass-produce products"; we may talk of the "automobile industry" or the "paper industry". But is that even what the word industry means? In the

Webster's 1828 dictionary there was only one definition for the word "industry". Let's take a look at it:

> *INDUSTRY, n. [L. industria.] Habitual diligence in any employment, either bodily or mental; steady attention to business; assiduity; opposed to sloth and idleness. We are directed to take lessons of industry from the bee.*

Words change meanings, do they not? Industry is not a bad word. The word has been stolen from us by despots and tyrants bent on profits at all cost and on colonizing the mind of the world.

Earlier generations succeeded by using their minds, wisdom, reason, logic, and INDUSTRY; that is something we need to keep in mind.

In the area of cooling, refrigeration, etc., the mind determined to move off-grid generally defaults to providing these benefits using some concept of alternative energy like solar, wind, or a combination of the two. The default instinct is to conclude that the *power* provided by alternate energy sources will be used to provide electricity for lights, freezers, refrigerators, and maybe even TV's and game consoles. It is so difficult for the average person to conceive of a life without these things that this type of thinking is really just a default. My constant harping on this issue is because we are not just talking about philosophy or some kind of "cultural" preference. This gets down to the basics of "Are we going to be able to afford and accomplish this change in life and living?" Because when you add the overwhelming cost of doing this type of thing (moving to alternative power) to the idea of buying land, building a house, building barns and out-buildings, planting gardens, buying or making equipment, purchasing tractors, etc., you can see why most people convince themselves that this is either not doable, or at the least it will take several generations to get it done. I tell most people I counsel, *"If you are like me, you cannot afford to go off-grid. Going off off-grid is your only real option."*

Basically, the philosophy that most people bring to moving off-grid is the idea of *moving to the Promised Land while taking Egypt with them.* I say we move towards the Promised Land and leave Egypt behind us.

When I talk to people about moving off off-grid, the questions we normally get run along these lines:

How do you keep food frozen?
What about air-conditioning?
What about keeping milk, eggs, and drinks cold?
How do you keep food from going bad in the heat?

It is important to note that not one of these things would have even been a question in the minds of our great-great-grandparents. Prior to the ready availability of cheap and easy grid power, none of these things were a problem or a serious concern. People lived generation after generation without even considering that it might be a good idea to freeze meat for years on end, or that you might want to drop the temperature 30 degrees during the day, or that somehow ketchup and mustard (which were invented as preserved food products) need to be kept a degree or two above freezing. It is an interesting and almost unknown fact that almost every kind of food we eat in our diet today was first invented as a means of preserving a harvest (and this fact can be translated from almost any culture):

Ketchup – is a means of storing tomatoes.
Cheese, Sour Cream, Yogurt – are all a means of storing milk.
Jellies, Jams, Raisins, and Wine – are all a means of storing fruit.
Mayonnaise – is a means of storing eggs.
Ham, Bacon, Sausage – are a means of storing pork.
Sausage, Jerky, Pemmican, and Broth – are all a means of storing beef and other meats.
Pickles, Relish, Kraut, etc. – are all a means of storing vegetables.

The list is really endless. Almost any food you eat, or any food you order from a restaurant, exists because some Agrarians somewhere decided to make use of their brains and their wits to preserve the harvest. Every time you eat one of these foods, whether you know it or not, you are confessing that your ancestors created and lived a way of life that is far superior to the plastic, artificial, virtual life that most earthlings live today. You are cruising along on the fumes of a far superior culture – and maybe you don't even know it.

We want to learn the old ways, not just because they are old or because they are historical, but because they work and because they are *sustainable.* I do not mean "sustainable" in quite the way the modern eco-friendly folks do, though there is something to that as well. I mean "sustainable" in its literal meaning. We learn these ways because we will be able to continue in them even if the grid beast collapses and dies. We can continue in these ways without undue intercourse with a corrupt and dying world, and without being stained or harmed by too much dependence on what the world calls "necessities". Again, it is all about dependence. As you will learn in this chapter, there really is no valid reason to keep food frozen to 0 degrees for long periods of time. Your great-grandma didn't need a 48 inch fan or a 48 inch plasma TV screen, and neither do you. Your great-granddaddy didn't need a perpetual 72 degrees in every room he entered and every minute of his life, and neither do you. The point is that we ought to get past that thinking, and when you do so, you will find that *most* of the costs of moving off-grid are eliminated when the myths and bulwarks in the mind are eliminated. If you realize that you can do the things you want to do with hard work, with industry, and with your own labor without paying $24,000 for an off-grid solar power system, then you will have just saved $24,000 and all you have to do now is learn to replace *stuff* with skill and know-how.

As I have said before, when it comes to the biggest bulwarks in the mind - I would say that freezers and refrigerators are way up there, and since we have been talking here about these things, the question arises - how *do* you store the food you produce? Well first, I'll tell you how the old-timers did it - the folks who first settled this land...

THE ROOT CELLAR

Root crops and many other food products were kept in a root cellar. The root cellar was usually the first project started and the first completed on the land, and for good reason. When folks first came into my area of Texas they were facing a sometimes harsh climate (especially during the heat of summer), and though there were oaks and other trees for building, the days could get downright difficult during the sweltering summer days while the homestead was being built. So the first structure constructed was almost always a hand-dug root cellar. There is one of these, probably originally built in the 1930's (before electrification), still existent up at the front of my property. These first excavations were basically wide trenches; the width depended on how it was to be used. If a young couple or young family planned on living in it while they were building a house, the trench may be as big as 4 to 5 feet wide. Sometimes the original hole was dug only 5 or 6 feet deep. So you can see it didn't take long to build. These earliest "dug-outs" were really just rock-lined trenches that were covered with heavy branches and beams; then some of them would have been covered with 6 to 12 inches of dirt or sod. That was it. The family would live in there for a time while the homestead was being started. Usually the next thing to go in would be the gardens and animal pens, and then, only after food production was up and running, the barn would be built. Food production and preservation came *before* the house. Imagine that. That is shocking for most people to comprehend, but because we idolize our comfort in ways our forefathers never did, we usually think of the house as the first and most important structure. But, if we knew better, the concept of building the house last wouldn't be shocking at all. Many of our ancestors got their wisdom from *the* source:

> *"Prepare thy work without, and make it fit for thyself in the field; and afterwards build thine house"* (Prov. 24:27)

We shouldn't be surprised that modern man has managed to get it totally backwards.

So, after the fields, and the gardens were prepared, and after the outbuildings were complete, the home construction would begin. In our historical scenario, after the house became livable, the family would move into it and the "dug-out" would get a door and would become the first cool storage or root cellar. When the barns and the house were built, sometimes they would have a larger root cellar dug up underneath them, and here is where your quick foods and your condiments would be stored. Remember, ketchup and things like that were not foods that were originally designed to make french fries taste better. Ketchup was conceived as a way of storing tomatoes from the harvest. We have moved so far away from common-sense agrarianism that even many modern encyclopedias err in claiming that ketchup was created solely as a condiment, ignoring that it was designed to make use of the harvest and to preserve it for a long time.

As an illustrative aside, and to prove the point, here is a recipe for ketchup (or Catsup) from an 1801 cookbook:

1. *Get the tomatoes quite ripe on a dry day, squeeze them with your hands till reduced to a pulp, then put half a pound of fine salt to one hundred tomatoes, and boil them for two hours.*

2. *Stir them to prevent burning.*

3. *While hot press them through a fine sieve, with a silver spoon till nought but the skin remains, then add a little mace, 3 nutmegs, allspice, cloves, cinnamon to taste.*

4. *Boil over a slow fire till quite thick, stir all the time.*

5. *Bottle when cold.*

6. *One hundred tomatoes will make four or five bottles **and keep good for two or three years**.*

Ketchup, as originally designed and when made for that purpose, will maintain quality at moderate temperatures for years, so the idea that you need to store condiments in a refrigerator is really a very new myth. While it is true that you don't want to let Mayonnaise get really hot, it is a myth that it must stay refrigerated at 35 degrees in order to stay good. Mayonnaise was originally a product made from eggs and oil in order to store the egg crop at root cellar temperatures. Mayonnaise is perfectly fine at these moderate temperatures. If you were to take everything out of the average refrigerator that doesn't need to be kept in there, as you looked into the cavernous emptiness of this industrial creature, you would be left with this strange and bizarre epiphany... that most Westerners keep and feed a money sucking refrigerator for a single primary purpose – so that they can have cold drinks and so they do not have to walk a few feet (or lift up a hatch door) to a root cellar or other cold storage to get their condiments or leftovers.

Not long ago I saw a $2100 refrigerator in a store, and I'll bet that it would cost every bit of $300 a year or more to power that monster with grid electricity. As I thought about this, I did some quick figuring. The price of most of these big, new refrigerators is generally figured into the price of a new home construction, or, they are bought using credit cards or store credit. This means that in its lifetime, with interest included and after all other things are taken into the equation, the owner of that refrigerator will likely pay close to $10,000 for a box in which to store cold drinks and cool mayonnaise, and for the ability not to have to walk to the root cellar. And the owners might even write me some day and tell me that separation and moving off-grid "takes too much time and money", etc., or, "we just cannot afford it right now". Listen, my whole cabin AND root cellar cost less than $10,000! The point is that the cost of doing things the way you are already doing them is WAY more than you can afford, and it is all because of some myths people have believed, and because of colonization in the mind. A root cellar, even a very simple one, is a much better idea, and it is more conducive to freedom and not slavery.

A root cellar is a glorified hole in the ground. It capitalizes on the fact that, only a few feet down, the ground stays a moderate temperature year around. When it is 100 degrees Fahrenheit here in Central Texas, it is generally between 50 and 60 degrees Fahrenheit down only 4 to 6 feet in the earth. When it is 4 degrees Fahrenheit in Iowa, it is still likely in the 50's only a few feet underground.

Some of the folks I know started their root cellar experience with a small hole in the ground, maybe 3' x 2' and only a few feet deep. It took them less than an hour to dig. Condiments and things would be put into coolers and dropped into the hole in the ground, then the holes would be covered with a board and some hay bales, etc. for insulation. By adding a bit of ice to the coolers, this mini root cellar would keep milk cold for a week or more. One young couple I knew used this method to keep milk cold for a baby and a toddler for quite some time. As a simple and quick solution, it works great. I read a story about a family that dug a small root cellar (maybe 5' x 5') right under their kitchen. They put a trap door on it and they put some shelves on the wall and a ladder down into it. They were able to keep all their condiments and almost everything else they used to keep in their refrigerator in their mini root cellar and it worked just fine for them. So, in short, you do not need a refrigerator. I am not saying you cannot have one, or even that you should not have one. A refrigerator can be just fine as an intermediate step, or so long as you know that when you move off-grid you will have to power it somehow; and so long as you know that if the world "system" is interrupted, your refrigerator (no matter how it is powered) will likely be one of the first casualties. If you are not dependent on it, and it doesn't stop you or slow you down, then there is no problem with having one. My point is that the prevailing myth is that you absolutely need it; but you do not *need* it.

WHAT ABOUT FREEZERS?

This is a question I received even when I visited Homestead Heritage, a large, conservative, agrarian community near Waco, Texas. Homestead Heritage is a religious community of Agrarians who also run several homesteading schools and classes. I have been there several times to visit and to take classes in woodworking (woodworking without power tools). While the good folks at Homestead Heritage are Agrarian-minded; and while they produce much of what they eat; and while they have many very valuable old-world skills; most of them are still on-grid, so to them, I was a bit of a curiosity. When I told them that I have lived off-grid for many years, one of the first questions I received was "How do you run your freezer?"

It is a natural question. Agrarians like to store and preserve food, and freezing food is an easy way to preserve it, so the question is totally understandable. First I must confess that freezers are nice to have, but if you were to read the top agrarian or homesteading writers in the homesteading magazines, you would think that freezers were actually an absolute necessary fact of life. Open up almost any book on preserving food today, or go to almost any Internet website about preserving, and you will see copious instructions on how to prepare food properly for freezing. And I must admit, as an intermediate step, freezers can be very helpful if used for other than long-term storage. I like to use the freezer mainly for temporary meat storage (until it can be eaten or processed and put in the smokehouse or root cellar). One of the few mixed blessings about living where I live is that it often doesn't stay cold for long, even in winter. So, while it may be freezing temperatures when we start butchering a pig or a goat, it may very well be 60 degrees by later that afternoon. We cannot do what so many northerners are able to do. We cannot just leave the meat out to age for a few days or a week, because the meat would not last very long. So for us, the freezer is a great way to keep the meat chilled until we can get it processed. And when you talk about bulwarks or road-blocks in the mind, here is where I have to face facts just like everyone else. I do like steak... and pork chops too. I don't eat them very often. Like my ancestors, we generally get fresh grilled meat during the late fall and winter during butchering season. But I really, really like grilled meat. I really have had trouble imagining giving up fresh meat every once in awhile, especially when I have a bunch of cattle and pigs on the hoof, and since a nice ribeye steak doesn't cost me anywhere near what it would cost in the store. Up north, winter is the good meat-eating time (for meat eaters, of course). Northerners can hang a side of beef in the barn and cut it up and use it at their own pace; but down here we have to design and plan for the ability to keep and store meat without freezers. Freezers are just an intermediate step, and they can be helpful. Are they necessary? Well... no, they are not.

Canned meat can be stored in the root cellar or in a cool and dry room built underground (the root cellar has high humidity), and when a cold-smokehouse is built, meat can be smoked and cured for long-term storage. Some folks who are new to the concept of "canning" are often confused by what we mean by the term. "Canning" usually means to preserve a food product in glass jars by means of pressure canning or water-bath methods (there is much more detail and history of canning and food preservation in Chapter 14).

Meat can also be "potted" - where it is cooked and then stacked in a large ceramic crock. Each layer of meat is then covered with its own grease or lard until the whole crock is full. Meat preserved this way, and kept fairly cool, can last for months and months. Meat can also be dried and then re-hydrated for consumption. Some of the old timers would cut beef or venison into strips and dry-smoke it, then hang it until it was bone dry. It could then be dry stored until it was needed. The night before it was to be used, it would be soaked in water until it had totally re-hydrated, then it could be cooked and used like normal fresh meat.

Lewis and Clark, and most of the inland explorers in the 18th and 19th centuries survived on what is called "pemmican", a native food that combines dried ground meat, fat (or grease) and dried and ground fruit or berries. Here is a short Wikipedia explanation of pemmican:

"Traditionally pemmican was prepared from the lean meat of large game such as buffalo, elk, or deer. The meat was cut in thin slices

and dried over a slow fire, or in the hot sun until it was hard and brittle. Then it was pounded into very small pieces, almost powder-like in consistency, using stones. The pounded meat was mixed with melted fat with a ratio of approximately 50% pounded meat and 50% melted fat. In some cases, dried fruits such as Saskatoon berries, cranberries, blueberries, or choke cherries were pounded into powder and then added to the meat/fat mixture. The resulting mixture was then packed into "green" rawhide pouches for storage." (Wikipedia)

For my family, for now, most of our meat preservation comes by way of canning. I want to stop here and make a comment about canned meat. I will engage in a longer conversation about the sustainability of canning later on in the chapter of Food Preservation, but for right now I want to deal with the issue of canned meat. I have heard many ignorant persons (people who have never tried it) make sarcastic and negative comments about canned meat. I can tell you from my own experience, as a meat lover, and as someone who eats canned meat several times a week, that canned meat is very, very good. If you like beef stews with big huge chunks of steak in it, then canned meat is for you. If you like beef stroganoff, or pork and rice, etc., then you will really like canned meat. The first canned meat I ever had that didn't come from a store was when I stayed with some folks up north and they made some venison stew. The lady of the house went into the storage pantry and came out with some quart jars of venison, and some jars of tomatoes and other vegetables. Not thirty minutes later, we were being served some warm, incredible smelling stew. And it tasted *exactly* like beef stew. It was tender and delicious. I went home and told my wife and now these types of stews are a regular on our menu at home. My favorite regular meal right now is pork and rice from our canned pork. I don't know why so many people have such a mental block about canned meat. It is easy and it preserves very well. We have been living off-grid for many years now, and as time goes by, we are learning about more and more ways to effectively can meat - even hamburger and ground sausage, sausage patties, and bacon. Our "standard" breakfast

168

around here consists of fried bacon that my wife has fried and then canned, with fresh eggs, fried potatoes, and tortillas or biscuits.

Canning, however, is somewhat of an intermediate step for us. As we head even further off the grid, we intend to move more towards curing, cold-smoking, drying, and potting of meats - but for now we are canning most of our meat.

COLD HARVEST

For thousands of years, cultures throughout the temperate zones have engaged in the seasonal harvesting of ice and snow. When one thinks about it, it makes perfect sense. It is only the entropy of our minds and of our creativity that keeps us from seeing the obvious. The Persians, the Hebrews, the Greeks, the Romans, and the Chinese - basically every advanced culture - engaged in the yearly harvest of "cold" for use in food preservation. Frozen ice would be mined from mountains or harvested from frozen lakes or ponds, then stored in cellars, caves, and dugouts. The harvested snow or ice would be packed in, or covered with, insulative material like wool, sand, skins, fat, dirt, or sawdust. Later, when the weather turned warm and the ice was needed, it would be uncovered and used.

The Persians were the ancient masters of year-round cold storage, and they were a desert people. Four-hundred years before Christ the Persians had perfected ice and cold storage by building structures called *yakhchals*. Persian engineers built large domed buildings throughout the country (even in the deserts) over subterranean basements or pits. The thick walls of the domes (sometimes 6 feet thick at the base) and other brilliant engineering concepts, kept the buildings cool, and funneled all hot air out through holes near the tops of the domes. Ice would be harvested from nearby mountains during the winter, and used to fill the yakhchals before the hot weather made it impossible to transport the ice very far. During the summer, the ice was used to preserve food, to provide cool drinks for the wealthy or for royalty, and even to make a type of ice cream.

This basic process - harvesting snow and ice during the winter for storage throughout the warmer seasons - has gone on for centuries all over the world. It was a basic, logical, and unquestioned practice in just about every culture north and south of the tropics. In America, particularly in the South, you will find the relics of this ancient process in the ever-present antique "icehouses" in small towns and big cities all over the land. In my home state of Texas, the term "icehouse", even today, is slang for a beer house or a beer hall, because beer used to be stored in the old icehouses before industrialism and electrification brought the advent of the personal electric freezer and refrigerator. The public icehouses of Texas were in use well into the 20th Century, and many of them still stand today. Probably hundreds more are still in existence on private farms and homesteads throughout the South. The point is that people lived for thousands of years, for centuries on this continent, without electrification and without modern air-conditioning, freezers, or air-conditioners.

Here is a quick snippet from Wikipedia on ice and ice storage, with some interesting tidbits of history for discussion:

> *"In 1790, only the elite had ice for their guests. It was harvested locally in winter and stored through summers in a covered well. Ice production was very labor intensive as it was performed entirely with hand axes and saws, and cost hundreds of dollars a ton. By 1830, though, ice was being used to preserve food and by the middle 1830s it had become a commodity. In the 1840s, it began to be used in the production of beer, and by 1850 it was used in urban retail centers. In 1861 the icebox was developed, and by 1865 two homes out of three in Boston had ice delivered every day." (Wikipedia)*

I disagree that only the "elite" had ice in 1790, since we have already established that Wikipedia has (and most modern historians have) a bias against the fact that most of the people in 1790 were middle-class (not "elite" or rich), landed, and surprisingly comfortable. While it is true that ice harvesting on a massive scale was very expensive, and the very wealthy did have the ability to use servant labor to store up large quantities of ice, small-scale harvesting for a single household had only the cost of personal labor, and it was quite common for the "regular folk" to harvest some ice to be stored for summer use and for food preservation. Almost every homestead had root cellars for food preservation, and many of these homesteads harvested ice from their own ponds (and snow from the ground) and stored it in well insulated holes dug deeply into the ground in a corner of the root cellar, or alternatively, in old or unused covered wells. By the mid 1800's personal icehouses existed throughout the country, for people from every economic level, and ice and snow harvest was a regularly scheduled event in the lives of homesteaders and farmers. There was even an episode of Little House on the Prairie where a girl gets locked in the ice house as a prank.

Let me say, before I get too deep into the topic of icehouses, I do not mean to allow ice to remain as a crutch for weak minded people. Humans are perfectly able to live good and productive lives without ice. It is not my purpose at all to infer that ice is a necessary element of life. Many billions of people have lived their lives in the tropical zones (and elsewhere) and they have never even had a concept or mental image of frozen water. We often become weakened by what we become used to, and we need to recognize that some of the crippling comforts of life may someday be lost to us for a period of time (or perhaps forever) if there is ever a drastic and permanent change in the reality we experience in this world. If you were to be kidnapped off of the streets of London (as many were) as a young child in the late 1700's, and sent to the tropics as a slave or a prisoner to work in the cane fields, then it is very likely that you would have had your last experience with frozen water. That is just the way things go (and have gone), and it is only the lazy colonized minds of modernists today that causes them to hysterically pronounce (like Scarlett O'Hara or some coddled princess) that if they do not have cold drinks they will surely die. You can live without ice or air-conditioning, and if things go really badly in the next few years or decades you will very likely have to.

What I am teaching in this book, and in this chapter, are not details about how to do things. I am not providing a blueprint for how you should live your life or what you should do to avoid pain and discomfort in this life. From the very beginning I have been talking about decolonizing the mind, and how to think differently. The point is that many of the ideas and concepts I am mentioning in this book were second nature to humans for thousands of years. We've been hoodwinked by a society that wants to keep us comfortable so that we will keep consuming and keep feeding the machine with our lives. It would be wrong of me, then, to merely give you a formula on how to stay comfortable when the system around you fails. Instead, I am hoping to teach people how to think so that they can live a lifestyle of survival and preparedness in their own generation, and then hand those skills and that knowledge down to the generations that are to come. If we learn to think properly, then new and unexpected problems won't cause us undue stress or pain. When the mind is decolonized it begins to work more naturally and more in tune with reality, rather than being in tune with the virtual reality that is today's world. It helps in our decolonization to recognize a very painful fact: The solutions I am describing ought to be absolutely obvious and logical to the reasonable mind. That we have not thought these thoughts before now merely exposes how unreasonable our world has become.

For our purposes, I have revised and adapted a common saying:

> *Give a man a fish, and he'll eat for a day. Teach a man to fish, and he'll eat for a lifetime... but he'll get tired of fish. Teach a man to THINK, and he'll not only eat well, he'll prosper (Michael Bunker)*

THE ICEHOUSE

When I was a young, dumb, college student, I traveled around Texas quite a bit. A longtime favorite experience for college guys was to stop in to the "icehouse", which, as I have said, is a Texas name for "beer hall". Out of curiosity (and as a history buff) I began looking into the history of these icehouses, and I was very surprised and fascinated with what I found out. As I have mentioned, it has long been the practice of almost every culture in the temperate climates to harvest ice and/or snow in the winter, and store it throughout the warmer months. In the northern states (and even in some of the northernmost of the southern states), ice would be harvested from ponds or lakes, and stored in large icehouses. But in many areas of Texas the ponds or lakes do not freeze hard enough, often enough, or deep enough to produce very much ice. So the very industrious people of the area would get ice a few different ways. In some cases they would make their own ice during the winter. Even here in Central Texas it can get quite cold in the winter, if only for a few days. Only a year or two ago it got down to eight degrees Fahrenheit one morning here at our cabin, and there were many, many days during that winter where the temperature was in the teens and twenties Fahrenheit at night. That is plenty cold enough to make a whole lot of ice if you are prepared for it, and if you diligently pour water into pre-fabricated forms made for the purpose. But that wasn't the only way to get ice. A very nice form of trade developed between Texas and some neighboring states and territories in more northern regions. Ice would be shipped down in wagons (and eventually by train) in large quantities and it would be stored in the well-built icehouses. Not long after Texas won her Independence, all the way up until rural electrification almost 100 years later, ice was a regular commodity in almost every town and city in Texas.

There is nothing that is un-agrarian about trade or buying or selling ice. In fact, ice is nothing more than another crop that can be harvested for the benefit of people. The point is that the clear and decolonized mind has to be engaged in seeing *weather* (in this case ice) as a benefit. We, who live by God's grace off of the worldly grid see weather (ice and water) as a harvestable crop. There is no doubt that people who are living in the tropics or subtropical areas are probably not going to be able to use these ideas, but for most of my readers (probably over 95%

of them) there is a way to make, procure, store, and use ice. It is only necessary that we get creative enough to harvest what God provides.

In fact, for most of you who will read this, you already have virtually everything you need to provide ice for yourself and your family without electricity, refrigerators, or freezers. If you live in an area with significant snowfall, or with ponds or lakes that freeze over sufficiently, all you need to do is study and research how to build a good-sized and well-built icehouse. Then you need to put aside some time in the winter to harvest God's increase, just as you would harvest hay, wheat, or corn.

An icehouse is simply a well-insulated building, usually constructed at least partly underground, that is designed to store large quantities of ice with the least amount of melting or heat transfer. Generally, a good icehouse will be a building within a larger building, creating a structure with very thick insulated walls. The icehouse I have been studying for our own homestead would be partially in the ground (about 4 to 5 feet), built into a slight grade or a hill. The outer structure would be made of thick, slip-formed, stone walls, basically like a large smokehouse. Inside the structure, a second "building" would be built, allowing for at least two feet of space between the outer walls and the inner walls. That space will be filled with an insulation material (in the past sand, hay, cotton, wool, or sawdust was used). At the top, air venting is provided to allow the heat to easily exit the structure. And here is where it gets interesting...

Even in the best insulated building, you are going to have some ice melt in the summer. This melt water has to be removed, because water will cause the remaining ice to melt faster. The melting ice is not a disaster though, in fact, it is necessary and a great bonus! The floor of the icehouse is designed to allow water (cold ice melt) to run off through gravel into a drain pipe. That pipe runs into a "spring house", which is another, smaller, nearby, insulated building. The cool water runs through the pipe (which is underground) down into a trough in the spring house. It fills the trough with very cold water, and things like milk, cheese, and other cold-storage items that keep well with refrigeration, are stored in the cool water. This springhouse, if it is insulated well enough will keep at a very cool temperature, even in the summer, so it becomes the "refrigerator" where meats and other items can be stored. So the two structures together, the icehouse and the springhouse, become a single unit designed for assisting in food preservation and storage.

The construction and usage of the icehouse and the springhouse is quite simple. The real tricky part (especially in our environment) will be making and storing enough ice during the winter to last through the warmer months. This is where the "process" is important, and for us this process will likely require some intermediate means, and a lot of testing. We do have freezers right now, so we can make ice provided we have enough good, clean, water, but making ice in this way is very slow and inefficient. Our freezers do not run for long enough to make very much ice at all. Because of this, I am also considering buying a used industrial ice machine. This machine could be used with our current off-grid system (utilizing solar power and the occasional generator), and, in a short amount of time, an ice house could be filled up with ice. Having a high-speed, high-capacity ice machine could give us time to test different ways to make and store our own ice without power. It could be a good "intermediate step" for us. One of the things we will be testing is block ice forms, as we try to see how much ice we can freeze at what different temperatures. I am considering getting some different sized forms made out of stainless steel, and then testing at different temperatures and for different lengths of time to see what would work.

What we learn from this process is more than how to make and keep ice. We learn how to think like our ancestors thought. Ask yourself, what would Great-Granddad do?

HOME COOLING AND AIR-CONDITIONING

As I mentioned, staying cool and somewhat comfortable in the old days had more to do with intelligence, common sense, and building design than it did using brute force and money with electricity and machines. Modern air-conditioning is a "brute force" form of solving a problem. It is saying, "I don't want to think about nature, geography, and how things work in the real world. I just want to be cool... RIGHT NOW!" So the brute force of energy, money, and machines are brought to bear to temporarily cool what naturally ought to be a hot space in the summer. Yet in nature there are naturally cool spaces and naturally warm spaces. There are areas that receive more wind and cooler breezes, and there are areas that are naturally stagnant and sometimes oppressive. Animals have learned how to seek out shade and naturally cooler areas, in order to stay more comfortable. In this section I am going to be discussing some general cooling principles.

On our land here in Central Texas there are different areas with sometimes radically different atmospheres. When I first built my cabin, I knew nothing about any of these concepts I am discussing. I looked at a spot I thought would be geographically handy for a cabin, and I built a cabin there. I spent no time scouting, testing, examining, or experiencing the location. I did not wait for seasons and weather changes to see how things changed throughout the year. I wanted a cabin, and I wanted it where I wanted it, so I built it. The following comedy of errors is added for your enjoyment and also for your education. Laugh away, but learn from my mistakes because I can tell you that I learned more from my building mistakes than almost anything else I have done since moving off-grid. The *one* thing I did do correctly, is that I oriented the cabin north-south, which is probably the proper orientation for the location. Almost every single other thing I did was wrong, so let's get to the comedy:

I built our sleeping quarters into the south end of the cabin, which is fine for winter, but which is not really good for the 7-8 months of the year when it is warm, considering the other mistakes I made. Then I put our screened porch on the north side of the building, meaning that since our prevailing winds are from the south and west, we would only rarely get a breeze on the front porch. Then I made sure not to put any south facing windows on the cabin, meaning that we would almost never get a breeze in our sleeping area. To make sure I couldn't easily fix this mistake later, I built a storage shed and a huge water catchment system that would block any winds even if I did happen to have a south facing window... which I don't. The only windows I put in the cabin were two very small (2' x 3') windows, one on the east and one on the west side of the cabin. Then I put these tiny windows about 3 feet off the ground, insuring that any slight breeze that did accidentally sneak into the cabin would pass harmlessly a foot or so above anyone who happened to be lying in bed. But wait... I'm not done... I put a large sloping shed roof on the cabin (which was actually a good idea), with the slope going from 10 foot high on the north side, to 8 foot high on the south side. But then I closed in the roof and ceiling, not allowing any of the hot air that "stacks" up near the roof to flow outside, even though it would naturally want to flow out, provided there was a vent or a window up there... which there is not. Then, I painted the whole thing barn red, which is a very, very dark color, because I liked the barn red color of northern farms. What I didn't consider is that a dark color is probably not a good idea when you live in Central Texas and you have hot, warm, or temperate weather for 8 months out of the year. Aren't I a genius?

But I did learn from my mistakes, and so can you. Had I followed my own advice and built a large root cellar first, I would have stayed nice and cool that first couple of years while I was building our farm and gardens. I would have had time to walk the land and experience the seasons and the changes. I would have learned about the prevailing winds, the water flow, erosion, etc. You can learn a lot about your land by going and experiencing it during different seasons, different times of the day, and different situations. This is one reason I suggest people consider temporary housing (a tent, camper, small cabin, or root cellar) when they first move to their land. I will discuss this all more when we get to the Building chapter, but take the time to experience your land in every season and every type of weather. Then you will know just where you ought to put your home, and just how you ought to build it.

There are many ways to build with cooling in mind, and I will discuss them in greater detail in the chapter on Building, but let it suffice for now to say that there are things that everyone should just naturally know. You should naturally know that it is cooler (sometimes 10-20 degrees cooler) in the trees than it is out in the open. In addition to providing shade, trees breathe and transpire water which makes it feel a lot cooler in the midst of them. Had I located my cabin 50 feet to the south of where it is today, it would likely stay 10-15 degrees cooler inside during the hottest days! You should also know that it is cooler underground than it is on the surface; and it is also often cooler 12 to 15 feet above the ground (because of breezes), than it is on the surface. Breezes and wind pass more readily through a long thin structure than they do a large square one. Taking all of these facts into account, a one -story square box on the ground level built out in the open and away from the trees is likely to be the *hottest* and most difficult to cool structure you could possibly build. And guess what? That is generally what homesteaders end up building, because that is what they know.

When you think of cooling your structure, think of these things:

1. Having your home built completely or partially underground can solve a lot of your cooling problems. Underground, banked earth, or combination buildings keep much cooler and are more temperature steady than other types of structures.

2. Build your structure in the trees, if you can. Also consider planting fast growing trees around it as soon as you possibly are able.

3. Build for a breeze. Learn where your prevailing winds come from and how they travel on your plot of land. Then build your building to make the best use of the most prevalent winds. Build yourself a large, screened, porch and make sure that porch will catch a breeze. Also, consider building your structure either a) tall, in order to be

able to catch a breeze when you are upstairs, or b) narrow, like a "shotgun house", so that wind is funneled through the house like a wind tunnel.

4. Watch the sun, and see how it is going to affect your building. Build so that you reflect as much of the sun as possible, except in the winter. Try to use smart building concepts so that the sun doesn't overly heat up your building during the hot months. This is where study and research will pay big dividends. By the time you begin to build, you should know exactly where the sun is at any time and during any season of the year.

ROMAN AIR-CONDITIONING

As I mentioned in the early chapters, the Romans had air-conditioning back in the 4th and 5th centuries. Many of the wealthy citizens were able to pay to have cool mountain water diverted from the city's aqueducts and piped through their houses where it was used in a variety of ways to cool the stone or brick structures.

Another method that the Romans utilized to cool their homes was by installing underground air pipes to create *actual* air-conditioning. Hundreds of feet of ceramic pipe would be laid several feet underground with the far end coming up out of the ground as an air intake. The temperature of the ground at that depth would likely have been around 50 to 55 degrees Fahrenheit, which would often be 40 or more degrees cooler than the ground level air during the summer. The air would be piped into the house with an air vent placed at the lowest level of the interior of the house. At the top of the home, a convection chimney would be built and painted a dark color. As the air in the convection chimney heated up, it would rise pulling air from the house and sucking air in from the air register and from the hundreds of feet of underground pipe. This air would enter the house at a fairly strong speed with temperatures, as we have said, up to 40 degrees cooler than the ambient air. You talk about air-conditioning! This was a cool way to cool a home.

It has been hundreds of years since people have actually, on any large scale, tried to build using these methods, so some trial and error will be necessary. The point is, it is possible, and it is important for us to consider these things.

On a recent trip down south of here to Fredericksburg, Texas, we had the wonderful opportunity to tour around the area. Fredericksburg is an old German colony founded in the 1840's in South Central Texas. Some of the "old European" building styles can still be experienced in and around this wonderful village. At an old homestead in Fredericksburg we were led from a ground-level kitchen into a partially underground basement or root cellar. We were told that this small room had once been "brewing room." Outside, on that hot August day, it was nearly 100 degrees. The brewing room was built about 5 feet underground and extended about 2 to 3 feet up above the ground where windows near the roof allowed any warm air to flow straight out. The walls of the structure were mainly made of stone, and were about 2 feet thick. The temperature in the brewing room was a very pleasant mid-70's. It actually felt air-conditioned in that wonderful room. The Germans used it as a brewing room because German ales could be brewed, fermented, and stored in the room year 'round.

BACK TO THE SOUTH

In my studies I learned that many of the plantations in the Old South were built with natural cooling in mind. If you look at pictures or watch any of the old movies of the Old South, you'll notice that most of the plantation houses had a similar building design. The bottom floor had very high ceilings, and usually there were at least one or two underground root cellars or basements built beneath the first floor. The high ceilings allowed the heat to rise and high windows that went nearly to the ceiling would allow this heat to pass out instead of "stacking" into the room. The bottom floors generally included a very open floor plan, with lots of windows and very thick walls. This kept the bottom floor much cooler than the outside air. The second floor of these plantation houses generally started more than 12 feet up in the

180

air. According to my research, there is almost always a minimum wind speed of 5 to 7 miles per hour at 12 feet above ground level even on a "still" day, meaning that there was a near constant breeze for the second floor. All of the bedrooms were placed upstairs for this reason, and there were large balconies with French doors and large windows that would allow for this constant breeze to pass through. During particularly stifling heat spells Southern folk would sleep out on the balcony so that they could catch the breeze. As a bonus, the high second story was also usually above the "bug line", so most flying bugs (like mosquitoes) wouldn't find their way up there.

Now, earlier in the book I asked the question: In those pictures of the Old South, why did the people generally wear heavy clothing, and why did they seem cool and collected, even during the heat of the summer?

Because they knew how to keep cool!

All of this is to prove to you that we don't need to invest money, time, and effort into addictive, corrupting, industrial cooling systems. The more we use our brains, wisdom, and a good knowledge of history, the more money we save and the better will be our choices. As I've said several times before, you probably cannot afford to go off-grid when it comes to food preservation, air-conditioning, etc., but you can afford to go off off-grid.

OTHER APPLIANCES AND TOOLS

A short word about electrical appliances and tools... Much of what I have to say has been covered earlier in the chapter on going off-grid, and much more will be covered in the chapter on Building. But since I am concluding the couple of chapters on electricity (and how not to use it), I want to say a few things about "other" appliances and power tools.

Many years ago we bought some battery-powered 18 Volt power tools when we were building our barn at our old on-grid homestead. I had a choice between buying some really nice and expensive cordless power tools, or some really cheap ones. I decided to buy the cheap ones and figured if they got me through that one project, they would have been worth the price. Four years later we were still using them. The original set came with a drill, a flashlight, a hand vacuum, and a circular saw. We bought a second set of batteries a few years after the original purchase. A couple of years ago, while working on our root cellar project, I was irritated that the batteries weren't lasting very long, and we had so many things going on that I needed to have another set of batteries on hand charging, so I went to town to buy another set of batteries and a second charger. It was going to cost $59.99 for the batteries and charger; but then I discovered I could get a whole second set of tools with batteries and charger for $99.00. I bought the whole second set. This allowed us to have a second set of tools, so we could have more people working at once. This gave us a second flashlight too. Later I bought a car charger so I can charge the batteries in my truck whenever I go to town. This allows me to charge batteries (for the most part) using power I am already paying to produce (that is something to remember... every time you drive your car, you are producing many times more electricity than the car needs. Using driving time to charge batteries is a good idea). Since I purchased my first set of these tools, they have created dozens of other tools and accessories that will run off of these same 18V batteries. We use our 18V flashlights almost every night and every morning since we are up before the sun. We are not dependent on them, but they do come in handy. We milk the cow by these lights as well. The point is that, as an intermediate step, some cordless, rechargeable, power tools can be a good investment. But...

Once again we must apply our philosophy to the use of intermediate means. What will happen if the system crashes and soon I am unable to charge or use these cordless tools? They will become useless to me. So here is what I do: Every time I use one of these tools, I deliberately stop and ask myself. How will I do this task or chore if and when I don't have access to this tool? Then I ruminate on it and force myself to remember what solutions I come up with. Later on, when I am in a flea market, an antique or junk shop, or at a garage sale, I look for "old-timey" tools (like hand drills, hand saws, planes, etc.) that will allow me to continue working and growing even after I am unable to use power tools. But, it is not enough to own some old tools. We need to know how to properly use them, maintain them, and sharpen them. For this reason, I have taken several courses at Homestead Heritage in Waco, Texas, in order to learn how to work using non-electric hand tools. And, I have to tell you, what I have learned there has been well worth the money. There are likely similar schools and classes near you, or maybe you can contact an old-timer who still builds furniture or cabinets in this way who will teach you. There are many ways you can begin to learn and practice these old skills and I do suggest that you begin immediately. It will likely be too late to acquire and learn to use these tools after an emergency has made them necessary.

We also use a few electrical appliances or tools in the kitchen. We have a few blenders, an electric juicer, a coffee grinder, etc. that currently we operate using our off-grid power. Our process, in mitigating our risk when it comes to kitchen appliances and tools, is the same as the one that I used with power tools. Every time we do something, we ask, *"How will we do this without power?"* Then we set out to procure both the tools and the know-how to be able to continue our work without electrical or other type of power. We now have an old hand powered coffee-grinder, a large butter-churn, a cheese press, and a hand-operated food processor. We have all kinds of other "antique" hand tools for the kitchen, and we are looking into buying some fruit processing equipment (peelers, juicers, presses, etc.). I also make my family use these things regularly so they are used to them and aren't hesitant to use them.

This process can seem overwhelming at first until you stop and figure that all of the hand tools we have purchased, _all of them put together_, cost less than a single new refrigerator, a dishwasher, or a new electric stove. And we will never have to pay for electricity to power these hand tools.

My friend, the Agrarian blogger Herrick Kimball said recently, *"SIMPLE, people-powered machines are best"*. Most of them do not break down, and will work dependably for years with only some cleaning and a spot of oil now and then.

OLD PATHS

Looking towards the old paths is not a melancholy dream, or some fantastical wish for a mythical bygone paradise. We don't look to the past as if it was the perfect, idyllic, pastoral utopia. We know it wasn't perfect. We look to the past for a few great reasons: Because the Bible tells us to (Jer. 6:16); because there is wisdom and reason in learning these old and valued skills; and because the way the world has chosen, though it seems to be right for a time, has wrought nothing but damage, destruction, intellectual and spiritual entropy, and mental colonization. The product of the modern way of doing things is spiritual emptiness and sadness, is fraught with disappointment and unrealized expectations, and creates a crazed urge to fill the void with consumption and "stuff".

May we all start looking backwards with hope and joy. Our political mottos might be: *Building A Bridge To The Past,* or, *Agrarianism: Change We Can Believe In... Because it Worked Before.*

CHAPTER 8
LAND... OF THE FREE
(LAND PART 1)

LAND, A LONGING IN THE HEART

I would have loved to talk about land first. After all, we are "Back to the Land" proponents, aren't we? As homesteaders, our lexicon is steeped in the concept of "the land." We "work the land"; we "live off the land"; we see land and the blessings and obligations involved with working and tilling it as the central pillar of our philosophy. So why didn't I make "Land" the first category and chapter of the book? Well, because I have had to deal with the way the mind works today, and that is quite a chore. There were too many giants in the land to talk about the land first. Hopefully, having slain a few giants, we can talk about the good and plentiful land.

The thought of man working on a piece of land he can call his own has ever been the secret yearning of billions of men, although, if we stop to think about it, the concept of owning land is really a bizarre one when you consider how long the earth has been here and how short our own lives are in comparison. Though I believe in Total Depravity (the corruption of our desires and our nature due to the fall), I believe that there is a spark of knowledge of God's original plan for the earth in every single man and woman. Why do you think people take "vacations" from work? Seriously, why do people save up money and vacation days to go somewhere wild and unspoiled? Why do people go camping when they have time off from work? Have you ever been out in the wild, or on a trip through Amish country, or on a beach or a boat somewhere and thought, "You know, I cannot wait to get into a cubicle in a building somewhere in some big city!" Of course nobody but a fool would dream of leaving a homestead somewhere, someday, to get a grinding corporate job punching a clock. There is something universally extant in mankind that teaches him that he would rather be in nature than in some mind-numbing urban jungle. I know people who spend most of their lives thinking about two things: Weekends, and Vacations. Why is that? Why do people spend their vacations out on some hunting lease, at a lake, or camping in the wilds? Why do parents take their children on day trips to petting zoos and model farms or homesteads? What is the deal with camping? Why do people choose to spend their "free" time trying to get back in touch with the land, unless there is some connection between freedom and land? When people look at a picture of a beautiful Amish farm, they are generally overwhelmed with a feeling of peace, tranquility, and a secret longing for a simpler life. When the same people look at pictures of traffic, or cubicles, or cityscapes, they are often inundated with feelings of stress, anger, confusion, or hopelessness. These are not isolated feelings. If we are honest, we all identify with what I am saying.

In every place where urbanization really began to take root, a walk or ride in the country was soon the cure offered for city madness or stress. When urbanization and industrialization inevitably led to greater class distinctions (more rich people, more poor people, and fewer middle-class people), we find the rich buying country houses to "get away from it all". In Ancient Greece, Persia, and Rome; in 19th century Russia, England, and France; anywhere where urbanism had begun to predominate – the country house, villa, dacha, or retreat began to be common.

I am convinced that the perpetual command of God to work, till, and have *benevolent dominion* over the land is a latent urge and desire in every human put there by God. It is a faint reminder or our pre-fallen state, and, if you are honest enough within yourself to admit that it is there, it is plain and unequivocal evidence that we are correct in our Agrarian philosophy and ideas.

Modern man is lost without a compass, hopeless and confused in an increasingly urban world. Something in him, however faintly, detects peace and goodness in the concept of being in nature and working the land. I am not the only one calling men back to the land. I honestly believe that the conscience of man, *if it is still functional at all*, is calling men and women back to God's ordained way of living.

DEBUNKING SOME MYTHS

There are some great myths in the minds of many people when they hear about Agrarianism or Agrarians. Debunking these myths is necessary before we can get into too much depth talking about land and a right land philosophy. Here are a few of the most notable myths:

1. That there would be no cities, towns, or villages in an Agrarian society.

2. That under an Agrarian system, everyone will own land and have their own farm.

3. That when you live off-grid in an Agrarian system, you are expected to make or provide 100% of what you consume straight off of the land.

4. That business: buying, selling, trade, import, export, etc. have no place in Agrarianism.

If we are to have a right mind and a right land philosophy it is necessary that we debunk these myths. These myths are all interrelated, so I will deal with them corporately:

There have been cities, towns, and villages almost as long as there have been people. In fact, so long as there is sin there will be big cities. That is not the issue we are addressing. The idea of the small town or village is not incompatible with Agrarianism at all, in fact, when Agrarianism was the ruling economic system and philosophy of life, small towns and villages thrived and everyone benefited. It is only natural that there will be those individuals in Agrarian societies who are gifted with special talents, or who will be called upon to benefit the society and the community by expediting trade, barter, import, and export. Villages and towns were nothing more than places where Agrarians could go to commune, to seek services, and to expedite the exchange of excess materials or crops for other necessary items. Every region, every area, and every property is not conducive to growing or producing every single thing that might be helpful or necessary for life. Therefore, towns will always spring up to assist in trade between individuals or between different regions so as to equalize the availability of needful things. The main difference between the hyper-specialized commercial society (like in our current system) and pure Agrarianism, is that in a truly Agrarian society, everyone would have at least a garden plot and a few animals in order to help (as much as is possible) to ensure survival and to mitigate against shortages, scarcity, or an interruption in trade.

Every piece of land does not have every necessary mineral or resource. It would be nice if every farm was a complete closed loop - a perfect biosphere - but most farms are not. Some land is resource rich, and some land is resource poor. Your land may have a nice, sustainable woodlot, while your treeless neighbor may have a nice vein of salt or iron ore on his land. Not every farm, community, or every area will be able to produce everything that is necessary for survival and comfort; and it is good that trade and barter develop in and between Agrarian individuals and communities. The whole community is strengthened through these means.

Not every person in an Agrarian society will be a landowner and farmer. Although it is a high ideal, it is impossible. It has never been a workable solution - in all of history - for every man to own and farm land. Not every Amish man owns his own full-fledged farm. When you go to Amish country and you see Amish buggies, someone made those buggies, and someone is working on them and fixing them. But behind that buggy shop, you are likely to see a small farm, or at least a garden. Every community will need people who are good at building things, repairing things, procuring things, etc. Some men have skills and talents in management, while others are "small picture" folks, with an eye and heart towards artisanship in a very specific area. Even in the most successful eras of Agrarian history there have been landed folk and un-landed folk. There will always be employers and the employed. Even in the Bible the shepherds were shepherds, meaning that they were specialists that tended and herded sheep. Shepherding was an Agrarian profession. The Bible teaches employers to be fair with their employees and to not withhold their wages; and the Bible teaches employees to serve and honor their masters and to work for them as if they were doing the work for God Himself. There is nothing dishonorable about being employed in a trade or specialty. In Agrarian Europe 250 years ago, the average farm would have employed dozens and dozens of workers - shepherds, swineherds, thatchers, millers, sawyers, coopers, smiths, brewers, etc. How do you think most people came upon their last names?

Here is where many people can get confused. How can we say that specialization is good, when we have already named specialization as one of the primary causes of many of the problems in the society today? Is specialization good? Or is it bad? Some specialization in an Agrarian culture is a good thing, but when specialization becomes sub-human, in that it causes almost every human to become just a cog in a larger machine, then it has gone too far. The problem with specialization occurs when people throw off all responsibility to provide for themselves and their families from the land, and instead begin to rely on an unnatural and unsustainable system for that provision. When the farmer stops growing his own food, and instead puts all of his land and resources into growing a single "money crop", then he begins to rely inordinately on the system, and he begins to feed the system that will one day destroy him. As this type of system develops, eventually the farmer doesn't even know where his food is grown or who grows it. In fact, he is not a farmer at all... he is an "industrial producer." When problems happen, as they inevitably will; when people get sick from dangerous and unsafe foods; when the whole society grows sick from the un-Godly methods of commercial agriculture, there grows up a need for more specialists and bureaucrats: Food Inspectors, Government Agents, Purchasers, Middle-Men, Trucking Specialists; not to mention the need for more doctors, nurses, hospitals, insurance, socialized medicine, etc., etc. Taxes go up and up and up and eventually there will be a call for the government to step in and just run everything for everyone. All of these people and systems and government regulation become necessary to make the farmer (industrial producer), who once grew his own food, feel comfortable and safe in the environment and culture caused by hyper-specialization. The point is that when specialization is very limited, and when it focuses on Agrarian activities, art, and skills, it is a good thing; when it becomes corrupted, and is the single most identifiable element of the society and culture, then it is a very bad thing.

As an aside, the modern political dialectic between "conservatives" who are assumed to be for small government, and "liberals" who are assumed to be for big government is a load of hooey. All conservatives and liberals who operate in (and for) an urban, industrial, world system – are for big government. Period. It is like saying that one man (we'll call him a conservative) is for eating only 47 pancakes at breakfast, while another man (the liberal) is for eating 150 pancakes at breakfast. Can it be said that either man is for moderation and against gluttony? No. Neither the modern political conservatives nor the modern political liberals are for limited government. Urbanism, specialization, globalism, and industrialism require big government – in every case. One party is for slow poison, the other is for fast poison – that is the only real difference. I'll give you a very good example of my point about big government. When everyone drove a horse and buggy, if you were in a small "accident" on a rural dirt road, you were traveling at a very slow speed and it is very likely that no one was killed and there would be no reason to get policemen and insurance companies involved. No government other than that of morals, manners, good sense, and honesty, was needed. In fact, policemen in those days, when they were needed or available, generally dealt with crime and investigations or in enforcing criminal and civil laws. What happened when we paved the roads? Now you needed government to build and maintain roads and to own property once owned by private individuals. When industrial motor vehicles began plying the roads at high speeds severe accidents became commonplace – many of these "accidents" were fatal or required massive amounts of health care and action by insurance companies and other businesses that inevitably require more and more government oversight and regulation. The need for policemen multiplied and skyrocketed. Horses, which never needed petroleum fuels, maintenance, and government inspections, were no longer safe to use on the roads. The motor vehicle industry basically BECAME the country, and more than half of the economy (sometimes much, much more) became dependent on the production, repair, maintenance, and operation of motor vehicles... not counting the untold number of jobs created in order to scrape dead bodies out of cars, man ambulances, the need for paramedics, tow-trucks, etc.; and all of this required more and more government in order to keep it all straight. So... what happened to small government? If the so-called "conservatives" were for small government, they would advocate getting rid of motor vehicles and high-speed roadways and a return to horse power. But they aren't for small government – not at all. Agrarianism is the only philosophy, lifestyle, and political system for those who actually believe in smaller, less-intrusive government. A free and responsible Agrarian is a real conservative... everyone else, whether they like it or not, is a statist.

Back to my main point... In an Agrarian society, not everyone will own land. Some people will eventually become Agrarian specialists. Some people will not have the necessary ability to keep and hold property, while a few people may grow wealthy in land and holdings. We're not communists. We believe in freedom, and in a truly free society there will be some people who have more than others. But, what does all of this mean to you? As you move forward with your off off-grid plans you need to be thinking about what you want to do. What skills do you have and how do you see yourself living in the future? If it is not possible for you to become a land-owning farmer, it is still possible for you to go off-grid and to live life in Agrarian terms. Land ought not to be an idol. Many of the Pilgrims, the Puritans, and the Pioneers, worked for decades before they owned their own farms, and some never did. Some people were more than happy to live their lives as servants and workers, or as artisans engaged in some skill or trade. In many cases, these workers served on a larger farm, but it was likely that they also had a small spread for themselves and their families which they worked diligently to provide more for themselves and their loved ones. Others started up trades in small villages, working for themselves and helping the Agrarian society by focusing on a specific area of need in the community. As I said, there will always be those who acquire and hold more land than others and who are willing to employ others.

WHAT IS A FARMER?

People today have some very odd ideas about what a farmer is. Lately, there has developed an image of the farmer as the rich rural cowboy, riding huge tractors, each costing hundreds of thousands of dollars across thousands of acres of open farmland. I am sorry to tell you that this man is not a farmer. He is an *agribusiness-man* – an industrial producer. I can't help but snort with barely masked derision when these men claim to be farmers. If people do not see the farmer as a rich rural cowboy, they might instead imagine him as a poor, miserable, wretch, just struggling to make ends meet. Both of these views are, generally, inventions of the 20th century, and both are snapshots taken at different times during that dismal century of the fall and ruin of the farming culture and society. Here is how the system progressed (or actually *regressed*):

Historically, the farmer was considered a wealthy man, held in high esteem by the society and by other men - he was the *Gentleman Farmer*. There was nothing shameful or ignoble about working for a good, honest farmer on a good farm. The farmer was not only the master of his family, but he was the benevolent leader of a large, extended family of workers and tradesmen. The farmer was a lynchpin in the society. He was the benefactor of the Agrarian community and he was responsible for the happiness and survival of many. Many of the beautiful villages you see in the picture postcards of rural Europe actually began as small towns that sprung up on or near large farms and estates. In Russia, the villages were all on some privately owned estate. The community and the society was so intertwined with working the land that there was no real dividing line between "town" and "farm". The town was merely a location where specialized Agrarian trades and some commerce took place. The town was a place of communion and unity. It held the farming community together so that people felt that they belonged to some unit larger than just the nuclear family. The village was not *mercenary*; it didn't exist just for buying and selling and making money. The village was a place of *common ground*, which is why most early villages had a "green", often called "the commons". Almost everyone in a village or region felt that they were related, if not by common blood (though many of them were related by blood), at least by common purposes. The farm and the village community *was* the society.

THE FALL OF THE REAL FARMER AND THE RISE OF AGRIBUSINESS

At some point, when trade and mercantilism began to flourish, farmers learned that they had the opportunity to make enormous amounts of money if they would put all of their land, and all of their resources, into the production of just one product or crop... *"the money crop"*. Survival, Simplicity, Sustainability, Satisfaction – all of these were no longer the main point. Money became the main point. Farming, rather than being a life, slowly became "making a living"; it became a *business*. The millers, the coopers, the sawyers, the brewers, the thatchers, etc. were all let go – unless they were needed for the production and sale of the one money crop. Laborers stopped being neighbors and started being mercenaries themselves. Skilled laborers were no longer a part of the farmer's family, they became hired guns, contract workers. They often worked for more than one farmer, or for anyone who paid well. As specialists, these workers moved to town and opened up shop. Gone were the private plots and the family gardens. Any land that was not set aside and usable for production of the money crop (which could be either plants or animals) was sold off, and more land was purchased for production. This means that the village was no longer located on the expansive family farm. The village became independent – it became *government*, and its purpose became mercenary like the people who now lived there. Jobs left the farm and went to the village first, and eventually to the cities and the ports where trade was centered. When hard times hit, or when crops failed, or when the business changed, the farmers either suffered through it, or they went out of business – selling their land to speculators, investors, or agri-businessmen. The downside of specialization became a common reality. Revolving debt became necessary in order to tide the farmer through planting season or through any rough patches. Most of the farmers eventually closed up, sold out, and went to the cities. Bankers and government farm agents became the new lynchpins and masters of the community. Agri-businessmen and corporate farmers, aided by the bankers, grabbed up the newly available land and the maintenance of the soil, once the loving employment of those who were given benevolent dominion over it, was turned over to the new mercenary spirit. Governments began to learn that under a system of specialization and industrialization the money crop agri-businessmen had to be kept (as much as possible) from failing, so crop insurance and government subsidies were put in place. Government tariffs were imposed to keep the farmer from suffering through the "whims of the market". Before long, almost 100% of agribusiness was being run or directed by agents in the governments of the world. As a result, when you meet a man who calls himself a farmer today, statistically it is most probable that you are meeting a state-sponsored and tax supported agri-businessman, a government supported or subsidized hack, *not* a real farmer. There are some real farmers out there today, but there are not many. Keep this in mind when you hear statistics about how many people still farm. Keep this in mind when someone tells you that some bill or some tax is going to be "good for farmers".

When people ask me what I do, I either say "I am a farmer", or "I homestead", and the difference in the responses I receive is notable. When I say, "I am a farmer", almost inevitably the next question asked is, "Oh. What do you farm?" You see, the money crop system is so widespread that people have trouble conceiving of what the word "farmer" really means historically. When they say "What do you farm", they mean, "What is your money crop? What is your *Business*?" When I say, "I homestead", there usually is not any answer at all. Usually there is just a slight nodding of the head and a quizzical look, because "I homestead" is an answer that does not compute with most people. Colonization has taken its toll, and the mind no longer has a real concept of the sustenance farmer who works with his hands and raises most of the things that he needs from the land. That concept is an old faded dream, or a picture postcard from some bygone time. Maybe such a farm would be a nice place to visit, but really... who would want to *live* there? That sounds suspiciously like... work.

But what does all of this have to do with you buying land? This lesson is designed to give you a historical concept of what land is, and how our understanding of land has changed. Make sure you study the four myths given at the beginning of this chapter, and really ruminate and pray on what it is you actually want to do. It is always a mistake to jump into some new philosophy or way of life without knowing any history. Always remember that history is a lamp by which we may guide our feet.

OFF OFF-GRID LIVING... LIFE ON THE LAND

"Land," Mark Twain said, *"Buy it if you can because they aren't making any more of it."* There have been, it seems in history, as many philosophies about land as there have been philosophers. Philosophers, even the good ones, are just zealots with ideas. Some ideas are really good, and some are really bad, but all ideas are founded on some philosophy. One of the problems with philosophies is that they often get codified into law by brute force without any real reason (Biblical or otherwise) behind them. At first a new philosophy may be questioned and debated, but, as time passes and people become totally

trained in that philosophy, it may become an erroneous or *unreasonable maxim.* Unreasonable maxims become walls in our thinking, guiding us to conclusions that may be just as unreasonable as the philosophy that brought us there in the first place. Errors are often sanctified by the passing of time. This is why we say that the mind of modern man is "colonized", which means that he has accepted things as truths that are not truths at all, but are just learned behaviors - patterns and trails of thinking - that have become ruts out of which man cannot free himself.

Most people believe certain things merely because their whole lives everyone around them has believed those things. People accept things the way they are mainly because they have never experienced, or been exposed to, any other way. Unhappily, when I speak to people about land it is difficult to get them to think clearly on the subject because their thinking is based on a lifetime of accepting as truth that which was once just the crazy idea of an eager zealot. The modern, industrialized mind cannot even begin to consider that, for literally thousands of years the idea of being caged into a poorly built cracker-box house on a ¼ acre suburban lot literally 15 feet from a neighbor would have been laughable as a workable land philosophy. Most modern suburbanites don't know of any other way of living because the way they now live is all they have ever known. Most of the people who first start studying history are shocked when they learn that, only 150 years ago, owning "forty acres and a mule" was considered a bare minimum for sustenance farming. The Homestead Act of 1862 gave 160 acres of land to each person or family who could claim them, provided they stayed and worked the land for at least five years. By contrast, today, television commercials show excited, smiling couples, hugging one another in joyful bliss, ecstatic because they have entered into a thirty year mortgage contract to purchase a shoddily built, but gilded and trimmed, crackerbox house on ¼ acre of land. The voice over says, *"You always dreamed of owning your own home..."*

In order to properly think about land in our Agrarian journey to an off-grid life we have to be willing to consider things we have never before considered. Land has to be central to our thinking and our philosophy, but land cannot become an idol or we will surely fail in our Agrarian pursuit. Land is a means through which we can obey God, provide for our own, evangelize our families (first, and then others), build community, obey the commandments of God, and glorify Him in the work He has given us to do.

Land, like any other means, needs to be put in its proper place in our thinking. For too many people, land is the beginning and the ending of their off-grid planning, and they are crippled because they haven't ever examined any of their fundamental presuppositions or foundations concerning just where and how they want to live. This mentality can manifest itself in a few different and interesting ways:

1. Many people are married to a place or a region, without any real identifiable reasons why. Just like a man who has a favorite local sports team, even though he might have no real tie to that team at all, people grow fond of where they are and they act like they are planted in that place like trees. In fact, one of the most popular (but stupid and untrue) statements I hear is "Grow where you are planted." Well folks, we are people and not trees. We have legs and not roots. There is nothing wrong with being loyal to land and region if the reasons behind the loyalty are logical, reasonable, and/or Biblical. But, most of the people I talk to have a strange and unreasonable loyalty to an area or region and they cannot even begin to offer a logical and reasonable apologetic for their decision process. Unless you already own your land and are determined and committed to make homesteading work where you already are, there is no reason to default to one particular area over another without well thought-out reasons for your decisions.

2. If you do not already own your homesteading land, then please take the time to consider the "non-physical" or spiritual

ramifications of what you are doing. I know too many people who have land and resources, but no fellowship or communion. I cannot imagine ever again living my life outside of true Biblical community. Fellowship is too important to us to sacrifice it for our own self-preservation and carnal success. I said recently that I would rather live in a desert with friends and brothers, than in a carnal "paradise" without any fellowship or community.

3. Please do everything you can to defeat and destroy any concept you have of "The Perfect Homestead". Too often we idealize the Agrarian life until it becomes a wall we cannot scale or a picture postcard we will never realize. I have heard people wistfully describing the idyllic land they are looking for with dreamy eyes cast back into their heads. After their breathless description of rural bliss, I will say, "I have seen just the land you are describing... it is in a picture hanging on the wall in a restaurant in town". Life is not a postcard. If you are expecting to find the perfect little homestead with a year-round brook flowing through it, and a pond with geese, and a perfectly green pasture with the perfect red barn... etc.... etc... you are probably going to be sadly disappointed because the homestead you are looking for will either a) cost you a million bucks, or b) never live up to the dream you have concocted in your mind. You will most likely start with empty or overgrown land and you will most likely have to build your utopia there. Agrarianism is coming to love the land God gives us and to till it and work it according to our needs and the directions given by God. We build homesteads - we cannot afford to buy them.

Basically, this first part is an exercise in destroying myths and fantasies. When most people start on their journey they have unreal expectations, and their dreams and visions are based on false presuppositions and faulty or unreasonable assumptions. Unhappily, people forget or leave out some really important things when they begin their quest for land,

and they include some fantasies or myths that need to be dashed on the rocks. We need to have a realistic view of our land needs and desires, and we need to have at least some historical context through which we can view our situation.

Land is highly valued by Christian and Secularist alike, and will be tough to acquire in quantities sufficient to serve us as homesteads. If it were not tough we would not value it highly enough. Acquiring land, if that is your goal, will take some creative thinking; unless you are just rich enough to plunk down a sizable wad of cash on the perfect homestead. Good for you if you are, but most of us are just not in that situation.

In order to procure land in the world today, we must be willing to pray hard, work hard, and think hard. If the solution is just "plunk down the money and buy the land", you may never have money enough to pull the trigger. The longer you work in the world's slavish system, prices are going up and expenses are increasing. Your target is always going to be moving. I don't know how many people out there are working hard in the current consumer system in order (they say) to get out of it, but, in my experience, I have met very few who have really thought out their plans, and I have met even fewer who are not still operating according to some flawed presuppositions.

You need to be creative and to think in ways you are not accustomed to thinking. There was a reason that millions of men and women became indentured servants only a few short centuries ago. Do you think all of the original colonists came to the New World as rich men with just enough money saved up from worldly pursuits to plunk down on some land? Not so. Most of the original colonists were poor, and most didn't even have the money to pay for their transit. They were willing to work as near slaves for 5-10 years in order to become landholders someday, *if* the Lord did will it. Most of them wanted to be free from political and religious persecution. Being a rich farmer was not the first thing on their minds. Today, few people are even willing to even consider that most of their ancestors came to the New World indentured, and our society has trained them to rebel against any concept at all of servitude. Ironically, the same people who are brainwashed into rejecting out of hand any concept of voluntary servitude remain slaves to a debilitating commercialized money economy, having their souls sucked out at their "jobs" each and every day just because they cannot think outside of what they already know. In effect they say, "I will not be any man's servant!" and they are too deaf to hear their proud exclamations being drowned out by the rattle of their own chains. I know this, and maybe I am alone in believing it, but – knowing what I know now – if I had a choice between working for 10 or 20 or 30 more years in some soul destroying job, working for the Prince of This World's mercenary consumer kingdom in order to save up enough money to someday buy some land in the country; or placing myself in indenture, or serving as an apprentice, or even accepting voluntary slavery for 5 or 7 years in an Agrarian situation in order to procure that land sooner... give me my Agrarian chains. I'll trade in the industrial ones. I say this so that you will recognize that revolutionary plans take revolutionary ideas – and walking in the light requires that we recognize that we have heretofore walked in darkness.

If we are to succeed in this revolutionary plan of ours, we have to be willing to try new things and to think extraordinary thoughts. Our ticket to land ownership may be out there right now - we just haven't thought of it yet.

HOW MANY ACRES DO I NEED?

This ought to be one of the first questions you ask yourself. How many acres do YOU need? There is no "one-size-fits-all" answer to this question. If you desire to be a tradesman, or an Agrarian specialist, you may not need many acres at all. If you intend to farm, you will need more. Historically, there were different kinds, and therefore different sizes, of farms. For most of pre-industrial history, forty acres has been generally accepted as the most acres a man could work with just his family and a mule, ox, or horses for plowing. I was shocked to learn that, on a common forty acre farm, only five or six acres were tilled and worked for growing crops. Most of the rest of the forty acres was used for pasture, and the balance was for housing, barns, and other structures. I was very surprised to learn that so few acres were actually in tillage. But, when I studied deeper, it made sense. Most early farmers were not growing large amounts of "money crops" and a man and a mule would have their hands full plowing five or six acres in a few days, so those five acres would be intensively farmed and cared for. The rest of the land was generally maintained in pasture for the animals. Later, with the advent of the cash crop and industrial farming methods, larger farms became more commonplace. In my opinion, except for those who are ranching or running cattle in arid areas (where more acres are needed), most families will find anything over forty acres to be superfluous and unnecessary.

But do you *need* forty acres? Absolutely not. I have read of people who are successfully homesteading on as few as two acres, and there are a whole lot of people out there who are very successful with as few as five acres. With intensive gardening and crop rotating techniques, it is very possible (and maybe even preferable) to maintain a *micro-homestead.*

As I have said, there is no single answer to the question "how many acres" that will be satisfactory for everyone. In my family, we are trying to model our homestead, as much as is possible, on the successful small homesteads of the last several centuries; but there are others in our community who are very satisfied with much less land. I am absolutely certain that it is possible to provide almost all of the food that a normal sized family can eat, off of only a few acres. The answer to "How many acres do I need," is a fluid one, and the answer can change wildly depending on how we answer some pretty important questions: What kinds of animals are we going to own, and how many? What type of growing philosophy are we going to adopt? Are we going to be "row-croppers" or intensive gardeners? Are we going to feed our animals with hay? With bagged feed? With root crops? Are we going to keep full-sized animals, or miniatures? Do we intend to harvest from the wild, or is most of our food going to come from gardens and from domesticated animals? Are we going to need a woodlot, or are there other natural resources we can tap? Are you going to be a lone-ranger, or are you going to live in a community where you can specialize a little more and then barter and trade for other needful things? All of these questions will have a bearing on how much land you want or need. So you can see that having a plan is critical to our homesteading survival.

It is certain that there is plenty to think about! Maybe it is time for a walk in the country to clear your head? In the next chapter we'll look at some land ideas, and I'll offer some real-world examples for your edification.

CHAPTER 9
DIFFERENT STROKES
(LAND PART 2)

DOUG'S STORY

Doug was up before the sun. He didn't need an alarm clock. He was so accustomed to waking up at the same time every morning that he knew naturally by the faint light on the horizon and the sounds and smells of the morning that it was time for him to get started. He dressed quickly and headed to the small milk shed to meet Polly, his milk cow. She was waiting for him. He had separated her from her calf the night before, so she was full and very ready to be milked.

After milking he returned Polly to her calf and headed back to his small cabin for breakfast. By this time the sun was up and the morning was fully underway. It was shaping up like another glorious day on the land, Praise God. He needed to go move his small herd of cattle to the newly fenced pasture he had prepared. Doug had created a workable pasture rotation system on his 80 acres. 80 acres is a lot of land for a single man without children, but Doug had every intention of finding a wife and having a family someday, if the Lord were to will it, and he had arranged his property in such a way that it didn't take as much work as some people might think. He had cows, chickens, some sheep, and a few pigs. He had divided 50 of his acres into ten acre paddocks, so he could keep the animals rotating onto fresh pasture. Ten acres of his land was a woodlot and the rest, what wasn't used for his cabin, sheds, and gardens, was left in permanent pasture. Whenever necessary, he could turn animals out into this area if he needed to "rest" any other portion of his land.

From his land, Doug was able to produce almost all of the food he needed in order to survive. His garden was a large "truck garden" where he would produce enough to take a truckload of produce to the farmer's market every week during the growing months. He also produced enough "overage", primarily in meat, eggs, and wool, to be able to pay the balance of his land payment to Mr. Polk. Two days a week, Doug worked on Mr. Polk's ranch building or repairing fences, cutting brush, moving cattle, or basically doing any "grunt work" that Mr. Polk required. The arrangement was ideal for both of them. Mr. Polk was getting older, and he really needed a lot of help around his ranch. Doug had gone to work for Mr. Polk several years ago. After he had built up a good relationship with his boss and had shown him that he was a good and diligent worker, Mr. Polk had agreed to sell him 80 farmable acres in exchange for a handy, regular ranch hand. Doug agreed to pay cash, broken down into monthly payments, for 50% of the price of the land. For the balance, Doug agreed to work two days a week for Mr. Polk for five years. The two days every week were flexible. If he wanted to, he could work four days in one week and then take the next week off. He picked the days he wanted to work, and if he were to be sick or if he were rained out, he could make up a day or two the following week. This still left Doug with a significant land payment every month, but he was committed to paying off his land in five years. In order to ease the burden, Doug started by selling almost everything he had previously owned. He had hosted a garage sale that lasted nearly a month, and he liquidated virtually everything. He cashed out his retirement from his last job, and he turned everything he owned into cash. He also got rid of almost everything that caused him to make a regular monthly payment. After simplifying and paying off all of his debt Doug had enough money to build a very small cabin (12' x 12'), a small milking and storage shed, and to buy his seed and his first starter animals. He began with 4 pregnant heifers (one would be his milk cow to start), 14 hens and a couple of roosters, 3 ewe lambs and 1 ram, and 2 pigs – one female and one male. After building some rudimentary pens and a chicken tractor Doug had just enough cash left over to prepay his land payments for 9 months. His agreement with Mr. Polk was that, if some situation or calamity arose where Doug would be unable to make his land payments for more than a few months, half of the land would revert back to Mr. Polk until which time that Doug could catch up on payments. In a worst case scenario, where there was an economic crash or some other world-changing event, and if Doug became unable to come up with cash for payments, he would be allowed to keep the forty acres, so long as he was able to:

Stay loyal to his obligation to work two days a week for Mr. Polk for the five years, no matter what.

Provide a small percentage of his production of food and material to Mr. Polk.

By this agreement, Doug had resurrected an age-old method used by poor people for millennia to acquire land and eventually their freedom. Doug had entered into a gentleman's agreement that basically created a modern day system of indentured servitude, and he was glad to do it! In effect, he owned 40 acres from day one of his agreement, and he was working two days a week to acquire 40 more. He was protected in case of economic downturn or other worldwide crisis. He was still free for four days a week, and in the morning and evenings on his ranch work-days, to work on and enjoy his own farm. If things remained economically stable for five years he would own 80 acres free and clear, and he would be free to marry and start his family.

Interestingly enough, when Mr. Polk experienced some of the farm fresh eggs, beautiful vegetables, and grass-fed meat that Doug produced, he agreed to buy a good portion of his monthly food from Doug. Of course, no money had to change hands. Mr. Polk just took the value of the food he purchased off of Doug's land payment. This further reduced the amount of money that Doug had to produce from "off-property" sales.

John's Story

A few years after Doug started working on his homestead, his friend John and John's family moved down to live near Doug and to partake in fellowship with him. Doug had a wife and a young daughter, but he was not interested in operating a large farm. John was very talented as a woodworker, and he was also passably able to shoe horses and perform some other work with animals. Doug introduced John to Mr. Polk, who quickly agreed to sell John four acres adjoining Doug's land. John offered to pay cash for his land, but Mr. Polk convinced him to do some work in lieu of cash payments. Mr. Polk and John agreed on a sale price for the land, and then, whenever Mr. Polk had some work he needed John to do, he would subtract that amount from the land price. In this way, John was able to purchase his land outright in only a year or two, and he had the cash he had saved from the land purchase to use to start his own small homestead.

John studied a lot about how other people in the past (and even today) had built sustenance farms on only a few acres. He even traveled to a nearby Homesteading historical village in order to see how they had built, and were operating, a fully sustainable homestead on only three and a half acres. He was shocked and pleasantly surprised to learn that so much food could be intelligently and sustainably grown on so few acres. Before long, John and his family were providing almost all of their food and supplies from their small farm.

STEVE'S STORY

When Steve, another one of Doug's friends, heard what Doug and John had done, he contacted Doug for more information. He definitely wanted to move off-grid, and he wanted to have a garden and produce as much of his own food as he could, but his situation was troublesome and he had some concerns. He felt he had passed his "farming prime" (he was in his 60's), and though he was still able to work, he wasn't able to work like he used to. He was unmarried, so he didn't have the need for as much land, and he was very likely going to need help doing any building or construction. At his age, he couldn't see going out and buying a large plot of land in the country, most of which he would never use. However, very few people in rural farming areas are willing to sell just an acre or two. It was a troubling truism that the further you get from a city, the less people are willing to break up the land into small portions. Most of the land was in 100-300 acre sections or larger, and the smallest amount of land Steve could find for sale was 25 acres. What could he do?

Doug had an idea. He proposed that, with Mr. Polk's permission, Steve move onto a small portion of Doug's land. They would carve out an acre for Steve, and make him a small homestead on that acre. An acre is plenty of land on which to have a sizeable garden, and maybe even some chickens, rabbits, or bees. Basically Steve would be treated as a part of Doug's family and household, and he would work three days a week for Doug. In exchange, Doug offered Steve a lifetime "lease" on his one acre homestead. He could treat the land as if it was his own, and he would have friends, family, and neighbors to help support him in his later years. Steve had no real reason to own land, and he had no one to leave it to upon his death. He wanted to be an Agrarian and separate from the wickedness of the world system, so Doug's idea was a great deal for him.

As Steve's small homestead became more productive, he began to earn a little side money from his rabbits and bees, and when he was able to earn some money doing some other side jobs, sometimes he would "buy" work days back from Doug – in effect paying a low rent instead of working for his land. Doug and Steve worked out a rent payment price, so that on any of his scheduled work days if Steve didn't want to work, or had something else to do, he could pay for the privilege. They both found this to be an acceptable arrangement. Eventually Steve and Doug worked out a deal where Doug would take Steve's produce (primarily honey and beekeeping products) with him when he went to the Farmer's Market and the profit paid for Steve's "rent".

PAUL'S STORY

Paul was a young friend of Steve's. Paul was an artist, and although he loved Agrarianism and desired very much to live the off-grid life, he really had no intention or desire to operate a whole farm. Paul was a young married man who wanted to live his life working with his hands.

He wanted to engage in some Agrarian art: for the glory of God, for a living, and for the good of the community. Doug and Mr. Polk suggested that Paul consider blacksmithing. After some study and prayer on the subject, Paul agreed that blacksmithing may just be perfect for his future. Mr. Polk, Doug, and everyone else that could afford to do so, gathered some money together to send Paul to a blacksmithing course near a town only three hours away. Paul loved the course and found that he had a natural affinity and talent for blacksmithing. He was absolutely convinced that old-fashioned blacksmithing was truly an art form and it was something he wanted to pursue.

After the blacksmithing course turned out to be a success, Doug gathered Mr. Polk and everyone else together and pitched his idea. Mr. Polk would temporarily donate some acreage with country road access to the community. The hope was that eventually a small Agrarian village would spring up on that acreage, and that "outsiders" would also have access to the village to buy homemade, homegrown, traditional products. If it grew to be successful, it would be a great way for the off-grid Agrarians in the community to make money to pay for property taxes and other expenses. The first building in the village would be *Paul's Blacksmith Shoppe.* Everyone in the community would pitch in to build the shop and provide the equipment and material, and in exchange, everyone who was willing or able to help would receive discounted blacksmithing work for three years. After things were up and running, Paul would begin to buy the lot where the blacksmith shop stood from Mr. Polk. His home would be behind the shop, and he would keep a garden and some productive animals as well. Paul was more than willing to exchange his work for food and supplies, and usually, so long as someone was willing to buy the materials, he would barter for just about anything he needed to survive and thrive. He started by making some artistic decorative pieces for sale in a nearby town, but soon the "townies" were driving out to the blacksmith shop to buy his art, or to get him to do repair or fabricating work for them.

Within two years, Paul had completely paid off the land he purchased from Mr. Polk. He then bought the lot next to his blacksmith shop, and opened the first General Store, which his wife operated. The General Store, although it did sell items made and grown in the community to "outsiders" also served as a barter/trade center for those who lived in the new community.

THE COMMUNITY GROWS

During the fourth year of Doug's arrangement with Mr. Polk, some more friends decided to move into the area and to join in the fellowship. The Millers, The Parkers, and the Darnells all were prospective homesteaders. They all wanted to live off-grid, and they all were very eager for fellowship. The idea of living in a community of like-minded believers was a dream for all of them. None of the new families were able to find any homesteads for sale that were small enough for what they needed and could afford. Unhappily, most of the land for sale was usually over 100 acres. When smaller acreages came up for sale, they were usually priced unusually high compared to the local average per/acre price. Eventually, the new families decided to go in together to purchase 120 acres near Mr. Polk's ranch. The new homesteads were adjacent to Doug's 80 acres, and soon a community dirt road was built between the several homesteads. The new families created an agreement for the distribution of the land, and they each made payments to Mr. Miller who had agreed to purchase the land on behalf of the group. They only wanted about 25 acres a piece, so they would have 45 additional acres available to sell to anyone else who might want to move down to join the fellowship.

Not long after that, four single men, friends of Doug and John, got wind of the new (old) lifestyle and decided that they also wanted to begin an off-grid Agrarian life. Doug arranged for the men to meet Mr. Polk, and it wasn't long before the men were at work building a barracks on ten acres of Mr. Polk's land near the new community. None of the four men had any money to speak of, or yet possessed any real skills, so Mr. Polk made them a deal: They would each agree to work full-time for him for five years. Mr. Polk would provide room and board during those five years. Any of them that successfully completed their agreement by working the full five years, would, upon completion of their obligation, receive ten acres and the materials to build a small cabin and a small barn. They all found this deal agreeable and the community grew once again.

Mr. Polk, who had originally planned on just living out his retirement in town, became invigorated by what was happening out in the new community. He was excited to be able to help so many people, and, he soon learned that he was being helped quite a bit as well. Since he now had so much available labor, he purchased a herd of cattle and had his new field hands maintain and work them. Within a few years his herd had grown to the point that he needed to haul a bunch of them to market, where he sold them for a nice profit. Eventually, he became so captivated and enamored with the lifestyle led by his friends in the community; he became so convinced by their Godly worldview and their Biblical doctrines because they actually *lived* them; and he became so overwhelmed by their love for one another and their joy, that he decided to build a small house on his land and join the fellowship himself. He had always considered himself a Christian, but now he knew that he had missed it for most of his life. Christianity, he learned, is a life of obedience, community, diligence, and joy. It is a *life-lived*, not merely a profession of faith or the mental agreement to some system of doctrine, or some club you go visit once or twice a week.

The community slowly grew. Before long, the small village had several small shops, and had become a bit of a local attraction. There were also now several Agrarian tradesmen and women. There was a seamstress, and a shoemaker, and even a small restaurant. Word in the community was that Doug and Mr. Polk were helping a new family start a grain mill. What an adventure!

DIFFERENT STROKES

As I have said a few times before, not everyone who is living an Off-

Grid life needs to own a bunch of land and be a farmer. Many of you who are reading this got your names from Agrarian trades, and an Agrarian society will always need Carpenters, Millers, Thatchers, Brewers, Coopers, Sawyers, Shoemakers, Shepherds, etc.

This story was designed to get you to think in ways that maybe you have not thought before. All of these people in our story came to off-grid Agrarian living from a different background and with differing needs and desires. There is not just one answer, and unhappily that is pretty much all that the modern "off-grid homesteading movement" has ever really offered people. A good and workable land policy requires that we be open to new ideas and new ways of thinking. If you are looking to get off the globalist grid then don't be limited by the modern idea that you have to go get a Realtor and a hefty mortgage. That way may surely work for some people, but for some people it will never work. Your solution has to be crafted for you, and the more creative you can be, the better you might find your solution.

So how can all of this fail? My examples are all based on a few important factors. You must be willing to work, and willing to keep your word. This will all fall apart if you don't take it very seriously. I personally have had several people who have agreed, much like in the above examples, to work for me and study for five years in exchange for land, but I have never had one of those people complete their commitment. Generally, and it is an unhappy fact, most people are not really willing to work, and they are deceived when they think that off-grid living is just a picture postcard or some idyllic, pastoral dream. It is amazing to me that people are willing to put on a tie and go to a city to do the most de-humanizing and useless work that you can imagine, but when it comes to actually having the opportunity to live the life *they say* they dream of, they think it is too hard and they quit.

Working the land means getting up early, often before the sun comes up, and applying yourself to your daily tasks. Often those tasks are very physical, and very repetitive. Getting up to milk a cow may seem romantic the first couple of times you do it, but believe me, the romance of it goes away very fast. That doesn't mean that off-grid living isn't pleasant, or that we don't enjoy our work, because we do. I'd rather be doing this than anything else in the world. But if you are not absolutely prepared to give your life over to benevolently stewarding the land, and to daily fulfilling your obligations, then you are inevitably going to fail.

OPTIONS

There are options here for just about any situation. I know that every situation is unique, and it is a given that almost everyone thinks that their own particular situation is the only one that is unsolvable and therefore hopeless. I have met very few people who have actually examined all of the available options, or who have spent much time dreaming up new ways to make good things happen.

You see now why it is so difficult to answer the question "How many acres do I need?" I don't know, because I don't know what you are for, and I don't know what your hopes and dreams are. I don't know what you can afford, and I don't know how hard you want to work. I don't know what animals you want to raise, or what skills and artistry you are willing to acquire and perfect.

Now, some of you may be sitting back and scoffing sarcastically, "Yeah, all we need now is a Mr. Polk!" Well, there are Mr. Polks out there - it is just your job to find them. I've been very pleasantly surprised at how much God is willing to help those who truly seek to live this life with an honest and sincere heart. Let me give you a very recent example of what I am saying...

A month or so ago my daughter (who as I write this chapter is sixteen) came up to me and asked me if she could seek a job cleaning someone's house a couple of days a week. She had come up with a whole plan of how it was going to work, how much money she was going to make, and what she was going to do with the money. I gave her my rules for the endeavor, and I told her that her mother and I would have to approve of any job, and that our family rules and community *ordnung* (rules and order) would still apply. If she could not find a job that would work around all of those rules, then she could not get a job. Well, she plowed into the challenge. She had a friend make her some business cards, and she put up signs in the small towns around where we live. She had other members of our community begin to ask around, and before long, there were some opportunities. One job in particular she really wanted, but the lady of the house was not willing to work around our very particular rules of order. Tracy was heartbroken, and she felt like our rules might be keeping her from ever getting a job. I sat her down and explained that our God is completely sovereign over everything in her life. If God wanted her to have work, he would send the perfect job for her in His own time. Our job is obedience, to keep moving forward, and to not take our hand off of the plow. We pray to God and let Him know our wants and desires, and if He sees fit to make them work out, we praise Him for it - if He doesn't, we praise Him for that too. I told her what I have told literally hundreds of people in counseling over the years. I said, "Tracy, if God wants this for you, there is nothing you could do to stop it. While it is nice to have the signs and the business cards, He can send someone out of the blue to you whenever and wherever he likes." She smiled at me like a sixteen-year-old does, and agreed to be patient. Well, not two weeks later, Tracy and her mother were picking up Mesquite pods on the side of the road when an old man drove up to see what was going on and to ask if they needed any help. My wife explained what they were doing and they had a short chat with the man, explaining how we process and make coffee and flour from the seed pods. When he was getting ready to drive off, he asked off-hand, "Hey, by the way, do any of y'all want to clean my house for me? I'll pay you."

That really happened, and it worked out just fine. The man had two houses he needed cleaned fairly regularly, and he was willing to work around our rules and regulations. The greatest thing to come from the experience was to see my daughter's faith grow. She learned to lean on

God, and to seek obedience and diligence in His Kingdom first.

I know that this story didn't have anything to do with land, but it was given for your encouragement. This doesn't mean you sit back and wait for someone to "miracle" you some land. It does mean that you need to be aggressive, creative, patient... and you need to have faith. Don't be afraid to ask questions or to make offers; and don't be afraid to have rules either. If you are truly willing to work, and if you truly want to live this life, and if you are truly committed to doing it right, I am convinced that there is an opportunity out there for you.

PROPERTY TAXES AND OTHER BOTHERSOME DETAILS

When I write and talk about living off-grid, inevitably there are people who will use some pretty troubling logic to try to dismiss what I'm saying. One of the arguments goes something like this:

> *You will ALWAYS have to pay property taxes, so you'll ALWAYS need money, which means you'll ALWAYS have to work and have contact with the "system", which means you'll ALWAYS be, in some ways, hooked to the grid. So why bother?*

I really have no problem with the question "what about property taxes?", unless it is asked, not in search of a real solution, but to dismiss off-grid living altogether. This is an example of how "some" truth, and some bad presuppositions, can be added together to come up with an absurd result.

To conclude that it is better to stay on the grid (where, by the way, you will pay property taxes – even if you rent), despite all of the horrible negatives involved with that worldview and lifestyle, and despite the fact that living such a life is unsustainable and perilous, just because if you move off-grid you will have to pay property taxes, is foolish. The idea that I should keep living a life in the urban or suburban sewer because no matter where I live I'll have to pay property taxes is an example of some pretty scary logic. That is like saying I should live in my outhouse since I can't escape having to go in there every once in awhile.

It is true that so long as our system remains corrupt and in its current condition we do have to make property tax payments. But property taxes are not the same everywhere. There are areas with very low property taxes and very limited government intervention, and there are areas with very high property taxes and very high levels of government intervention. In general, if you live in an area where the government believes it ought to be able to control every area of your life, then you are probably also living in an area where property taxes are going to be high. Property taxes have to be high in those areas in order to pay for all of the government busybodies and pencil pushers necessary to make your life miserable. It is a delicious irony that property taxes are almost always in a direct relationship with the amount of "government". The lower the government intrusion level, the lower the property taxes. Isn't that great? The problem is that people idolize those areas that, because of some natural beauty or carnal benefits, have both high taxes and a high level of governmental intervention.

It is probable (unless you happen to be independently wealthy) that you will have to do something to produce enough money to pay your property taxes. If you have been wise in choosing the location of your homestead, hopefully this will not be a very large amount of money. Where I live in Texas, it would be very easy to pay our property taxes for the whole year by working for one or two weeks (per year!) earning cash. Unhappily, with the reality of *ad valorem* taxes (taxes on the value of the property), the more you improve and build on your property the more your taxes are going to be. It is good, then, that homesteaders have so many good and viable options when it comes to making a small side income. Here are only a few ideas:

1. You can grow a "truck garden". A truck garden is where a farmer grows some type of produce for sale locally. You can be very creative in marketing and selling your produce. Talk to local restaurants and grocers to see what you would have to do

to sell directly to them. You can also sell your produce at a farmers market, or directly to the customers on the side of the road (provided it is in an area where this is both safe and allowed).

2. You can open up a small store, either on your property or in a nearby town, for the sale of items or products you make or gather from your land. This type of store could be open only a day or two a week, or even just seasonally. You can also discuss the option of selling items in local stores, or on a consignment basis.

3. You can build useful things or create art. Many early Agrarians were also artisans. Consider learning a skill or trade, or practice any natural artistry you may possess. Your creations can be advertised in the newspaper, or by word of mouth.

4. You can do day labor, fence work, clean-up work for local farmers or ranchers. This type of work can be seasonal, perhaps in the winter when there is not much work to do on your land.

Recently I took my family to a nearby farm and we spent several days in their "pick your own" (or "u-pick") blackberry orchard. We made most of the blackberries into blackberry jam. From our own peach trees (planted our first year on our land) we made the delicious peaches into peach jam and cinnamon/peach pancake syrup. Then, we arranged with some folks in a nearby small town to have a garage sale so we could divest ourselves of more accumulated "junk". We put the jams and syrup on the table... and sold out in hours! Later, almost every time we would come into town, people would stop us and ask us for more jam or syrups. Word of mouth did the rest. When we were in the butcher shop recently, almost all of the workers came up to us to put in orders for more jam whenever we could make some available.

The point is that, if your property taxes are reasonable and manageable, you shouldn't have to do much to earn enough money to pay your property taxes. If your taxes are so high that they necessitate you working full time (or even part time) throughout the year in order to pay them, then I hate to be the one to tell you this, but you are living in the wrong place. Consider relocating.

Which, by the way, brings us to a major point...

As I mentioned earlier, high property taxes are a product of a few variables:

1. Property taxes are high because there is a large city either nearby, or in the same county. It is a fact that rural people are taxed in order to pay for services enjoyed mainly by urbanites. If you live near a big city your property taxes are likely going to be very high so that the Smiths and the Joneses can have police protection because they live their lives in an artificial habitat that breeds crime and antisocial behavior.

2. Property taxes are high because you live near, or in, some area noted for its natural beauty. Since most people are dead on the inside, they require natural beauty and life *on the outside* in order to make them feel more complete. Unhappily, the more carnal and depraved a man is, the more he is likely to sell out everything else in order to live somewhere with natural beauty. This is not to say there is anything at all wrong with beautiful areas of the country. It is to say that beautiful areas attract busybodies and politically loathsome people who move there and then decide that they ought to be able to tell other people what to do. Paradise-on-earth is expensive, and if you choose to live in one of these areas, you will pay through the nose for the privilege. It is far better to build a paradise where the busybodies aren't.

3. Property taxes and government intervention may be very high because the area is subject to natural disasters. If you live in an area where there is likely to be a major earthquake, or that is probably going to be destroyed by a hurricane, it is likely that the government may require you to build to certain "codes", and your property taxes may reflect the idea that the government feels the need to protect you or to come and save you if things go wrong (and they will).

4. Property taxes are high because of poor governmental management, and some really bad political philosophies. You may live in a rural area, far from any big city, where there are no tourist attractions, and you still might have high property taxes. Why? Because the locals have some very socialistic and tyrannical ideas about who owns the land. In this case land covenants may restrict what types of animals you can own, and what you can do with your land. The local governments may require that you get approval and licenses to build on or improve any of your property. My general philosophy is this: If I have to ask permission from some local governmental body in order to build a shed, then I really don't own my property at all, and this is not a place I want to live

I receive communications from people all the time who tell me that they live in the most beautiful area in the world and that the soil is so productive they really don't have to do any work. If you listened to them you'd think they lived in Eden. They ask me, "Why would you live in Texas? It's so hot, and there are bugs, and there are snakes, and it just doesn't seem conducive to farming." Well, that is really a cartoonish representation of where I live. I've traveled all over America and all over the world and believe me there are pluses and minuses in every area. It is easy to talk yourself out of a place that might be challenging to your flesh if you can only list the negatives about that place. It is also easy to talk yourself into some area that solely panders to your desire for comfort when you never consider the negatives at all.

Remember, the human mind is capable of rationalizing anything.

I have developed a list of things that are important to *me* and that are crucial to me living the life of obedience and diligence that I want to live. You should produce your own list as well, and then honestly examine how different areas match up to your list.

Here was my list:

1. I wanted to live in fellowship and communion with like-minded people. I'd rather live in a desert with friends and family who work together and serve one another than live in a paradise alone. If I lived on the most productive farmland in the world, and had the most beautiful weather and the most beautiful scenery, but I couldn't live my life in true Christian community with like-minded people, I would be miserable beyond words. Too many people want to call "independence" what is actually selfishness and pride. We know the importance of fellowship and we value how God has commanded us to live, so we put fellowship at the top of the list.

2. We wanted to homestead, homeschool, homebirth, and homechurch. This means that we wanted the freedom to live our lives according to our consciences without unnecessary and unconstitutional government intervention. We wanted to live in a place that not only encouraged our freedoms, but protected them by law. I know people who live in carnally beautiful areas, but who are not permitted to homeschool (or if they can homeschool, it is heavily regulated), or who live in areas where the government is well known for interfering in the family through regulation and heavy-handed behavior. It seems strange to me that someone would balk at living in one area because of snakes and bugs (which are everywhere in the world, by the way), but wouldn't think twice about living in a state that has shown a willingness to take away the children of parents who

don't "toe the line" of the modern society and culture; or whose government will force the parents to subject their children to indoctrination in beliefs contrary to their own.

3. We wanted to live as freely as possible - which means that we don't like intrusions and usurpations by meddlers and busybodies. We wanted as little government intrusion in our lives as possible. We value good government and seek to obey all Biblical laws and to be good citizens and neighbors, but we also want the freedom to build what we want, where we want, when we want, without codes and permits. We value low taxation and few if any limitations on our freedom to work and to travel. Though we are thoroughly non-violent and law-abiding, we want the right, if we choose to, to defend ourselves from predators (all kinds) without onerous government restrictions (this means good, pro-freedom gun laws).

4. We knew that we needed a sufficient amount of rainfall per year, both for our crops and gardens, and for water catchment. Land price is often directly related to rainfall, so we knew we couldn't afford to live in a farming paradise, but we didn't want to live in the Sahara Desert either. Somewhere in between worked for us.

5. We wanted as long a growing season as we could get, which meant that we wanted to live in the south, if possible.

6. We wanted to be sufficiently far away from any large cities but near enough to some medium and small sized cities so that we wouldn't have too far to travel for building supplies, etc. We wanted to be at least 3 hours away from any large metropolis, but were desirous of having some very small towns or villages fairly close by, so that when we move towards traveling by horse and wagon, we will be able to do so.

I learn a lot about a person when they explain their criteria for where they want to live. You probably have your own list running through your head, and some of you may be shouting *"SOIL! What about the soil!?"* Well, if there is anything the Amish have proven, it is that you can build soil anywhere in the temperate zones. If you receive enough rainfall, and you can raise animals, you can build soil. I am convinced that with proper care and with the proper application of soil amendments good workable soil can be built in only a few years just about anywhere.

I think location selection is critical, and I hope that you will spend the appropriate amount of time in considering what is important to you in your life.

Land is a crucial element of our philosophy. Land is a crucial element to our freedom. Not everyone will own land, but everyone ought to have an opinion and a philosophy about the land. Modern political parties and social and cultural movements that neglect a consideration of land and how important it is to life and living, build their houses on sand. In the long run their philosophies cannot stand. Any political party or movement that does not have a complete and consistent land philosophy and land policy cannot stand for true freedom. Land is not just crucial to our lives. The health and care of the land is crucial to the lives and futures of our children and their children.

One of the essential elements of my religion is the understanding that God gave us *benevolent dominion* over the creation. The modern consumer/industrial system not only rejects this concept of benevolent dominion, it turns it on its head and replaces it with a greed based malevolent tyranny. Industrialism and the consumer economy sees the land as nothing more than another thing to rape and pillage for profit, which makes it contrary to the teachings of the Bible, and of Christianity. Any religious philosophy that supports and enables modern consumer/industrialism is Anti-Christian and is contrary to the Word of God. That is a heavy condemnation of the foundation of modern society.

In the next chapter, we will talk about another topic that is essential to our lives and our future... Water.

CHAPTER 10
WATER

"Water is life's mater and matrix, mother and medium. There is no life without water." Albert Szent-Gyorgyi (Hungarian Biochemist)

LIFE REQUIRES WATER

Many people have a mental image of the pilgrim, the pioneer, or the settler; standing as a solid and immovable force (like a stone wall) against the relentless tide of destructive forces: hunger, drought, challenges, heartbreaks, and disasters; but, while this image does represent one pixel of the snapshot of pioneer life, all-in-all we cannot say that it is precisely correct, especially not if we are able to look at the bigger picture. In order to be successful, homesteaders and settlers had to be flexible... like water:

"Nothing in the world is more flexible and yielding than water. Yet when it attacks the firm and the strong, none can withstand it, because they have no way to change it. So the flexible overcome the adamant, the yielding overcome the forceful. Everyone knows this, but no one can do it." (Lao Tzu – Chinese Philosopher)

As the saying goes, water is the *medium* of life. It is both life-sustaining and destructive. It gives buoyancy to ships, and with the same force it smashes them against rocks. It has given both hope and dread to cities of every size and in every age. It has served as both lifeline and currency. It is boon and bane. One might be doomed with the lack of it just as easily as one might be buried and swept away by the overabundance of it. It is everywhere primary, everywhere necessary, and it is everywhere the first and last maxim of life and living outside of God. It is used in the Bible to represent the Alpha and the Omega of spiritual life (Jesus Christ, the Water of Life.) Water is both secular parable and religious metaphor, and as a vivifying force it is both shadow and reality.

If irony is your thing, in our own day and time, the city of Los Angeles, California, perched on the edge of the largest body of water in the world, is actively perishing from a lack of water and must pipe billions of gallons of water from the Eastern Sierras and the Colorado River in order to stave off what is an eventual, inevitable disaster.

In every age of the earth it has been recognized that life requires water. "The Romans realized, as have every civilized people since, that living in cities is impossible if the water supply is not reliably clean and fresh" (Frank and Francis Chapelle, The Hidden Sea: Ground Water, Springs and Wells). Likewise, in arid rural areas around the world it is common to see abandoned homes and dwellings, and over each one of them an epitaph might be written: "They ran out of water." There is no category of survival more elemental and important, and, sadly, there is no category over which we have less control, than that of water. Whenever I walk on my ranch I have an ever-present reminder of the importance of a diverse and well-thought-out water supply system. At the front of my property, along the county road, are the ruins of an old homestead that was probably built in the beginning of the 20th Century. Based upon the look of it, and on my knowledge of the history of the region, and after seeing all of the other abandoned homesteads around the area that date from the same period, I would guess that that old homestead failed because of a lack of water. It stands as a very real reminder to me of the importance of the "mater and matrix" of life.

A RUDE AWAKENING

When we moved to Central Texas from West Texas we had no idea that we were in for a rude awakening. Where we used to live in West Texas (which is a semi-arid desert) we were accustomed to living in a place that only received about 15 inches of rain a year (and sometimes much less). However, living *on the grid* we were not attuned to the reality of water. You see, although we lived in a desert, we lived on top of one of the largest aquifers in the world, and because we had grid electricity, we felt like we had endless amounts of "free" water. Sometimes I would put the garden hose on a garden or a tree and just leave it there, forgetting about it until hours later when I would come out and find the whole yard flooded. Who cared? I didn't. I had enough money for the electric bill and, after all, water was "free". Because we were not really farmers, rain seemed like more of a nuisance than a blessing; it made the roads muddy and kept us inside for days on end, and since we had endless amounts of "free" water coming out of the ground, we thought, "Who needs rain?" Right. We had no idea how ignorant and foolish we were. We had no idea how precious water really is, and, living in the middle of a desert had really not taught us anything about the value of water.

In 2005 we moved from a semi-arid desert to the rolling hill country of Central Texas. Rather than expecting 15" of rain a year, we could expect 26" or more. We automatically assumed that water would never be a problem for us. Our first few months (which happened to be spring) were a bit of a shock to us because we were not used to humidity, and it seemed like everything was wet all the time. My cattle tanks were full and it seemed like there was water everywhere.

Then summer came.

We have since learned that that summer was a particularly brutal one. The temperatures were over 100 degrees almost every day and not a drop of rain fell... month after month. We had to drive over 30 minutes each way to a nearby State Park for our drinking and cleaning water. We didn't have a well but we were trying to drill one for ourselves. After over a month of drilling in the brutal and dry heat with a small drilling machine we had gone down only 80 feet. A friend told us that we might already be to water, so we prayed for the best, cased the well, dropped a pump down there and started pumping water. It pumped water for a few minutes... then it went dry. There was no water down there. The well was a dry hole. We hadn't reached water.

The only water in the hole was the water we had pumped down there as part of the process of removing the drilling material "waste" and dirt.

At that time we were building our small cabin, so we built a catchment system to catch the water off of the roof, which was fine except for the fact that it almost never rained. We had a couple of downbursts towards the end of the summer, and a little more in September, then it stopped raining altogether for a very, very long time. Drought had come to Central Texas.

We continued to drive to the State Park or to town sometimes twice a day for the next 10 months. One of my cattle tanks went totally dry early the next summer as we pumped the water onto our gardens. Water became so precious to us that when we would drive to a city and see people watering lawns we would be shocked, appalled, and depressed. Every drop of water became a symbol of life to us. Every gallon of water had to be hauled by hand, and the constant trips to the State Park or to town for water became a financial drain. We seriously wondered if we were even going to make it. God taught us a very valuable lesson about what is truly valuable in this world and how much we take for granted His gifts and His providence. We have learned to highly value water. When the rains finally came in August of 2006, I remember that a bunch of us just went out and stood in it. It felt like life coming back to dry bones. I cannot fully express the feeling of appreciation and relief that came upon us. As I write this, we are still lingering in mild drought conditions, although we have received some good rain since 2007. The land, though, has not fully healed from the brutal drought that started during the fall of our first year of life here on our ranch.

There is a truism that this understanding will help us all to recognize. We do not value anything aright until we are able to see the situation clearly. Until our minds are decolonized we will always take valuable things for granted.

"And he cried and said, Father Abraham, have mercy on me, and send Lazarus, that he may dip the tip of his finger in water, and cool my tongue; for I am tormented in this flame" (Luke 16:24)

There is an old saying that survives from the depression era. It is said that when the dust bowl conditions hit; when the wells went dry, and when the rains failed, and when drought and the greed of industrial farmers and producers forced many homestead farmers from their land; many farmers would, upon abandoning their farms, write messages on the walls of the living rooms they were leaving; messages for others to find. This is one:

"Thirty miles to water, 10 miles to wood, and 6 inches from hell"

Water is more valuable than Gold, because you can live without Gold

Not long ago I was helping a friend of mine pick up a wood burning stove that he had purchased from a man who had put an ad in the paper. The man might have identified us as survivalists, or maybe he just liked to talk, but he indicated that he was very serious about the dangers out there in the world today. He talked about (and showed us) some of his preparations for "when it all comes down" (his term for *the crash*). He seemed to think that our biggest worries ought to be about boogeymen, bandits, and terrorists, but in any case he had rightly determined that the world is not as safe and dependable as it pretends to be. He spoke as if he had realized that the "grid" system of life was in a tenuous condition and that it is destined to collapse.

One of the things he told us was that "the terrorists" were going to attack our electrical and water systems. Ok, I thought, so what was he doing about it? I looked around. I know a little something about survival and preparedness, so I examined his situation according to his thesis. He was obviously on grid electricity and grid water. It might be true that he had stowed away a generator or two, but, as I have shown many times in this book, the system of petroleum delivery in our modern world is subject to interruption at any time. I want to pause here to again make this point, and it goes back to our overall philosophy...

Congratulations if you have seen the problem, but if what you plan to do about the problem (your solution) is destined to fail are you that much better off? If you recognize that our systems that deliver power (for example) are vulnerable, are you really better off by trusting in backup systems that require industrially produced and scarce products?

So, as this man talked to us about the threats we all face as a modern society, we looked around and saw that with all the roof lines available on his property, not one had a gutter or any semblance of a mechanism to catch rain water. Do you see the *disconnect* between what people *say* they believe, and what they show that they believe by their actions? I never believe what a man says to me... not ever. I believe what he shows me by his actions.

There is very little doubt that someday there will be an attack on our already dwindling fresh water supplies. It will either (and most likely) come from government, in a move to seize water resources and to limit the individual's right to water from his own land, or it may come from some so-called "terrorist" group, or some combination of the two. Where any future attack comes from and just who is ultimately responsible for it I cannot tell you, but there are three things you ought to know about the current industrial water supply:

1. It is *already* poisoned. If you are living on unfiltered and un-purified city or county water then you are already being poisoned *every day.* If you didn't already know that, then you need to do some research, because this book on off off-grid living is not going to be big enough or long enough for me to catch you up on the dangers of city water supplies. Heavy metals, dangerous and caustic chemicals, toxins, fecal matter, etc. exist at some level in almost every urban and suburban water supply. Think about it.

2. It is highly susceptible to attack. Although the post 9/11 focus on possible terrorist attacks has increased the security of some elements of the water supply in some of the bigger cities, the security measures that have been implemented are hardly foolproof and are generally considered by more than casual observers to be more cosmetic than actual.

3. The system of mechanized water delivery is tenuous at best, even if there is never an attack. With very few exceptions, city and surburban water supplies require electricity or other source of power for pumping, distribution, and purification.

One of the most glaring realities that urbanites and suburbanites face every day is that they may wake up in the morning with insufficient water, undrinkable water, or no access to water at all; and it can all happen without notice.

Not long ago, Coleman, Texas, which is only twelve miles from my ranch, had a serious water situation. During what was called a "random" sampling, a water test expert detected dangerous levels of toxins and fecal matter in the water supply. The word went out for everyone to boil their water. Stores and restaurants were informed that they could not provide water or ice for drinks. Usually, when a disaster happens (like when the power goes out, or if an ice storm is expected to sever power) people have an opportunity to fill bathtubs and other containers with water. In this case, however, the water already in the pipes (or already stored in the house) was already contaminated. In fact, who knows how long the water had been toxic? The response was quick, but how long was there a problem before a "random" testing caught it? And what about notification? If someone did not listen to the radio, then he or she would never have known that there was a problem. And this situation is not an isolated incident. This happens in cities around the country virtually every day. When this understanding is added to what we already know of the state of the power supply system (a system that is required to pump water to city dwellers), a very stark reality becomes apparent. No one can be sure that there will be water when they turn on the faucet. No one can be certain that the water that comes from that faucet is not already harming their health. In short, when the "water of life" is pumped and piped to you by government bureaucrats, do you really think you are safe?

I could go on and on, but the point is that you cannot trust water that is provided to you by government. Ever.

SOURCES OF WATER

There are several ways to procure water for an off-grid life, and I will discuss a few of the methods and then give you some positives and negatives to think about:

1. A water well (either deep or shallow)
2. Surface water (lakes, streams, ponds, tanks, etc.)
3. Water-Catchment (we also use the term "catchwater")
4. Water from the air (Air-wells, dehumidifying systems, etc.)

In the modern world water can easily be taken for granted. Most people, despite the fact that they use it every day, have no idea how much water they use or require. If you plan on living off-grid you will need water for your own family use (for drinking, washing, cooking, cleaning, etc.), and you will need water (and larger amounts of it) for keeping animals, watering gardens and trees, etc. Your long-term water plan needs to provide for sufficient water for every conceivable need.

On average, modern urban and suburban dwellers use about 100 gallons per person per day! Most of that water is wasted. Getting your mind around how much water that is in a week, or in a year, goes a long way towards illustrating the depth of the problem of industrial colonization. Smart, efficient, off-grid agrarians may use anywhere from 5-15 gallons per person per day - usually less than ten. For my family of six, I figure our absolute minimal needs for personal use (not including gardens or animals) at six gallons per person, per day, which adds up to almost 14,000 gallons per year, and remember, this number does not include the water needs of animals, gardens, or trees.

WELL WATER

Most people, when they first begin to consider their future off-grid lives, if they think of water at all, believe that it is absolutely necessary that they have a well. Of course people who still rely on city or county water may not even be thinking about wells at all. Many rural folks around where we live still rely on the county water supply, since our underground water availability runs from "spotty" to "non-existent". All that said, I would still say that 95% of the people who ask me about our off-grid life here ask me if I have a well. I do not have a well. Remember... our well was dry. A water well is a good thing, *so long as it works.* If the land you buy has a working water well, then that is a great start. Your next job will be to diversify, because I need to warn you - a well isn't always as dependable as most people think. Wells often have problems. Wells can cave in; the water can dry up or go bad; the pumping system or mechanism can break or stop operating, etc. Having access to a well is a great thing, but always be careful not to depend too much on it. Most of the people who homesteaded out in the Great Plains a century ago failed because of the failure of water wells and because of their dependence on them. **They failed because they did not diversify their water supply.** We said earlier that the epitaph could be written for most homesteading failures in arid rural regions in the past: *They ran out of water.* Under it we might find written, *"The well went dry."* The well didn't always run dry though. Sometimes the well caved in, or became contaminated, or the system of drawing or pumping the water failed. In any case, the over-reliance on one source of water doomed many aspiring homesteaders, just as the over-reliance on pumped, chemically treated, government provided water will likely be the doom of most modern urban consumers when the industrial system does begin to fall apart.

Today, a good well in an area that has a pretty dependable aquifer at a reasonable depth can cost you between $3,500 and $5,000, and that is before you ever pump a single drop. That price does not include pumps and pump supplies, getting power to the pump, etc. If you plan on going non-electric using a deep-well hand pump you will still probably spend over $1000 for the pump and all of the pipe and other supplies you will need. A hand pump is more dependable than an electric pump though. Some people choose to use both, and it is possible to have both an electric (12V or AC) pump and a hand pump in the same well hole. Again, the well is susceptible to cave-in or contamination, especially if it is not properly and carefully cased, and there is always the possibility that the well can run dry during a period of extended drought. Here in Central Texas, the digging of water wells is speculative at best. There have been three wells dug in our community: One was successful, though it is a very low-output well. The other two were dry... failures. One of the dry wells cost $2,500 even though it never provided a drop of water. My point is that depending inordinately on a well can be a very dangerous thing. A well could be a good solution if used in conjunction with other water solutions. This is what we call *diversification*. Have insurance - In my opinion, you ought to have at least two different water sources, and several different ways to pump or deliver the water, in case of emergency.

SURFACE WATER

If you happen to procure a property with a very large lake or pond that has good, clean, water - then you are way ahead of the game, but you will likely pay a very hefty price for the privilege. One of our neighbors has a four acre pond with a pump that serves his house. The pond has always, even through our most recent drought, held enough water to provide for his needs. In this case one would only need work out a delivery and purifying system (purifying is usually only necessary for any personal use and drinking water) to feel pretty comfortable about the availability of water.

If there is enough water running through the property during heavy rains, a large tank, pond, or lake can be built. This can be an expensive process if you have to do it all from scratch, or if you have to pay someone else to do it. Here in Central Texas it can cost upwards of $15,000 to hire a crew to come in and build a new cattle tank (that what the locals call a small man-made pond, primarily used for watering cattle) that may be less than 1/4 acre in size. In our community, one of the residents has been working to build a tank without professional assistance. He rented a backhoe and is doing all the work himself. It still will likely cost him several thousand dollars in backhoe rental costs before it is all done, but it will be well worth it in the future. Always remember that these costs are generally one-time costs, and if your water plan can provide you with dependable water year-round, then it may be worth it for you to spend the money up front.

Of the two tanks we have here on my property, one went totally dry during the drought that started in 2006. Always remember that surface water can also be tenuous during drought conditions. This is another reason to diversify.

WATER CATCHMENT

This, to me, is the ideal solution for most situations. When we were in Western Australia in 2002 we noticed that virtually every roof line, no matter how small, fed water into gutters that ran into personal cisterns - even in the big cities. Almost every drop of water that fell from the sky was caught and stored. This, it seems to me, is the way we ought to live. It is a great philosophy for several reasons:

1. Rainwater in most rural areas is pure and clean. It only must be filtered because of the material that gets in the water from the surfaces it lands on (such as roofs and gutters); but, as it falls, it is pure and perfect. As a child, I was taught by a lot of fear-mongers and disinformation specialists to think that all rain was poisoned by pollution and was harmful for me. This is absolutely not true. Rainwater, especially in rural areas, is pure water. Pollution does affect rainwater in highly populated areas, but most off-grid Agrarians do not have to worry about polluted

rain.

2. Catching rainwater shows and displays our complete reliance and dependence on God and not on the systems of men. We rely on God to provide us with the rain necessary to maintain us. When we rely on rainwater we show this dependence and we are more likely to remember to pray and give thanks to God for His provision. City people do not usually think of God when it comes to turning on or off a faucet. People who rely on rain directly for daily use water are more likely to pray for it, and to thank God for it.

Although we live in Central Texas, there is plenty of water (many, many times more than all of the families here in the community could ever use) that passes through our property, especially during heavy rains. The primary philosophy of water catchment is to utilize as much of this water as possible, not only by catching it from roofs into cisterns and tanks, but by catching runoff water into tanks or ponds. The man-made lake, tank, or pond I mentioned in the previous section is actually a system of water catchment.

I have heard that in some states and regions it is not lawful to catch or store rainwater. You ought not live in any place that considers it the right of government to restrict land-owners from catching rainfall.

For the same amount of money that you would spend on digging a water well and procuring pumps, etc., a structure can be built and a tank purchased that will supply you with a good percentage of your water needs. You can catch water off of any roofline or building (barns, outhouses, sheds, etc.), but if you do not yet have a building off of which you can catch water, a simple shed roof can be built for the purpose very cheaply. This covered area can then be used to store equipment and tools out of the rain, or as a protection for equipment or livestock.

My cabin area is 610 square feet, but it has 710 square feet of roof line. This means I catch somewhere around 350-400 gallons for every one inch of rainfall. That is not a lot, but it adds up to over 6,000 gallons of water a year. Not enough for all of the needs for a family of my size, but it is a lot of good water, and it helps. We have since built a second structure that has a roofline that will catch about 420 gallons of water per inch of rainfall and are currently building a third structure which will (Lord willing) catch more than 600 gallons per inch of rain. Considering the rainfall average for our area, this will bring our total capacity to close to well over 20,000 gallons of water per year, *provided we are able to store all that we catch.*

Two of the homesteads here in our community have roof lines that are capable of catching between 1200 and 2000 gallons per inch of rain fall. This capacity would provide an average of 18,000 to 31,000 gallons of water a year in an average rainfall year. For a small agrarian family, this ought to provide most of the necessary daily use water. This would have to be augmented for watering large gardens or for watering animals, but if used in combination with other surface or subsurface water projects, this method ought to be very successful. I plan (if the Lord blesses and wills) to catch the water off of every roof line we build. Some of the younger and smaller families in our off-grid community are subsisting on the water caught from the roofs of goat sheds, farrowing sheds, outhouses, campers, etc. Every building project in which you engage ought to have a water catchment component.

It is also our plan (if the Lord wills), to expand our surface water projects, enlarging our current cattle tanks and even building new ones when we are able. In my opinion, the new agrarian homesteader ought to focus his/her resources and time on water catchment resources first, before considering wells or other means of procuring water.

WATER FROM THE AIR

It is possible in most places that have ample humidity, to produce water from the air. This would fall under the category of "intermediate" or "ancillary" means in providing water, and ought to only be considered as a plan to diversify the overall water plan. Let me give a few examples: Many of you know that air-conditioners, freezers, refrigerators, etc. will produce water from the air in high humidity situations. This is why you will see water dripping from your A/C unit in the summer when the humidity is high. This process is called "condensing" and the water is derived from the process of "condensation", which builds up because of the drastic temperature transfer and differential between the freezing cold in the tubing and the warm, wet, air surrounding it. Using this theory, some companies have developed low energy usage machines called "air wells" which are machines with condensers that condense water from the air and then catch it and purify it for consumption. This is something to look into for anyone who lives in a high humidity environment and who produces their own electricity via alternative power. Several of these units could be powered by solar or wind power to provide water - although it would be very expensive and it would still be subject to failures and problems. Before we went completely off-grid, I considered purchasing one or more of these units (or manufacturing one ourselves) and putting it in a special root cellar built for that purpose. For example, a couple of automobile air-conditioning compressors could be powered by solar power in an underground room with high natural humidity. The water condensing off of the compressors could be caught and stored for later use. Such an arrangement would provide two benefits: First, it would create a cool, dry space which is ideal for storing dry goods or some vegetables and crops. Second, it would produce a good supply of pure drinking water. I figured that up to 10 gallons a day could be produced in this manner. Water can also be gathered in small amounts from anywhere (either natural or man-made) where natural condensation appears regularly.

In the past, many ancient civilizations (the Persians, for example) were successful in building large structures designed to produce and capture moisture from the air. For those who are looking to live totally off of the grid, it might be worth your time to study these old processes and techniques.

WATER STORAGE

Water storage is more important to your survival and success than is food storage. As we have discussed, storing water in ponds, tanks, lakes, etc. is ideal. Water can also be stored in man built tanks and cisterns. We have a 2,500 gallon above ground storage tank for our cabin and we have another, slightly smaller tank for catching water from the roof of our newest structure. We just recently completed construction on a 5,000 gallon underground "ferro-cement" cistern for a cottage we are building. Someone who is handy and who can do some simple construction could build a cistern with much higher capacity out of wood and/or concrete. At our ranch, as an intermediate step, we have also considered purchasing an inexpensive 20,000 gallon above ground plastic pool for temporary water storage.

The homesteads in this area 100 years ago used below ground, rock-lined cisterns for water storage. A neighboring property used to have an old house on it. When a new owner purchased the property he allowed the men in our community to tear down the old house for any materials we could salvage from it. As we were tearing down the old house, we uncovered a large, hand-dug cistern behind the house. It was probably 20 feet deep and 6-8 feet in circumference. One-hundred yards away, and somewhat lower than the house, was a man-made cattle tank. Water from the tank was pumped up to the house by a windmill (which still stands, unused), where it was stored in the rock-lined cistern. I am pretty certain that the old abandoned homestead (the one I told you about at the front of my property), has a cistern somewhere underneath it. It will be interesting to find out someday when we get the time to do some work up on that portion of the land.

I am still studying ways to further enhance and diversify our water system here on the ranch. Off-grid water is an important issue, and I imagine we will be studying and adapting our system as long as we live here.

There is no way to guarantee ourselves water. No civilization in history, no matter where it was located in relation to water, has been able to guarantee itself plentiful, good, drinking water. What we can do is make sure that our plans are wise and that we are making use of diverse sources of water procurement and storage. Diversification means that we ought not to have all of our eggs in one basket, and we should not rely in any way on the world for the delivery or purification of our water supply. In the end we believe that God is sovereign over water, which is why so much of the Bible uses water as parable and metaphor. Rightly viewing and valuing water helps us understand those parables and the metaphors, which is how it really ought to be.

CHAPTER 11

FOOD, PART 1

CULTURE, THE LAND, AND FOOD

This topic will take several chapters to cover, so I will start again with philosophy before getting into specifics on different kinds of food production. Food preservation will have its own chapter.

Earlier in the book I pointed out that the foods that we eat, for the most part, are faint representations - faded memories – of our Agrarian heritage. Most of the foods in our diet, at least when we are not eating pre-packaged or frozen industrial foods, are based on (or derived from) traditional Agrarian food preservation techniques. Ham, bacon, sausage, jerky, bologna, cheeses, yogurts, jellies, jams, krauts, pickled vegetables, condiments (like ketchup, mustard, and mayonnaise), raisins, and hundreds of other foods we eat every day, even many liquors and malted beverages, were originally invented as ways to preserve the harvest and to make longer term use of seasonal food supplies. Many regional or traditional foods are indicative of the heritage of the people who settled in that region of the country. Today, if you travel the world and sample what are now considered "exotic" local foods, you are likely partaking of the ancestors of many of our own modern foods. Throughout Eastern Europe diets may be heavy in pork products, fat, cheeses, and foods made from fermented vegetables or grains. In parts of Russia, where the growing and harvesting season may take place in as little as four months, you will find people eating ample amounts of dried fish, and pickled... everything. From the wines and cheeses of places like Spain and South America, to the fermented milk products, dried meats, breads, and fruit of Africa and Asia, food in the lesser "industrialized" world has not changed significantly from what was eaten by kings and paupers hundreds of years ago. The point is that prior to the age of industrialism and mass transportation, different regions of the world were very much identified with their location on the earth and what could be produced and preserved from it. There is a universal truism found in the Bible that it would be well for us to ponder:

> *"But godliness with contentment is great gain. For we brought nothing into this world, and it is certain we can carry nothing out. And having food and raiment let us be therewith content"* (1Tim. 6:6-8).

If we are to be content with food and raiment (clothing), and if these things are derived from the bounty of the earth, we can conclude that our happiness and our contentment relies very heavily on our philosophy of the land and on our benevolent governance of it. We abuse or neglect the land to our own spiritual and physical detriment. In abandoning his Agrarian roots, man has abandoned his connection to the land, and with it has cast out his peculiar local heritage and culture. Instead, man has adopted a rootless, amorphous, and temporary international culture - defined alone by man's insatiable and fruitless hunger for more; more personal peace, affluence, and comfort. Benign cultures were defined by those peculiar practices particular to a people whose culture developed from a close, personal, and mutually beneficial interaction between the people and the land. Relationships, celebrations, and even diet were defined and restricted by land and growing practices, and all of life was governed by what (and when) the land would produce its bounty. By definition then, the culture was a representation, brought forth from the divine gardener, of a piece of land - *the good ground* - from which the progenitor of all men had been derived. Each culture was the product of not just the morality and laws the people had accepted for themselves, but of the types and quantities of crops that would grow readily in the local soil, along with the animals indigenous to that place which could be used for food.

Our ideas of what the ideal life should be will naturally change as we become more attuned and informed about what is truly and eternally good for us, and as our knowledge matures as to what a perfect God wills for His people and His land. Just as all people are not the same (some are bad soil, bad trees, or bad fruit) and all men and women are designed for different purposes, we should recognize that all lands, regions, or cultures are not the same and should not be forced into the same mold. The globalization and industrialization of food, diet, and production is as destructive as the globalization and industrialization of anything else. The world system has determined that all men and women are to be assimilated and systematized until they are all equally dependent consumers of industrially produced globalized products. I watched a documentary not long ago about how a major potato chip manufacturer struggled in trying to introduce potato chips into the Chinese market. It seems that the directors of the multi-national snack food producer did not know that, for the most part, the Chinese were not "snackers". Because the Chinese culture, other than in a few large cities, was still basically agrarian, the people still engaged in agrarian eating practices. They did not eat three large meals a day but instead ate many, smaller, healthier meals; and they did not eat "junk food" between meals from boredom or from craving. The snack manufacturer soon realized that even if they were to pump shiploads of potato chips into China, they still weren't ever going to create a market there without some serious re-thinking of their plans. You see, the availability of salty snack foods wasn't going to make the Chinese want to eat them. That kind of thinking works in America, but not in China. In order for the market to change, the *culture* would have to change. Covetousness and greed would have to be sold in China *first*. China was going to need an infusion of Western-style consumerism. Massive amounts of advertising were utilized to convince the Chinese that they needed to want *the good life*. The Chinese needed to be taught to want to be like Westerners. Potato chips were portrayed not as junk food, but as a symbol of prosperity and a sign that an individual was progressive and forward-thinking. Potato chips would become an indicator of Western-style aggressiveness and ambition, and snagging a bag from a street-side vendor was portrayed as proof that prosperity and advancement had arrived. Potato chips were portrayed as progress. Potato chip and snack food factories were built in China paying wages that would be sufficient to allow the new, upwardly mobile and ambitious workers to afford *the good life*. Eventually, the tactic began to work, and potato chips have become one of the fastest growing food items sold in China. China being invaded by snack producers may seem like a fairly harmless alteration of the ancient culture of China, but, in a kind of "butterfly effect" (where small changes in a system may have far-reaching - and possibly devastating - effects on the system) the overall results may prove to be more destructive than anyone may think. Introducing a westernized snack-culture and the industrialized method of eating to the people of China will likely have dangerous rippling effects in the culture, economy, and health of the Chinese people. We can probably guess, but only time will tell how harmful the effects will eventually be.

If Globalism and the "Potato Chip Revolution" were successful in corrupting and sowing the seeds of destruction in a traditionally agrarian culture, it seems logical that *Localism* and a Regional Food Revolution might be successful in building an agrarian culture. It may seem overly simplistic, but if millionaire marketers with all their college degrees and computers concluded that picking up a bag of chips was *cultural* and not gastronomic, and that it would support and expand the industrial processed food culture, then NOT picking up a bag of chips ought to have the opposite effect here. Maybe it won't work on a worldwide scale, but it absolutely will work in your home.

In all things I believe that traditional and local is usually better, and this philosophy will be reflected in all of the subsections I write about food. We should focus our efforts in studying and learning what will work well where we are. As you probably have discovered, I put a high value on a good philosophy and right thinking in engaging in an off-grid plan. As we grow and learn, some practices, means, and methods will develop (or re-develop) which are highly successful, and others will be abandoned as failures. Ideally, even in our small communities, we will begin to see the development of a peculiar culture particular to our region and lifestyle. Traditions, practices, feasts, etc. will become more local (because hopefully we will have already cast off the more globalist/consumer ones), and we will once again begin to be defined by our regional agrarian culture. The family will once again be connected to the land and associated with it. Man will again have legends and the stories of building and working the land, and he will have a sense of history that is more in line with reality and less the result of globalist, statist, industrialist propaganda.

RE-LOCALIZING AND THE DEVELOPMENT OF LOCAL AND REGIONAL CULTURE

I am a product of the South, so my examples will be derived from what I know the most about, though they can be applied to any area or region anywhere.

Once upon a time, when the South was still agrarian and predominantly Christian, even within the South there were many, many, diverse and discernible cultures. Though there was an over-riding general Southern culture (Christian Agrarianism) and set of values, from town to town you would have found a grand diversity in how these values were practiced. Every small town had different festivals and celebrations. One village might have "The Watermelon Festival", while another town celebrated "Okra Days". Here in our area in Central Texas, the two big festival days for us are The Fiesta de la Paloma (the Feast of the Doves) in Coleman, Texas; and Santa Anna Funtier Days (which celebrates the Old West heritage of the area) in Santa Anna, Texas. As our Christian community here (if the Lord wills it) grows and expands, we will likely develop our own special days and festivals, and these ought to develop organically. In our small community, we already look forward to "First Wednesday" which is our monthly community work day where we all gather together to work on some project for someone on their land. But the point is that our desire in our off-grid agrarian lives is to live our lives more locally, and to do so it all has to start with us.

A good place to start in our endeavors to re-localize will be in looking into what types of food and crops are indigenous to, or adapted well to, our area. Those products that may not be indigenous, but which have developed here and succeed here are great, and if they can fit our criteria, then we ought to pursue them; but if we can reclaim those foods and crops that are indigenous, and that really thrive in our local soil, then we would be foolish not to focus on them. It has been a shocking (perhaps it should not have been) thing for me to realize that the crops that I have grown over the past 8 years that have done the absolute best, are these:

Okra
Black-eyed Peas
Green Beans
Squash
Sweet Potatoes
Greens (Mustard, Collard, Spinach, etc.)
Peaches

Now, let me see... that looks like a southern menu if I ever saw one! Why should I be shocked that these foods grow well here in the south? I shouldn't be, but I really was. There is a reason that these foods are identified with the South - and sometimes we are too slow to figure these simple things out - I know that I am. I have eaten these foods all my life, but because I was so "in the world," they never became a regular and traditional part of my diet until recently. Likewise when I talk about meat animals, I have learned that there are animals which do well and thrive in our environment, and some which struggle and do not do as well.

In my off-grid plans, I really focus on these locally successful animals and crops, and naturally our diets have changed to represent what grows well here. Our minds and hearts need to become more local. Live wherever you want to live, but if you plan on living as an off-grid agrarian - then really *live* there. Make it your home and you will find you will more readily succeed in your endeavors. Rather than spend your time in the world, partaking in the world's culture and society, put those things behind you and live your life among your local friends and family. This book is about Off-Grid Living, but more specifically it is about *successful* Off-Grid Living. Our mindset is critical to our success, and a right philosophy of life and living will immeasurably assist in that success.

OFF-GRID VS. SUPER STUFFMART

Our topic in this chapter is food, and I will be getting to the specific categories of food in later chapters, but it is necessary that we discuss a few things first. If we formulate our plans according to the failed ideas of the old consumer system, or if we remain entrenched in our colonized thoughts and ways of doing things, then the product of our efforts will naturally reflect the errors in our presuppositions. The "grid" system of food production and distribution is no more reliable or safe than is the system of grid electricity or grid water. It is evident that the JIT (Just In Time) system of large industrial farms, trucks, and grocery superstores has provided a mirage of what looks like success and prosperity. You will remember that Ancient Rome had a JIT food delivery system, and when things crashed the people ended up eating other people. I remember many years ago I took some visitors from Australia into a huge chain grocery store here in one of our bigger cities. Australia is no backwoods third world country, but my Australian guests were completely awed by the sheer amount and variety of goods available in the store. One of our guests exclaimed, "Wow! This is the most decadent country in the world! This is Rome!" And he was right. It is possible today, at any time of the year, to buy big, beautiful red tomatoes, figs, pineapples, bananas, papayas, guava, watermelons, and fruit and vegetables of every imaginable type and kind. *Season* has no real meaning to the worldling any more. The readily available and inexpensive smorgasbord of goods might even, if we are not careful and aware, convince us that food is not a problem in America and that maybe it ought not be high up on our list of important concerns. How wrong we would be if we fell for the mirage and succumbed to such a superficial con. The questions we must ask ourselves are these:

1. Is the food that I see in such plentiful quantities and evident quality *really* good? Or does it just look good?

2. Is the system which makes such plenty readily available and cheap *good*? Or does it engender slavish dependence and weakness.

3. Is the system that delivers and provides for such ample bounty trustworthy and reliable? Or is it subject to interruption or cessation if tragedy or catastrophe were to strike?

4. Are the prices of these foods realistic? Or do they reflect the practice of "price shifting", where the real costs are (by sleight of hand) really moved over into higher taxes, higher fuel and material costs in other areas, or higher health care costs from our dependence on nutritionally deficient and chemically laden foods?

The plan is, of course, to stop buying food at these stores and to start growing our own food, but it is necessary that we spend a little bit of time in identifying what is wrong with the current system. Why? Because when we have more information we are strengthened in the inner-man, and we are more likely to stand firm against the flow of modernism that seeks to punish or isolate those who do not agree with the status quo.

When we very first started down our road towards off off-grid living, I received a ton of resistance from friends and family. Had I known then what I know now, I would have had better answers to give them. Back then I knew I wanted to grow my own food – I just hadn't really examined all of the reasons why my way was better, safer, and wiser than the modern methods. My parents would say, "You are losing money. It takes more money for you to grow tomatoes than it does for me to buy them at the store", or, "You're spending money on gardening, watering, seeds, plants, canning and preserving materials, etc., and for half of that money you could have bought already canned and preserved food from the store." Well, when I was ignorant, and when I looked at those facts according to the evident presuppositions that they had offered, it seemed like they were right. I instinctively believed that growing my own food made me freer and less dependent on the store, but back then I did not know enough to argue that, when all things were considered, they were actually wrong! It doesn't cost more money to raise my own food, not when I consider gas costs, taxes, health issues, and all the other ways that costs are "shifted" from the price of grocery foods into the other "stuff" I was being forced to buy from the industrial system. In reality, the more we moved out of the system, the more we realized that the whole modern food production and delivery system was an elaborate con game. I did not know then that foods could be genetically modified or actually grown differently and unnaturally in order to make them LOOK better, even if their actual quality and nutritive value was less. I didn't know that a huge, red, rich, ripe, store-bought tomato may have as little as 1/3 of the nutrition available when compared to a small and comparatively less attractive home grown heirloom tomato. This is not to mention the fact that most of those beautiful store tomatoes were grown with toxic chemical fertilizers and additives, and that even many of the "organic" varieties were of poor nutritional quality. I did not know that everyone is eating 2 to 3 times more food today than they were 60 years ago because of the anemic quality of the food, and because of the insane ways that food is processed and transported in order to make it look a certain way in the store. I did not know that obesity, diabetes, cancers and other health problems were skyrocketing, not just because of the ubiquitous reality of snack foods in the American diet, but because our bodies are screaming for nutrition and it takes more food to give us less of what our bodies need. I did not know that scientists and industrial producers had figured out how to grow big, beautiful, consistently sized products out of depleted and abused soils by manipulating the genes in the seeds or by hybridizing the plants. I was surprised to read that several Greek philosophers claimed that most people only ate 2 meals a day, and that they (the philosophers) felt like that 2 meals a day was gluttonous! They suggested that people (back then, when food had more nutrition) who ate only 1 large meal a day lived longer more healthy lives. One philosopher was shocked to hear that some libertines were eating as many as... (gasp!) 3 meals a day! Since then I have learned that today we have to eat so much bulk because our modern foods have less than 20-30% of the nutrition due to massive soil depletion and wicked food growing practices.

I know now that I need to grow and process my own food, not just because it is safer, more reliable, and healthier, but because it really is cheaper too. I know now that when I look at the bounty that *Vanity Fair* (the world) provides, that it is actually a hologram and not real at all.

All free men and women ought to be working towards simplicity, self-sufficiency, and sustainability in our food supplies. This means that each family ought to focus on producing as much of their own food supplies as possible, and at increasing that supply each year by learning better techniques, by learning new skills, by working harder, and by diversifying. Start by trying to figure out how much of your food you produce now. Maybe if you are new it is 0%, which means that you are currently dependent on the world system for 100% of your food supplies. These worldly food supplies grow worse and worse each year; worse in total nutrition, worse in toxins and poisons in the food, worse in every possible way other than in the way they look. As I said earlier, modern commercial farmers will tell you that they have learned to make food *look* better, by making it worse for you and by reducing its overall *actual* quality. I was reading the *Growing Great Garlic* book written by Ron Engeland, and in it he claims that smaller garlic that is a little less appetizing to look upon is actually more flavorful and probably better for you, but the commercial buyers and restaurants want the bigger and more robust looking garlics because they sell better.

This means that their overall actual quality is diminished in order to make them more commercially profitable; and this is an organic, gourmet garlic grower telling it like it is. If organic, gourmet growers are telling you this, what do you think is happening to the non-organic corporate grown industrial crops? The point is that you should be lowering your dependency on the industrial/commercial food system starting immediately, and working to lower your dependence every year. Independence is the opposite of dependence.

ABUSE

As I have said before, this is a very difficult book to write because every single reader is in a different place and comes to the information with a different mindset and a different set of presuppositions. Some of you may know all of this, and you just can't wait for me to get to the nuts and bolts (or meats and veggies) of off-grid food planning. For some of you, every bit of this, especially the philosophy, is brand new to you and it is like trying to learn a new language. Some of you have begun your move off-grid and you are looking for secrets or tips to help you along your way, while others of you may not be convinced that moving off-grid is a good idea at all. I have said it before, and I will never stop repeating it... this book is a philosophy book, and not a "how to" book. I am trying to teach people how to think, and not what to do. If you know how to think, you will learn what to do. This section is critical because sometimes we do not know an enemy until we know what he is done and what he is capable of, and sometimes we misidentify our own problems and errors because we think we already know all of the relevant information.

Maybe you never thought of yourself as an abuser, but, at its root our current system is all about abuse. Most of you may be unfamiliar with the real meaning of this word, and you have seen it applied to so many things that, in many cases, it has lost its real meaning.

ABUSE is *AB*normal *USE*.

Abuse takes place when any person, place, idea, or thing is used for something other than (or contrary to) its intended and natural use. Our world is a wreck because of abuse. Our society has grown wicked because of abuse. Our culture is freefalling because of abuse. Our land is being destroyed because of abuse. Our soil is depleted because of abuse. Our food is toxic and grows lower in nutritive value every day because of abuse. Our health is weakened because of abuse. The concept of family is decaying because of abuse. If we are honest we will admit that almost everything we do, and almost every principle by which we do it, has changed over the centuries. Now we must conclude that most of the things we do are abusive, and all abuse is sinful.

Like water, food is a representation of many things. The old saying "junk in/junk out" has never been more applicable. So many of God's parables and stories revolve around the growing and preparing of food, because so much spiritual truth can be derived from the holy process of doing it right. The Bread of Life is not genetically modified. Manna from Heaven is not hybridized, sterilized, or "enriched." If we want to reclaim our birthright and see our bodies and our land healed, it is necessary that the strongholds in our minds be overturned. It seems so simple to say, but when it comes to food - nothing could be more evident: Just because something looks good, doesn't mean it IS good. Just because our enemy has given us depleted bleached bread and a circus, doesn't mean that those things are good for us. It is our fault that we have fallen for such an elaborate con, but, once we have been enlightened, it is our responsibility to do everything in our power to repent and fix our situation. We cannot continue to support industries that rape the land and destroy our soil. We cannot continue to participate in a system that rewards greed and elevates thieves and murderers for killing us. We cannot stand by and see animals abused, the land abused, our health abused, our freedom abused, and God's creation abused without doing all that we are able to do to fight against it. Unhappily, much of this evil has been done in the name of, and with the support of, those who call themselves the "Children of God". The greatest destruction of topsoil in the history of the world has happened during the so-called "Christian" era. Abuse is Sin, plain and simple. Every time a thing is used for purposes other than what God intended that thing for it is sin. When we participate in it, we sin. When we give it credibility, we sin. Apathy is sin. Complacency is sin. When we enable it, we sin. Getting a right view and a right mind about food requires repentance *first*. We aren't going to fix the whole system at all, and we surely aren't going to fix our own problems overnight. We have work to do. We need to educate ourselves and we need to put our hands to the plow - but first our minds need to be changed. None of us, having learned the truth, ought to ever look at the current world food system with the same eyes.

Maybe you cannot grow a crop right now, but you can go to a farmer's market. Maybe you cannot start a garden right this minute, but you can seek out a local, organic, or natural grower. Maybe you cannot break free from the supermarket overnight, but you can get started... today. Repentance in this case is about movement and direction. This is something for you to think and pray about.

In the next chapter we will begin our discussion on the different categories of food, starting with a discussion on meat production.

CHAPTER 12

FOOD, PART 2

What we call "meat" today (generally the muscle, tissue, and fat of animals) has been a food staple for humans for many thousands of years. Our word "meat", which is derived from the Old English word *mete* (meaning *food*), has not always been restricted to identifying the edible flesh products of animals. Historically and Biblically, the word "meat" was used to represent all types and kinds of food. Basically the progression of the meaning of the word (to most people) has gone like this:

1. First, it was general term meaning *all food.*

2. Next, it began to represent all food except that which is derived from plants or trees.

3. Next, in some cultures (such as the Jewish culture), it began to mean edible animal flesh except fish.

4. As individual terms for the flesh of birds and fish developed, in some cultures, trades, or segments of society, or in most situations, the term "meat" took on the meaning of "the edible flesh of mammals".

So we will understand one another, in this chapter, unless I indicate differently, I am going to use the second definition of the term. I will be referring to all the edible flesh of all animals, even fish as "meat". I will also be including eggs (such as chicken eggs) in this chapter on meat. In most cases, unless I am speaking very generally (as in the 2nd definition), I will indicate what type of meat I am speaking of within the discussion.

As I have mentioned before, this chapter is not meant to be a "how to" on the different kinds of animals, nor is it a manual on raising, breeding, or processing animals for meat. When we started on our own path of off-grid living there were notoriously few books on homesteading, and on the "how to" of living off the land. The late Carla Emery's *Encyclopedia of Country Living* was our only book back then, and we used it almost every day (and I still recommend that everyone have a copy of it). Since then there have been literally thousands of books published on homesteading, animal care, pasturing animals, food production, food preservation and processing, etc. Do take the time to procure good books, and study hard to learn the "how to" of managing your farm. But always remember that the philosophy that informs many of those books is not a good one.

I do not plan on spending the time to provide an in-depth or exhaustive history of meat, although it would be a fun project for me to undertake. I am concerned that to do so might invite unnecessary controversy which might take away from the overall philosophy of the book. In most cases, the history of food can be related without inflaming emotions or creating opposing or warring parties or factions, but our understanding of the history of meat (and of eating meat) is often very much intertwined with some of our most cherished and firmly held beliefs. Of all the categories of food, our historical concept of meat is very uniquely tied to our personal understanding about God, the creation of the earth, the age of the earth, and it is indicative of any religious, philosophical, or cultural beliefs upon which we order our lives.

By way of warning and full disclosure I will first say that I do (very gladly) eat meat. I live in a community of meat eaters, and this chapter is about meat raised and used for food. If you have serious problems with man using animals for food, just go ahead and skip this chapter. I am also a Christian, and I am of the belief (contrary to many modern Christians and Jews), that man has eaten meat since (at least) the fall of Adam, and that animals were raised and killed for food even before we see the first mention of the practice in the 9ᵗʰ Chapter of Genesis. I say this, not by way of argumentation, nor do I intend to prove such claims in this chapter (this is not a Biblical commentary), but so you will know what historical beliefs inform my worldview.

MEAT: A VERY, VERY, SHORT HISTORY

Paleontological and archeological evidence shows that men have engaged in the practices of hunting, gathering, husbanding, and butchering animals for food as far back as such sciences can determine. The domestication and management of animals for meat was an evident practice in every ancient civilization, and most of the animals that are used for their meat today were first domesticated by these early civilizations. Sheep, Goats, Cattle (bovine animals), and Pigs have been raised, herded, and particularly and purposely selected for their meat qualities for thousands of years. The ancient Hebrews living in Egypt prior to the exodus were able to maintain their cultural separatism and religious identity specifically because they were shepherds, and because the Egyptians of that time considered all shepherding an abomination (Genesis 46:34). In most instances there still exists today both domesticated and wild (or feral) versions of many of these same animals that were domesticated by the ancients; except, perhaps, cattle – though the pure Texas Longhorn is probably a fairly close version of what were once wild *taurine* cattle from the Iberian Peninsula (modern day Spain, Portugal, Andorra and a small portion of France). Originally, this domestication and specific breeding for meat purposes was a very good thing and produced very hardy and more passive animals that produced large quantities of high-quality meat. Over the last 200 years though, industrialization of meat production, genetic engineering and manipulation, and abusive selection criteria have produced unviable and probably unhealthy meat animals that bear very little resemblance to their wild ancestors. Keep this in mind when I discuss the peculiar species because most homesteaders do not take into account that many of the animals they are choosing by default may be structurally weak, genetically altered or inferior, and unlikely to produce well or keep producing outside of the "factory" meat production system. For example, what we call the "commercial" or "industrial" meat cow today will very rarely live more than ten years (even less if an optimum environment, including supplemental food and nutrition, is not made available). Since these cows often do not reproduce until they are two or three years old, and since they take an inordinate amount of time to "breed back" (or get pregnant again after calving), it is probable that the average meat production cow today will only produce 4 or 5 offspring in her productive life. Compare this with the pure Texas Longhorn cow which will usually have her first calf in her 2nd year, and will likely produce calves well into her 20's. It is not out of the ordinary for a pure Texas Longhorn cow to produce 20 calves in her productive lifetime. I say this to emphasize the fact that all animals are not equal, and all animals are not even really "natural" representatives of their species. You must also be careful when you are getting information from people who earn their living as industrial farmers or ranchers, or who have a vested interest in pushing or selling modern industrialized or commercial animals. In an earlier chapter I mentioned that there are "lies, damned lies, and statistics", and that saying is true. But the saying, "let the buyer beware" is even more applicable. People engaged in industrial agriculture have had millions of dollars and many decades to create animals (using selective breeding, hybridization, genetic engineering, etc.) that *seem* to do well under the commercial conditions the agri-businessman requires. They have also had millions of dollars and many decades to learn how to "fudge" the numbers and manipulate the statistics. I told a man one time, "If you think used car salesmen are a bit shady, go talk to a modern beef producer." All of these industrial meat vendors also join "associations" that pay millions of dollars to create marketing programs for their products. There are accepted maxims in modern agri-business that are completely not true in a more natural setting, which is to say that what they are pushing will not work on an off-grid, sustainable farm.

The history of animal husbandry and meat production is a very interesting topic, and I encourage you to do your research and carefully select all of the animals you choose to bring to your off-grid homestead.

MEAT PRODUCTION

The production of meat on the off-grid homestead is a fascinating, fun, and sometimes difficult prospect for the small farmer. When most urbanites think of the traditional family farm, they think of cows grazing lazily in green meadows, chickens scratching for bugs around the farmhouse, maybe a few geese or ducks in the pond, and pigs wallowing in the mud to stay cool. Most people, however, do not really think about what is actually happening on the small homestead. The animals you see (or dream about) on your farm are pieces in the meat-production puzzle. They are, each one of them, being managed – from birth to butchering – for the purpose of providing meat, fat, and edible protein for the family; unless they are intended for sale, trade, or barter. On the small farm even the milk cows are being managed during their lives for eventual culling and use as meat. Farmstead animals are not "pets", as most city dwellers see them. While the pig in the book *Charlotte's Web* was eventually saved from the butcher block, we need to remember that 1) that was a fiction story for children, and 2) the rest of the animals (except maybe the rat and the horse) eventually went under the knife. On our farm, we must constantly remind ourselves that our animals are to be benevolently and kindly managed for their ultimate purpose, which is to be utilized for food and other useful materials for our family. We advocate neither of the common extremes:

1. We do not humanize our animals by growing overly or idolatrously fond or affectionate of them. We care for our animals, but we do not treat them like people (actually, many very sick people treat animals far better than they treat humans). We know what these animals are for, and we always keep their purpose in mind, because too many people slide into an unhealthy or unproductive relationship with their animals (they think of them as "pets" or as family members) and then they have difficulty with (or outright refuse) the necessary slaughter of the animal when the time comes.

2. We do not become abusive or callous towards our animals. We do not give them the names of food or meat products (like calling a pig "Bacon", or a cow "Hamburger") just because we think it is funny, or because it makes it easier for us to remember what the animal is for. It is fine if others want to do this with their animals, but we do not do it here. We try to maintain a healthy respect and love for our animals, which results in a proper mindset and proper order.

We believe that these animals are given to us for our service and for our use, and we believe that we are called to exercise benevolent dominion and to engage in the right management of them. We do not use the word "humane" when discussing the proper treatment of animals, because the word "humane" means "like human" and we believe it is wrong to treat animals as if they are humans. Sin is the abuse or maltreatment of any part of God's creation, or the abnormal or un-Biblical use of an animal or created thing for purposes other than its natural or commanded use. We constantly keep in mind that abusing an animal is sinful, just as humanizing an animal is equally sinful.

RAISING MEAT ON YOUR HOMESTEAD

One of the greatest things about homestead meat production is that the animals generally act "naturally" and, if properly managed and cared for, will naturally fulfill their purpose. Having animals on your farm is also the best insurance policy against hunger or starvation. The safest and best way to store meat for your family is on the hoof. Healthy, well cared for animals grazing, rooting, or scratching on your property, are absolutely perfect examples of emergency and survival food storage. This book is about survival, and you can do a lot towards increasing your survivability by having a well planned and executed meat production system.

Begin by thinking about what type of land/pasture, etc. you have (or will have) available and ask yourself specific questions about how you will provide protein for yourself and your family. Selecting the right species and choosing the right animals for your homestead is not as easy as it might seem at first. You cannot just say, "Well, this is a farm, and all farms have cows, chickens, pigs, etc., so I must have cows, chickens, pigs, etc.). We don't do things one way just because they have always been done that way. Every kind or species of animal is not good for every situation. You must first look at the availability of pasture, crop land, water, shade, woods, etc. and then work from there in deciding how many animals (and of what kind) your homestead will support. If you are living, or if you are intending to live, on a small homestead (less than 5 acres), you will likely want to focus on smaller animals that reproduce quickly. In that case consider pigs, rabbits, goats, sheep, chickens, turkeys, quail, and other small game birds. Also remember that there are often smaller, "miniature" versions of most of these animals.

Do not do anything because "everyone does it". Because of tradition, you may feel inclined or obligated to have a milk cow, but, if you have a very small farm, it might be better for you to milk goats or sheep and utilize them for meat as well, unless you are absolutely sure you are going to be able to produce enough food and harvest enough water to support a large milk cow. If you do have pasture and produce enough feed to keep a milk cow, as a by-product you would get a calf every year that you could grow and butcher for meat. If you choose to keep goats for milk, then you will want to maintain a herd so you can always butcher some goats for meat, and you might want to look into a good dual-purpose goat breed. If your homestead is larger, then you might want to consider having cows – both for milk and for meat.

The point is that our situation and our intelligence ought to dictate what animals we choose to have and how we select those animals. On our farm, we have been very careful to study and do research in order to learn what will do well where we live, and to learn the history of both the animals and our region. I will share with you what we have done, not because I think you should do what we do, but because it will help you to study the thought process that went into our decisions. I will also discuss the different categories of animals in the order that I think you ought to acquire them.

CHICKENS, EGGS (OR IS IT EGGS AND CHICKENS?), AND OTHER FOWL ANIMALS

For the smaller homestead, raising birds is an excellent option. One of the few generalizations that I am willing to make concerning homestead food production is this: If at all possible everyone should own chickens, and preferably chickens that will both lay eggs, and that will get broody on occasion and hatch out new generations of chickens. Our chickens have, in the past, during times when we had very little or no money, kept us in eggs and meat through those tough times. I do not know what we would have done without our chickens. After a disaster or in the event of a major or extended economic or social disruption, having chickens could easily save your life and the lives of your loved ones.

Make a decision on your meat bird production based on the availability of space and feed. If you will pen your animals then you need to provide enough other farm space to grow and harvest most of their feed. If you will free-range your animals (which I recommend), then you need to study pasture management and pasture rotation so that you can do this without constantly having to buy feed and supplements. Many, many new homesteaders have written to me in shock and dismay at the price of feed grains for their animals. Feeding animals with store-bought feed has become one of those automatically accepted maxims that we off off-grid folks cannot afford to buy into. It is true that when you first get started, and for some time after that, you may have to buy feed, but you really need to have a plan in place to feed these animals without the store-bought feed at some point. If a disaster strikes, or if a long-term disruption occurs, you may not be able to purchase feed from the feed store. What will you do then? Also remember that, so long as you are buying feed from the store, you are invariably relying on a system that is untrustworthy and unsustainable and you are also having to earn money somewhere else (or doing something else) to pay for that feed. The easiest time to plan your break from the feed store system is when you are first getting started. It is much harder to separate from that system once you have invested in too many animals, and therefore you literally cannot afford to separate from the feed store.

At our old homestead in West Texas (before we moved to Central Texas) we produced quite a bit of our meat by raising turkeys, geese, and chickens. Eggs are considered meat in our economy, so I will include them in the conversation. All of these different types of fowl have different positives and negatives; some will produce a large quantity of both meat and eggs, while others will produce one resource more than the other. Since I believe you should have chickens, I'll assume that you agree. Do your research and find a good dual-purpose bird (one that is good at producing both meat and eggs) that will also do well in your area. Chickens are easy to keep and raise and they do not require a lot of care once they are adults (after a couple of months), and they will naturally do most of the things they need to do without your help. If you can free-range your chickens they will learn to get most of what they need nutritionally from what they can find on your land. Some supplemental feed may be necessary, and most people find that their chickens lay a lot more eggs when they are supplemented with nutritional grains. Again, if you can grow grains on your own property, you will be way ahead of the game and you will not find yourself spending a large amount of money on chicken feed.

The first structure we installed here on the ranch was a chicken coop. I built the first coop out of a dilapidated hunting blind we found on the back of the property. I put a new floor in it and built it into a small, workable coop and moved our 50 or so chickens into it. We built a fenced pen around the coop with some old hurricane fencing that had been donated years earlier. We are still using this coop as our main chicken coop today. We had egg production immediately (since our chickens were already producing), which means that we had protein growing from the land almost from day one. You may have to start your chickens from chicks, or by hatching your own with an incubator, but you still could be producing eggs within 5-6 months of getting started (depending on the season). If I were starting today, I would put in a chicken coop and get chickens started even before beginning to think about where I am going to sleep. How many chickens you will need is really based on the size of your family and how many eggs you eat (By the way... EAT MORE EGGS! They are very good for you, no matter what the modernists say.) We do not eat eggs every day, but on the days we do eat eggs, my family of six will eat up to a dozen eggs for breakfast. We also often have egg sandwiches or omelets for other meals during the day. We do not keep commercial snack foods around, so an egg burrito or an omelet is often our version of a quick snack. We usually keep between 30 and 60 producing hens. During the winter, when the hens are usually not producing as well as normal, we still will generally receive more than 6 eggs a day, which allows us to have eggs at least every other day. Eggs are good and wholesome and provide a large portion of your regular daily nutrition. Eggs can also be stored for longer term use. They can be dried and powdered, waxed, larded, stored in waterglass (sodium silicate), etc.

Once you have successfully started chicken and egg production on your land, you might consider diversifying into other types of fowl. In the past, in addition to chickens, we have raised turkeys, geese, and guineas. Each type of bird has very particular attributes that you will need to consider when you are deciding what types of birds to keep. With turkeys, you can raise large amounts of very good meat, but they are not as rugged and hearty as chickens. We suffered through a lot of mistakes and bird loss when raising turkeys, although I know people who have successfully raised turkeys for many years with no problems. We eventually were able to raise quite a few for eating, but they are certainly not as easy to raise and as "hands off" as are chickens. Male turkeys, like male geese, can be very territorial, and you will have to put some attention into fencing and housing. We raised geese for many years, and really enjoyed it, but having a male goose (or many male geese) around can be quite a challenge, since the goose is very intelligent and often will see you as competition, predator, or mate. There is a reason our language has the phrase "getting goosed" in it. I have been "goosed" many times, and it is something you have to live with if you decide to raise geese. Historically, geese were a very popular homesteading animal, and in Europe the ubiquitous flocks of geese, often seen being herded down roads or from pasture to pasture by young "goose herds" were evidence that the goose was a very common food item there. In America, where there were very large tracts of land and farms were generally larger, the goose fell out of favor as a flock (or herd) animal. Eventually, the mass industrial production of turkeys (for holidays and special meals) basically doomed the goose as a popular form of food in America. The point is that geese are "flock" animals who like to stay together, and as such they are herded quite easily; they thrive on green pasture grasses, and they reproduce well and plentifully.

Geese are quite good at reproducing and hatching out offspring, though the goslings we had would often drown in very small amounts of water or they would get trampled to death. Turkeys, though, are a whole other issue. Most (but not all) breeds of modern turkeys that are available today will NOT reproduce naturally. They are almost all born through AI (Artificial Insemination), and will require AI if you plan on hatching out eggs. There are some very good breeds available (like the Midget White, for example) that will still reproduce naturally, though they do not get anywhere near the size of modern commercial breeds.

Both turkey and goose eggs are edible and taste much the same as chicken eggs, though they are much larger. Larger eggs mean you need fewer of them to make your omelet!

I want to revisit a topic I have really hammered on throughout this book. It is a very common tactic for modern homesteaders to engage in bulk purchasing and processing of meat birds. What I mean by this is the practice of buying a large number of young birds, raising them to butchering age, and then slaughtering them all to fill the freezer. I've done this before, I still do it, and there is nothing wrong with it so long as the homesteader knows that this is not a sustainable practice, and is basically just the industrializion of home meat production. As far as producing a large amount of meat, possibly cheaply, in a short amount of time for storage, as I said – there is no real problem with the practice – but too often homesteaders truly believe they are going to be able to maintain these industrial practices under survival circumstances, or if the economic or social situation were to deteriorate. Believing this would be a huge mistake. The negatives of bulk buying just for butchering are these:

1. This system prevents us from developing (or adapting) animals to our particular situation, climate, etc. The age old practice of raising a herd and then culling selectively allowed the animals, through time, to become adapted well to our area. Bulk buying and butchering practices short-circuit this natural system of adaptation since all of the birds are killed at the same time.

2. This system relies on the false-idea that there is always going to be someone out there selling bulk birds or hatching eggs. This is a false premise. If one relies on the bulk buying and butchering system, what will happen when the system collapses and the homesteader has butchered all (or most) of his animals?

3. Since this system is designed to happen fairly rapidly in order to maximize yield per animal, the ancillary benefits of having animals as a part of the homestead permaculture system are lost (think of the constant need for manure, bug control, etc.)

SOME PIG: THE POOR MAN'S GOLDEN GOOSE (MIXAPHORICALLY SPEAKING)

Some folks have problems with eating pigs, and if you do, then just skip this section - but for the rest of us the pig is the answer to a whole lot of questions. Pigs are easy to keep, they reproduce fast, are cheap to buy, and they are clean if they are allowed to range and fend for themselves. On top of all of this, they produce an enormous amount of meat in a very short amount of time.   No homesteading animal produces more meat (and more types of meat) in a shorter time for less money than the pig.   We have been raising pigs for almost seven years, and our problem is not "how will we have enough meat?", but "where do we put it all?"   Pigs are excellent citizens in an animal/pasture rotation system. They plow up the ground, deposit very rich manure, and do great benefit to the soil.

Most of the problems you hear about pigs are not really problems with the pig as an animal, but are conditions brought about by the mass production of pork by industrialized processors.   The modern commercial pig is an unhealthy monstrosity. Modern commercial pigs are sickly, weak, and are generally not a good source of meat. When people exhort you to make sure you cook your pork well, you should know that bad pork is the product of the way pigs are raised today. I recently read an article where a writer was interviewing a modern commercial pork producer, and the article literally made me feel ill. The pork producer talked about how sickly the animals are (all of them), and how susceptible they are to diseases. He said that his animals were so susceptible to disease that they were only permitted to be in contact with one particular human for their whole lives! He said if another human were to come into contact with his animals, all of his pigs would die! And this man is raising meat that he hopes that you will buy and put on your table for your family to eat. It's sickening. But this is the product of modern industrial pork production and not the product of some intrinsic flaw in the animal. The fact that wild and feral boars are reproducing at an alarming rate; a rate so high that it is said that there are over 3 million feral hogs in the state of Texas alone, many times more than could ever be controlled by wide-scale hunting, should prove to you that pigs, as a species, are not sickly and weak animals. If you buy your pigs from a homesteader (preferably not from a commercial meat breeder, and not from a commercial meat *breed*); and if you make sure they are healthy and strong pigs who have been raised in contact with nature, with access to soil and good water, then you should have no problem raising strong, healthy pigs. Do not buy your original stock from any commercial producer... ever. Do not buy pigs that are kept inside in a sterile environment, without access to dirt and mud. Do not buy pigs that are penned in tightly together, and that have never been able to run or walk around. It is an absolute truism that a dirty pig is a happy pig, and a muddy pig is an ecstatic pig. If you can find someone who raises and sells pastured pigs, you will have really found a homesteading gold mine. Be willing to pay more for pigs (and for pork products) that have been raised naturally.

Virtually anywhere you go in the world (except in the Middle East) you will find the pig as a central animal in almost every homesteading plan and as a primary article in the homesteading diet. Pigs are valued for their meat, for it is from the pig that we derive such agrarian delicacies as bacon, ham, and sausage, as well as other delectable eatables. Pigs are also valued for their fat because they produce copious amounts of it, and because it can be used for food preservation (as in "larding"), for lighting, for fuel, and as a food supplement for other animals. Possibly more importantly, the pig is a miraculous producer of meat from the excess or waste products of the rest of the homestead! Do you have excess milk from your milk cow(s) after you have set some aside for drinking, for cheesemaking, for yogurt, and sour cream, etc.? The pig will be glad to turn that beautiful (or even spoiled) milk into meat for you. In fact, I have read that many small homesteading farmers raise pigs all the way from birth to butchering weight purely on milk and pasture! Do you have excess eggs, turnips, beets, potatoes, grains, or greens? The pig will be more than happy to turn those things into more meat for your table or your smokehouse, and more fat for your larder. The pig absolutely loves root crops, and one of the great things about root crops is that they can usually be left (or stored) in the ground or root cellar until they are needed by the pig. Root crops are some of the easiest and cheapest crops to grow, and the pig will thrive on them.

Our homestead currently produces enough meat for us to never buy meat from a store again, and much of this bounty is thanks to our pigs.

CATTLE

The word "cattle" comes from the word "chattel" which identifies any property or value that is moveable. Bovine animals, because of their intrinsic value and portability, became synonymous with "money", or "portable wealth", thus the name "cattle" was adopted and applied for these animals. In Ancient Greece and Rome, the term "cattle" was often used interchangeably with the word "money", and most dowries were based in cattle currency. In the Bible, the term "cattle" may still refer to any valuable, moveable animals.

In America, and particularly here in Texas, the word "cattle" means bovine animals, which most people erroneously refer to as "cows".

Writing or talking about cattle can be difficult in English, because in English we don't have a word for a single bovine animal (the word "cattle" is plural)! We only have words for the single female cattle (cow), or the single male cattle (a bull or steer). It is technically wrong to say, "I came upon *a* cattle in the road", even though we do not have a word for a single animal where we have not identified the sex of the animal. Originally (and Biblically) the term "ox" was used to identify a single bovine animal, but since that time the term "ox" has come to mean a bovine animal that has been trained to pull and work and that has reached five years of age. So when you read about an "ox" in the Bible, it does not automatically mean an animal that plows or pulls a wagon. It merely meant "a single bovine animal", where the term "oxen" meant more than one bovine animal. Again, the world "cattle" in the Bible, meant all valuable, moveable (or herded) animals – and usually referred to sheep and goats.

In America, most people will call all single bovine animals a "cow", even if that is not technically correct. If you say, "I saw a cow in the road", you may be right, but then again you may be wrong; and if you are talking to a person who owns cattle they will automatically assume that you saw a female version of "a cattle" in the road. So bear with me because sometimes talking properly about cattle can be difficult.

For those of you who are new to this, a quick primer on how I use the terms, so that there will be no confusion:

A *heifer* is a female bovine animal that has yet to birth a calf. In some societies and cultures, an animal is considered a heifer until it has birthed two calves, but in our community, once a heifer has qualified by birthing a calf, she is called a *cow*.

A *bull* is an intact (or uncastrated) male bovine animal, presumably capable of impregnating a female bovine animal.

A *steer* is a castrated male bovine animal.

An *ox* is a bovine animal trained to pull or work, and that has reached five years of age.

Being so readily identified as moveable money, cattle have long been symbols of wealth and prosperity. In the Bible, and in the world, having many cattle has traditionally been a sign of power and prestige. I personally believe strongly in owning cattle because of their inherent value and many uses, but I do not believe that homesteaders ought to automatically assume that they must own cattle in order to succeed. This is not true at all. All decisions about purchasing and raising cattle need to be carefully studied, and only after thorough consideration concerning how much land will be needed, how much feed can be produced, and what utility the homesteader will receive from the animal. As I have said before, some homesteaders on smaller land parcels may not want to own cattle. Some beginners wrongly assume that they can own a single milk cow and that by doing so their milk concerns will be solved. This is hardly the case. Every milk cow must be routinely (yearly) impregnated so that she will produce new calves and continue to produce milk. Most milk cows must be "dried up" for at least a month or more before they drop a new calf. Cows also may get infections or diseases (like mastitis), causing the milk to be undrinkable for a period of time. Any homestead that relies on milk from cows will need at least two milk cows if they plan on having an uninterrupted supply of milk, and they will need a bull (or the seasonal access to a bull) if they plan on getting their milk cows pregnant each year. Seriously study your needs and your available resources before you decide what kind of (and on how many) cattle you will own.

Cattle are valuable for their meat, for their ability to produce milk and fat, and for their importance in producing manure for fertilizing fields, crops, and gardens. As I have said before, not all cattle are the same and not all cattle will thrive on every type of land or in every region. Being in Texas, we have settled upon the pure Texas Longhorn as our preferred homestead cattle. The pure Texas Longhorn is not to be confused with the industrial/commercial Texas Longhorns that are everywhere today. The largest Longhorn registries routinely register Longhorns that plainly and clearly have evidence of inter-breeding with modern commercial cattle. These registries encourage the breeders to breed for "meat and horn" which are what make their cattle more valuable to other commercial breeders. We are not interested in corrupting the breed in order to commercialize the animals, so we are not interested in impure Texas Longhorns. We especially ascribe to the philosophy and the practices of the Cattleman's Texas Longhorn Registry (the CTLR), a registry that is committed to maintaining the purity of the original Spanish cattle. In order for you to see the thinking and philosophy that went into choosing what kind of animal would do well here in our situation, I will discuss the pure Texas Longhorn and why we think it is the perfect animal for us. Remember, I am not trying to sell you on Texas Longhorns – not at all; I am trying to sell you on the right way to think about choosing animals for your situation. This is all just an example...

THE PURE TEXAS LONGHORN

True and pure Texas Longhorns are profoundly different from the commercial cows (actually European breeds) that are available today. So it is not just a few minor trait differences we are looking at, but actually the Longhorn is really "a whole different animal".

The pure Longhorn is a smallish example of cattle. The female rarely tops 800 lbs., while the Steer or Bull may get upwards of 1800 lbs.; but it will take him 5-6 years or more to do so.

The Longhorn thrives on stuff other cows will not even eat. They will eat weeds, thistles, scrub brush, etc. as well as grass when it is available. It is very common for our friendly and gentle Longhorns to come up to us with cactus spines all over their faces... and it doesn't seem to bother them a bit. YES, they do eat cactus pads, and they like it. The result of these traits is that you can generally keep three pure Longhorns in the same area where you could only keep one commercial cow. The commercial cow is designed (by humans) to live a fairly short life. Finding a 10 year old commercial meat breed cow is very, very rare. As I said in the beginning of this chapter, the commercial cow will likely only produce up to five or six offspring in their short lives. Contrarily, the pure Longhorn can live very long lives, and it is not unheard of to have a cow still producing a calf (every 10-11 months) well into their 20's and even into their 30's. The pure Longhorn "breeds back" (or gets pregnant again after calving) faster than any other breed of cattle. The old saying by ranchers is that the *"Texas Longhorn will calf every 9 months and 15 minutes."*

The Longhorn survived and thrived in the deserts of Texas and Mexico without any aid from (or crossbreeding by) man. The commercial breeds, however, are concoctions of man. The *true* Longhorn is a product of God. After hundreds of years living wild in Texas and Mexico, there were literally millions of pure Longhorn cattle free for the taking. This is what precipitated the "cattle drives" of western fame. I live along what was once The Chisholm Trail. The Longhorn literally saved Texas after the disastrous war of northern/industrial aggression.

So how is the meat?

Longhorn meat is higher in "good" fats, lower in what the world calls "bad" fat, and higher in protein than any other beef. It is naturally one of the tenderest examples of beef, even though it is also the lowest in saturated fats. After my first time eating some Longhorn hamburger I had to say it was some of the best hamburger meat I have ever eaten.

Longhorn steers can be made into oxen (and have for centuries). Longhorns can also be ridden and milked. We have been milking Longhorn cows for several years now, and although they do not produce a large amount of milk when compared to commercial milk breeds, they do produce enough for our purposes.

Longhorns are the only breed where almost 100% of the cow is usable and profitable. Not only is the meat great, but the horns are regularly sold for $400-$1500. The hides are often sold for $400-$700. On the Internet I have seen websites where you can buy Longhorn pillows, couches and blankets (try to buy an Angus blanket!) Industrious Longhorn owners have been able to sell the hides and horns for more than a whole commercial breed cow will sell for at market. This doesn't count the meat at all!

The main points for the homesteader in our area:

1. 3/1 ratio of Longhorns to a commercial cow in the amount of cows per acre.

2. There are no known cases (of which I have either read or heard) of a Longhorn cow ever having to have a calf "pulled". Ease of calving is a famous trait of Longhorns, and it is why many, many commercial breeders now have their cows bred to a Longhorn bull for their first calf.

3. Low feed costs and the ability to keep a cow on land that might not be good enough for a commercial cow.

4. Multiple uses of the Longhorn: meat, milking, riding, pulling, work, etc.

5. Easy sale of all the "parts".

6. Quality of the meat.

Many people are scared of Longhorns because they can look so frightening, but anyone who owns pure Longhorns will tell you that they are the gentlest cattle in the world. I know homesteaders who would not dare go near their Jersey, Holstein, or Angus bull, but we have never had an aggressive Longhorn bull, and most of our animals are so gentle you can walk right up to them and pet them. The old Jimmy Stewart quote that the Texas Longhorn is "meatless, milkless, and murderous" is not true at all – even if it is funny. It is the industrial mindset that caused meat producers to abandon the Longhorn years ago. The Longhorn is for the rancher or farmer who truly wants to live closer to nature, without chemicals, antibiotics, or supplemental feeds. At a meeting once, a commercial cattle breeder asked a pure Longhorn breeder what he fed his cattle during the recent drought. The pure Longhorn breeder looked at the man quizzically and said, "I don't know what you mean. I didn't feed them a thing. They fed themselves. If had wanted to feed cattle for a living I would raise Herefords or Angus or any of those other commercial breeds. I don't want to feed cows - that is why I raise Longhorns."

One last true story about Pure Longhorns... since this is a survival book. In the 1950's in South Texas there was a drought that virtually destroyed the commercial cattle business. Most ranchers were dumping their commercial cows because they just could not afford to feed them – and the glut on the market devastated the ranchers, because they were being forced to sell their cattle at historically low prices – often at a loss. One rancher had a herd of commercial cattle, and a herd of 300 pure Texas Longhorns. His Longhorn herd was able to make it through the drought, and even multiplied during those seven years. In a parallel to the Biblical story of Joseph in Egypt during the seven year drought, when the South Texas drought was over, this rancher was the only cattle raiser with ample cattle to sell for meat (the price had skyrocketed by that time). He was able to pay off all of his debts, pay off his ranch, and became quite wealthy. That is what I call survival! Many, many ranchers then swore that they would always keep a herd of Longhorns around "just for emergencies". Unhappily, memories are short. Today, it has recently been estimated that there are fewer than 4000 pure Longhorns left in the world.

SHEEP AND GOATS

Many homesteaders keep goats, and in my family we raised goats for well over a decade. We have only recently moved away from the raising of goats and are now raising sheep.

Goats are adequate meat producers, and, depending on the breed, you can really do well raising goats for meat. A lot of people, especially in our area of Texas, swear by goats. If you like venison, you will love goat meat. Our goat meat, when it has been processed and canned for long-term storage, is almost indistinguishable from beef. We have also made very tasty sausage from goat meat.

We have found that if goats are kept solely for meat purposes, a fairly large herd must be maintained in order to utilize goats as the primary source of meat. Many homesteaders are wisely considering goats primarily for milking purposes, or they are purchasing dual-purpose (meat/milk) goats. Some of the goats that are milked in our community produce more milk per day than our milking Longhorn does! And goat milk is high quality milk, said to be the closest in makeup to human breast milk.

The downside in raising goats (at least for me) was that they are very destructive. There is a reason that the Bible uses the goat as a "type" of the damned or of the reprobate (this is also why we never call our children "kids" – they are "children"). It is said that *"a fence that will not hold water, will not hold a goat"*, and this is quite nearly true. If you want to learn how to build and constantly repair fences, then get goats, because goats do not respect rules or fences. Some people love and are very successful raising goats, and I applaud and encourage them. We did it for a long time, and we have a high level of respect for those who are able to successfully manage a good goat herd.

We transitioned to sheep for several reasons, but primarily it was because sheep (when kept in a fenced pasture) are easier to manage, are far less destructive, and the meat breeds produce better meat faster than do goats.

Several years ago, my wife, our oldest daughter, and I, traveled to Australia where we stayed for about 6 weeks. While we were there, we toured an expansive "sheep station" (basically a huge ranch of over 4000 acres). The station was so big that the sheep were herded by dogs... and *helicopters!* The family that owned the sheep station invited us to stay with them and while we were there we were served a dinner of roast lamb. In all my travels I have never been more impressed with a "home raised, home prepared" meal. It was delicious, and I have never forgotten it.

Sheep have historically been raised for their wool, and if you are ready and able to process wool, there is really no good reason for you not to be raising sheep. The fact that an animal can produce such valuable material just by living is quite a testament to the value of the animal. However, I stayed away from sheep for many years for just this reason: because we were not ready to manage and process the wool from the animals. Wool-producing sheep must be sheared at least once a year and we did not know how to do it, or what to do with the wool once the sheep were sheared. Frankly, I wanted to eventually get into wool production, but I really wanted the sheep for their meat, for their temperament, for their ease of management, and because they wouldn't tear up my fences. Enter the "meat breed" of sheep... for us it was *The Dorper.* We received our Dorpers not too long ago and we have been very pleased with them. Dorper sheep are indigenous to South Africa, and they are very well acclimatized to our heat and to our dry summers. Best of all, the Dorper is primarily a meat breed, and if you do not want the wool the Dorper is kind enough to drop its wool naturally so you do not have to shear them! We have also discovered that the Dorpers are very easy to manage, they do not destroy our fences or our young trees, and the young lambs reach butchering age and size many months earlier than did our meat goats. For us for right now, Dorper Sheep are a very good solution to our needs and concerns.

RABBITS AND OTHER SMALL CREATURES

My children raise meat rabbits, and they do their own butchering. My oldest daughter is in charge of rabbit production, and she is doing very well with it. She has often trained other homesteaders in our community how to butcher different animals, and the rabbit is usually a good starter animal for learning how to butcher. Oftentimes these smaller meat producing animals are overlooked by the homesteader, but, particularly for those of you who will have smaller homesteads, the small meat animal is definitely something to consider. Rabbits, for example, reproduce quickly, and produce a very high quality protein. The only real downside is that they do not produce much fat. If you are going to raise rabbits for meat, you will definitely want to diversify by also raising some other animal that is better at producing fat... pigs for example.

CONCLUSION

There is no way that this chapter could ever be an exhaustive compendium of homesteading "how to" advice. I have tried to offer actual examples and more of a "real world" philosophy that can be adapted to your own circumstances; keeping in mind that, after a disaster or a collapse, most of the accepted maxims that have guided and informed traditional homesteading will not work. I have also not discussed hunting, fishing, or trapping – even though these are often viable and sustainable means of procuring meat for the homestead. Unhappily, if a systemic disaster were to last more than a few weeks, hunting, fishing, or trapping is not likely to produce enough food for a family to survive for very long. The examples given in this chapter are not suggestions for you. They are examples that show a process of thinking, and a philosophy of animal selection and management. I wanted you to learn *how* we decided to do what we do. My purpose is to show you what kind of thinking is necessary for true off-grid survival, and to help "decolonize" minds so that we might more effectively consider our needs when it comes to producing homestead meat in a sustainable way.

CHAPTER 13
FOOD, PART 3

SEPARATE, SIMPLE, SUSTAINABLE

The methods of acquisition, procurement, production, processing, and preservation of our food – every one of these things - have to be re-evaluated once we come to the right conclusion that the system we have trusted heretofore has gone wildly off-track. Once we admit that our lives have become dependent on a corrupt and unsustainable food philosophy, it is only logical that we will need to throw down all of our former opinions and start developing newer and more reasonable ones. Survival is going to require us to re-think everything. As I say all the time... *"It is not something that is wrong with our thinking when we are in the world... everything is wrong with our thinking"*. No previously held maxims can be exempt from re-consideration. The system we have discussed thus far in this book needs to be a framework for re-examining everything we have come to believe.

I have appreciated all the great comments and emails I have received while writing this book. I think one of the most interesting things to me has been that so many people have rightly identified that the philosophy of *"off off-grid"* living that I teach in this book is radically different than the philosophy they see portrayed in the off-grid or "survival" magazines, books, and websites, which all take for granted the unquestionable nature of the current system. Some materials assume that the system is stable and will never be interrupted; others assume that interruptions, even if they are severe, will eventually be corrected – and everything will return to "normal". A study of history shows that these assumptions are often very, very wrong. As I have said before, most people think of off-grid living as merely a way to avoid paying utility bills; or as a way to be insulated against temporary or short-lived disasters or emergencies; or as a preferable eco-friendly lifestyle choice.

Our philosophy includes all of those things, but those things are merely results or products of a life lived separately, simply, and sustainably. Because we choose to live separately, simply, and sustainably, we don't have to pay utility bills. Because we choose to live separately, simply, and sustainably, we are insulated, as far as God wills it, against disasters and systemic failures. Because we choose to live simply, separately, and sustainably, we walk and live lightly upon the earth, and practice benevolent dominion over it - improving it for our progeny.

The philosophy I am espousing in this book is *so* fundamentally different than what most people know or expect that it makes it necessary that I constantly remind everyone of those pre-suppositional differences.   First,   I   personally   believe   that   this   life (particularly *Agrarian Separatism*) is the one that God commands of His people. Second, I believe that this way of living is the only way to preserve and maintain the health and spiritual safety of our families *and our Christianity* in the face of a world bent on destroying both it and us. We believe that modern, so-called "Christianity" is apostate and has succumbed to the great deception promised in scripture, and that the modern, urban, industrialized culture is the bad and stony ground, and the way-side where true crops do not thrive. We believe that the simple, separate, and plain Christianity of the historic *Church in the Wilderness* is the true and historic Christianity that God maintains for a witness to and against the world (*Contra Mundum*). Our religion and our agrarian culture and worldview are not separate - they are one. Only the colonized and fragmented minds of modern man can live such bifurcated lives.   Our focus on separation, simplicity, and sustainability, means that many of the biggest features of what the world considers "off-grid living" are not going to be part of our long-term plans. Every single thought and idea has to be examined to see if it actually fits into our model. Every single process needs to be measured against these measuring sticks (and note that they are all interwoven and interdependent):

1. *Does it increase or maintain our separation?*   Does the

principle, idea, or act require more syncretism with the world, or less? If it does require constant maintenance and expense, is that requirement going to increase my dependence on the world and the world's vulnerable systems? Does any item, product, or practice require continued worldly input? Do I have to work away from my land in order to support it?

2. *Is it simple?* Is it less complicated and involved; less likely to break or break down and need worldly attention; less gaudy, ostentatious, vain, or prideful? Why do we do what we do, the way that we do it? As an example of the philosophy behind this question, I always ask myself this: How was this task done in the past? Why the change? If there was a change, what precipitated it, and what was the result of it?

3. *Is it sustainable?* How much continued cost, expense, outside material, money, etc. will it take to maintain or continue doing things this way? Can I produce it here, or can I produce what it takes to produce it here? Can I continue to use it/do it/practice it if the world system around us collapses?

Of course, for us, all three of these measuring sticks are founded on the over-riding principle *"Is it moral and Biblical?"*

RE-THINKING EVERYTHING

We have previously shown where our current systems of industrial food production and JIT transport and supply are not sustainable or safe. The alternative in the minds of most homesteaders or off-grid folks has usually been to engage in some combination of gardening, a pen-based animal system, row-crops, greenhouses, etc. While these things, each in-and-of itself may be helpful or beneficial in certain circumstances, I have determined that the usual alternative means of going off-grid in producing our food supply does not perfectly fit our new worldview and philosophy. The knee-jerk (or default) system of off-grid food production fails in answering one or more of the three critical questions

I have asked above.

So let us do some re-thinking...

Although the scriptures do mention some rotational, "seasonal", or *annual* crop farming, by far, when speaking of food products in the context of, or in relation to, God's providence, or in identifying blessed wealth, the Bible more often speaks about (or refers to) perennial crops or perennial food items. Crops such as wheat and corn ("corn" in the Bible usually refers to barley, but "corn" can refer to any seed crop) are discussed, but generally these are products used to make bread and other staples, therefore they are representative of basic sustenance and not wealth, prosperity, or success. In the Scriptures, a blessed land is said to run with *"milk and honey"*. The phrase "milk and honey" represents more indulgent food products that exist naturally without much added human work or management. They represent wealth and prosperity. When the Bible identifies the overflowing blessings and providence of God, we read about olive and almond trees, pistachio trees, dates, sycamore figs, apples, grapes, and pomegranates, as well as many wild or perennial root crops including garlic, onion, and leeks - foods which in many cases could be left or stored in the ground for a good part of the year. I think we can all agree that the original garden planted by God for man was most likely made up of fruit and nut orchards and other perennial plants, trees, and shrubs. I doubt very seriously that annual row crops were instituted until after the fall of Adam, but of course that is mainly speculation on my part. I do, however, believe that many crops which are considered annual seed crops today were actually perennial plants in ancient times, and in the original garden. For example, tomatoes, which are an annual plant in most of the world, are actually perennials in the Tropics, and all of the modern species of tomato are derived from a once perennial fruit. Logically we can determine that most "annual" crops are products that, through selection and adaptation, were annualized from originally perennial ancestors. I am not disparaging annual crops because in many cases we must rely on them and they can be very valuable to us and our survival. Please do not for a moment think that I am against annual staple crops. I am saying that if we want to re-think our food supply, we must begin to question anything that man has adapted to fit in with his industrial designs and plans. My point is that, based on the current way of thinking, annual row crops or annual planting is the *first and primary* default for almost everyone who attempts to grow their own food. Should that be the case? Should the common practice (and maxim) of planting row crops and focusing on annual vegetable gardening be our *primary* source of staple food? Maybe not.

Let's take a lesson from what we have learned before. As we mentioned in the previous chapter, historically, most *non-plant* food was stored "on the hoof", which is actually one of the Biblical means of storing and growing wealth and for being prepared for hard times. The Israelites were able to take their wealth and survival materials into Egypt because they were herdsmen. The cattle went with them. Biblical herdsman concentrated their efforts on animals that were fairly easy to keep, that reproduced well or copiously, that could be pastured on free or relatively free lands, and that did not require expensive care or feeds. *In short, it seems that a man's primary wealth was determined by that which he owned that was renewable, sustainable, and more or less perennial.* This principle seems to have applied to all manner of what was considered "wealth" in primitive cultures. A wealthy man would have had a land *"running with milk and honey"*, vineyards, and orchards; which means that he had many, readily available, renewable, and sustainable food resources available to him. He would have had orchards *and* vineyards *and* cattle *and* root crops that come up and produce all year or every year. Those who depended inordinately on annual crops (putting all of their eggs in one basket), as we see in the story of the Egyptians when Joseph and Israel first went into Egypt, were subject to drought, disease, and famine. We ought to think about that when we get started in our own homesteads.

So, although row-crops and annual vegetable gardens are a good source of food for our homesteads, our thinking ought to *first* be more inclined towards ideas like:

Primitive and Simple over Complicated and High-Maintenance
Perennial over Annual
Permaculture over Separate Individual High-Input Systems

PRIMITIVE AND SIMPLE

This category is going to be predictably and appropriately short. When I say that our food plans ought to tend towards that which is *primitive* and *simple*, I am saying that we ought to focus on what is indigenous, local, and natural *first*. Do some research and find out what the first inhabitants, colonists, homesteaders, etc. produced or gathered from the land *in the area where you plan on homesteading*. Read books written by, or about, primitive inhabitants of your region and you will find some great ideas that might help you. This doesn't mean that you must stop doing things the way you've always done them all at once. It means that you need to start transitioning to a more natural and sustainable food production system and you can learn a lot by studying primitive examples. This is how we "discovered" the over-abundant and invasive Mesquite Tree in our area. We learned that the pods were used by Indians and early settlers as flour for bread, as a sweetener, and as medicine. We read in an Almanac that Texans used the roasted Mesquite pod to make coffee when none was available during the War Between the States. For many years now my morning "coffee" has been Mesquite Coffee. It is delicious, has plenty of caffeine to get me started, and is basically free. We learned that our local (and also ubiquitous) *Optunia* (Prickly-Pear cactus) cactus was, and still is, a food staple for many people who live where these cacti grow abundantly. Then we learned that many of these primitive and simple food products are excellent (and in some cases superior) replacements for the more industrialized, processed, consumer foods that we had been trained to consume. For example, we used to buy lots of canned tuna from the store. Like most people, we would mix it with dill pickle relish and mayonnaise to make tuna salad for sandwiches.

Now we know better. We pickle the prickly-pear pads after cutting them into strips. After they are pickled and made into relish, they taste remarkably like the pickle relish you would buy from the store. I can't tell the difference. And we no longer buy tuna. We found out that our home canned chicken or turkey has almost the same consistency as tuna, so we mix it with the prickly-pear relish and it makes a delicious "tuna salad"... in fact, I enjoy it more than I ever did the old store bought tuna and pickle relish... and I hardly miss the mercury and other heavy metals that were abundant in the tuna.

PERENNIALISM (A WORD I MIGHT HAVE MADE UP)

In an ideal system we would initially focus our energy, from the very beginning of our off off-grid journey, on creating a program that utilizes all of our available resources to produce (as much as is possible) a perennial and sustainable food production system on our land. Now, this reality will likely mean that our diets will need to change. More of our non-meat food will need to come from perennial plants, trees, and crops. We will need to eat more indigenous (or wild) foods, nuts, and fruit and less of our diet will naturally come from annual row crops and annual vegetable gardens.

One of the first things any diligent homesteader will need to do is to PLANT TREES. Make it a priority. I mean, before you do almost anything on your land *including building a place to live*, you should plant fruit and nut trees that will provide you with food (If the Lord wills) year after year in due season. Our family has made a practice of planting trees every year, and the majority of those trees are chosen for some type of food production. I think setting a goal to plant 5-15 fruit or nut producing trees a year *every year* ought to be in every homesteading plan no matter how much land is available. Even if a small acreage were to get too crowded with trees, the oldest trees could then be harvested for the wood. Pecan, cherry, walnut, and apple trees provide great wood for woodworking, for building, and for firewood or wood for the smokehouse. Fruiting bushes and vines ought also to be planted every year so that their product can be used for valuable food, for people and for animals.

You ought not to worry about producing too much fruit or too many nuts. Remember that you will always be buying food for your animals - until you can produce enough on your own so that you can stop buying feed. Planting productive trees is just another down-payment on becoming independent of the feed store. When you begin to experience an abundance of these products, feed a portion of your crop to your animals because fruits and nuts are a great addition to a balanced animal diet. Rotted fruit is great for a compost pile or for your pigs. Fruit and nuts can be dried, powdered, canned, etc. pretty easily. It is a truism that in this current environment our diets are greatly lacking in fruit and nuts, so changing our diet to represent those items which are more permanent and perennial is just a good idea.

In addition to planting trees and plants for our food, we ought to immediately begin learning about, and eventually harvesting, whatever edibles are already being made available from our land. This is something that everyone talks about but almost no one really does. I went on a nature walk in the high-mountains of New Mexico a decade ago with an herbalist who illustrated how much of our environment is actually edible. She claimed (and I have no way to know if this is true, although it seems about right) that in *most* inhabitable environments, during the "growing season", up to 20% of the plants or trees you see are actually edible or useful for other productive purposes. This means that ideally (though maybe not practically), if you have five acres of land, up to one acre of that land is covered with edible (or if not edible, at least *usable*, growth. It is up to us to be diligent to determine what plants or trees that grow on our land actually produce some edible product (leaves, shoots, roots, fruit, nuts, etc.). Then we must educate ourselves on how to nurture and encourage these plants (and others that we might introduce) so that we can have a sustainable food source for the future. On our land we have identified several edible plants and products, though we probably have not identified even a small percentage of what is actually available. We currently harvest several products from our land: the prickly-pear cactus (pads and fruit); Mesquite pods for flour, coffee, and tea; some edible berries; and a few other edible "weeds" (such as stinging nettle and purslane) as greens. We intend to learn what other edibles naturally grow on our land, and we also are considering introducing some perennial and wild vegetables that we think will grow well and become sustainable in our environment.

Some plants, roots, berries, and vegetables - like sweet potatoes, bamboo, Jerusalem artichokes, mint, and strawberries – if left alone to multiply (which I don't recommend - everything should be managed) will become invasive and can produce beyond your wildest dreams. Encouraging this tendency in the proper place, in a controlled way, or in a portion of your property set aside for that purpose, will ensure a continued source of food for ourselves and our families. Many perennial ground cover plants generally used for landscaping under trees, in small raised beds, or in gardens are actually edible and can be used in salads or can be preserved for later use. We were shocked and pleasantly surprised to find out that, the year *after* we planted sweet potatoes in the spring and harvested them all (we thought) in the fall, the next year our garden was almost completely overrun with new sweet potato plants. We even had a larger crop of volunteer sweet potatoes then we had planted the previous year! Sweet potato leaves are delicious greens for salads, for stir-fry, or as an addition to soup and stews. Dandelion greens have always been a very healthy and delicious perennial vegetable. We had been so "colonized" into thinking that we had to grow annual lettuce plants every year for salads and sandwiches that we didn't consider how many other more natural and perennial plants would serve the same purpose. I won't recommend many materials in this book, but I do highly recommend you get a copy of *Perennial Vegetables* by Eric Toensmeier. His is an awesome introduction into a completely non-traditional (but historical and ancient) way of looking at growing food.

PERMACULTURE

One of the topics I talk a lot about around here, and one that you will hear me speak on quite often, is *permaculture.* The word "Permaculture" is a combination of the terms *Permanent* and *Agriculture* (therefore it ought to immediately have our attention). Permaculture is a philosophy and design theory that revolves around the idea of inter-dependent planning, planting, and design. The overall idea is one of simplicity and sustainability, but it goes beyond that. A permaculture plan is one that incorporates all of the sustainable ideas in a way where each area benefits and serves another area, in a type of *symbiosis* that is hard to explain, but easy to understand once it is grasped. For example, a permaculture idea of raising chickens might be a chicken coop and pen system where fruit and nut trees and bushes are planted so that they drop their fruit or nuts into the chicken pens. The coop might be designed so that the chickens (which produce heat, fertilizer, and carbon dioxide - all of which are necessary for healthy plants) have a portion of their "run" in a greenhouse. By going about their normal duties, they produce a large portion of the heat and CO_2 that is necessary for the plants to survive (especially in winter, when the chickens will spend more time inside). The plants produce oxygen and food for the animals, and the fertilizer can be used to boost the productivity of the plants. This is mainly just an idea to get you started on the overall philosophy, but modern pastured poultry and pasture rotation/animal rotation schemes are all based on permaculture philosophies.

Proper, intelligent, sustainable, permaculture design of the homestead can greatly reduce the overall workload and can reduce or eliminate many of the costs related to running the homestead. A few hours of planning and design can eliminate untold amount of cost and work on the homestead. Some permaculture ideas, though they will not eliminate labor completely, will certainly eliminate costs. Using chickens or guinea fowl in insect and pest control, using properly planned and designed orchards to produce food for our animals, and using animals to work and improve the fields and gardens, are all a part of permaculture design.

PUT IT ALL ON THE TABLE

In coming to a right mindset on these issues, it is necessary that everything we think be put on the table and debated. Our diets ought to change to better represent our location and our geographical reality. We ought to eat those things that grow well locally, and, as much as possible our diets should reflect those things that can be grown perennially, or that increase the sustainability of our homestead. From the species of trees we plant, to the types of crops we grow, we need to keep in mind how each choice is going to affect us - and how that decision will continue to affect us in the long run. If we get into the mindset that we are always going to be able to put in a nice annual vegetable garden, or some annual seed crops, and that somehow that that idea is a sustainable one, then we are likely to fail if things do not forever continue as they are now. From the day we start our homestead we ought to be thinking about some type of perennial or continuous food production, and never stop thinking about it. It is hard in this world of immediate gratification and a "get it now" mentality to plan for a crop that may not mature for many years, but we ought to always remember that this is exactly the way that God works, and our patience will be rewarded in due time. One of my greatest anticipations, and now greatest pleasures, has been to see the trees we planted in our first year here on the ranch produce fruit. Not only is this a great example of God's mighty works in and through us, but it is a profound picture of His providence and grace towards us - that He provides sweet and free fruit from the ground abundantly to all of His children who will reach out and take it.

GROW YEAR-ROUND

One of the solutions to many food production problems is to really work on and emphasize a year-round growing program. I was personally so colonized into the "spring annual garden" rut that I never

286

really spent much time thinking about using the whole year to grow food. In a conversation with a master gardener and homesteading teacher I discovered that in our area many of the staple "colder weather" crops are best planted in fall and harvested all winter instead of counting on these crops to grow up and mature in our short and unpredictable spring weather. Most people plant broccoli, cauliflower, cabbage and other crops in late winter or early spring for harvest before the heat of summer comes, but here in Central Texas, I have found that this is very difficult to accomplish because the heat of summer comes in early spring! Most of my early crops were just getting going good when the high-90 degree days would start... and eventually burn up my crop. The homesteading teacher told me that he usually plants these crops in the fall, and he finds that often (in this area) they will continue to thrive and produce throughout the winter. He also uses cold and hot frames, along with greenhouses to extend the growing season. The point is that, since I was operating on the accepted or common way of doing things today, I was missing out on about half of the available year in my food growing system. Every area and region is going to be different, so we shouldn't accept any "commercial standard" as the accepted or only way to do things.

In addition to our plans to add a greenhouse and cold-frames, we intend to do some other year-round growing of plants and vegetables that we have learned can be grown in our area throughout the fall and winter. We are installing double-dug garden beds and raised beds for these purposes, and we also will (if the Lord wills) be building some ½ acre and one acre pens for free-range animal and crop rotation. I learned by reading history books and old almanacs that the modern and ubiquitous "feed grain" animal feeding system is really just that... it is very modern. Historically, most subsistence farmers (homesteaders or farmers who grow all, or nearly all, of their own food) fed their animals almost exclusively on pasture and on seasonal root crops. Today, if I were to ask almost anyone to draw a picture of a farmer feeding cattle, he or she would draw a picture of the farmer throwing purchased hay to cows in pens, or pouring some type of grain feed or industrial feed cubes to the cattle. But historically, even as late as the early 1900's, this was not how cattle were fed. Cattle, as I have already said, were primarily fed on pasture, on bailed hay or grass from pasture, and on root crops. So in the old cartoons when you would see a cow lazily chomping on carrots, beets, and turnips, that mind-picture was there because the cartoonist knew what subsistence farmers fed their cattle. Root crops were used because they were very easy to grow and because they could be stored in the ground until they were needed. Some farmers would let the cattle graze on the greens and then later, maybe even in the winter, the roots would be harvested to supplement the cattle. All manner of farm animals: cattle, poultry, sheep, goats, pigs, etc. were mainly fed on root crops and not primarily on grain crops. The modern grain crop industry came about during and after the industrial revolution as large agri-businessmen found it easy to produce enormous supplies of feed grains on their expansive corporate farms. What followed was predictable and followed the normal industrial pattern.

In the beginning (the beginning of the industrialization of our food supply), feed grains were very, very inexpensive, sometimes only pennies a bushel. Because grain prices were so low, small farmers found that they could profitably raise cattle and other animals in pens, rather than on expensive pasture (which could, instead, be used to raise grain crops), and they could begin to make good money selling their animals into the industrial food production system. Later, as human food needs exploded due to the industrialization of the human food supply and the concentration of humans in cities, people competed with animals for the feed, and prices increased. By this time, unhappily, most farmers had changed the way they did business and the way they raised animals. They were now entrenched in the "pen system" of raising animals on grain feed. They couldn't figure out what went wrong, but when feed grain prices skyrocketed, they knew they could no longer operate small, diversified farms using industrial feed grains for feed. Pigs were sold off or butchered, and from that point on, pork production was consolidated by the industrial pig producers who specialized in *just* pork production. Beef production was "farmed out" to the corporate beef producers who raised cattle on huge tracts of land for short periods of time, then fattened them up in very small and tight feeder and stockyard operations. Once upon a time, local dairies bought their milk from small family farms, but eventually the dairies found it easier to operate their own, large-scale, industrial milk production systems based on feeding the cows cheap, bulk grains. There was really no going back for these farmers because as grain prices increased, they found that they could buy bulk, mass-produced, and nutritionally inferior food at the store for cheaper than they could grow and process it. "Economy of scale" pushed out the small producer and entrenched the large, commercial producer.

This industrialization process happened in every single category of food production. The corporations and marketing arms of the industrial system needed all food to be inexpensive, consistent, and mainstream. A commercial ham or package of bacon with a brand name on it purchased in Waukesha, Wisconsin, needs to look and taste *exactly* how it would look and taste if you bought the same brand and product in Jackson, Mississippi. This is what the corporate markets demanded so this is what the industrial producers provided. Eventually this became what the consumer demanded, because he didn't know any better. This process "mainstreamed", or actually "dumbed-down", our food supply and the tastes of the modern consumer. In the old days, pigs that fed almost exclusively on acorns and root crops produced far superior meat than those who were fed cheap and mass-produced grains, and everyone knew it. But all of these differences (and the ability to know the differences) were eradicated when the industrial producers took over the production of our food. We were all trained to like and expect what the markets provided - inferior and unhealthy food products. The pictures on the wrappers of industrialized food still show the pig, the chicken, or the cow munching on grass in a beautiful green meadow, even if the actual animal *inside* the package never saw the sky, never ate green grass, or never left the commercial feed pen. Differences between brand names are usually purely cosmetic, or are based on some differences in additives, not on differences in quality or nutritional value. Later in the game, chemicals and additives were introduced to increase consistency and to increase the visual appearance of the food – regardless of what had been done to it nutritionally.

Hopefully by now you have picked up on the industrial process and how things devolve under that process. Along with that process our food has been devalued and diminished, and along the way we have become weaker and unhealthier. Most people over 50 years of age today are on copious medications and they need more and more medical intervention as they grow older in order to maintain what they have been told is "the good life". But, what is the inevitable result of where we are headed? The inevitable destination and result of industrializing the food supply has been (and will increasingly be) socialized and Industrialized medicine, brainwashed and sometimes seriously intellectually challenged "consumers" and one day soon, societal collapse. So, what does this all have to do with grain crops vs. root crops? _Not much, and everything_. Not much if you plan on doing nothing about it. Everything if you plan on living off of the grid. To succeed and to survive it is needful that you learn the history of how every particular modern agrarian practice or process began. When you are dumping that bag of grain to an animal, you need to know where you are on the slippery slope of societal "progress". This doesn't mean that you cannot use bagged grain as an intermediate step, but it is necessary that you know how you got to where you are so you can make plans to escape. The price of bagged grain feeds will only increase until the world as we know it collapses. Prices for grain feeds will become untenable when petroleum prices do. When you cannot afford fuel for your car, you should know that the next domino will be the food/feed that you buy. We need to think differently today in order to survive that inevitable collapse. Which brings us back to our topic...

When you are planning your farm you need to carefully consider what crops you can grow easily and cheaply in order to supplement your animals. Hopefully you are considering a pasture system for feeding your animals, but if you are not, then you need to grow what it takes to feed them and keep them healthy. Our Agrarian ancestors planned their land and their farms so that they grew many root crops that were beneficial to both their animals, and to their selves. They focused their energy on foods that grew well in their region and that would thrive even in difficult times. Sure, they grew some grains and row crops, especially in places where products like dry beans, corn, and grains grow exceptionally well without chemicals or without extensive labor. Sure, they often had annual vegetable gardens, and saved seed. To deny that would be to deny history. But the point is that these products were often very small portions of the overall food plan of any subsistence homestead.

On our farm we do produce some large scale dry bean and seed (oats/wheat/etc.) crops. We do intend to use these crops in rotating fields (as well as rotating the crops in each field) as part of our pasture rotation system. We are also moving into intensive gardening of some vegetables and other staples in order to move towards 100% production of our own supplies. We are constantly studying and testing to find out what will grow well in our area and what will fit well into our overall plan.

MAKING A PLAN

One of the first things the potential off-grid family can do is to get an idea of *what* you use, and *how much of it*. As a part of that process you should also ask yourself *why* you use each item and what alternatives are available. Realize that many of the things you do, and many of the foods you eat, are part of your life, but not because of some deliberate plan or because of intensive study. Many of the things we do we do just because we have always done them. We haven't changed because our own thoughts and preconceived ideas and notions have never been challenged. For gardeners, this means that many people just grow whatever they feel like growing and in whatever amount the current garden size and condition allows. Many gardeners put more thought into *having* a garden than they do into what they will grow and how they will grow it. A garden and all growing programs, even for your small homestead, should be planned. Some old favorites, or things you just like to have around, may have to be sacrificed if they are not solid additions to an overall sustainable food supply plan. Crops that take up a lot of space, but only produce a small amount of food and only for a short amount of time are usually the first things that need to go. Some other crops that you may never have tried, or that may not currently be a part of your diet, may need to be adopted by you and your family. After much study and research, our family is adopting many traditional southern food products that were once more occasional, ceremonial, or "seasonal" in our old lives (like sweet potatoes, cooked greens, and dry beans).

PLAN YOUR FOOD STORAGE AS YOU PLAN YOUR FOOD PRODUCTION

We are going to talk more about food preservation and food storage in the next chapter, but it is important to mention here that you ought to plan your food storage program as you are planning your food growing program. Plan out what you will grow, and how it will serve you throughout the year. These are all questions you need to spend some time answering:

What is your food storage capacity, and in what ways (and in what amounts) will you plan on storing food?

How will your food storage capacity change, and in what ways will your growing program affect your food storage program?

What (and how much) do you plan on growing for fresh picking and how much for storing?

What do you plan on growing to preserve for the cold winter months?

What foods are amenable to what preservation techniques - and what output (labor and money) will be necessary to practice those particular techniques?

For storage purposes, I always try to pick out one major product every year, and I heavily focus on growing a lot of that one product that year. This is not a *cash* crop - it is a *cache* crop. That product ought to be a.) a major food source for the family - something you will eat a lot of, b.) something that stores or preserves well, and c.) something that you can produce *a lot* more of than you can consume in one year. For us, one year that product was green beans. The next year it was onions. Several years ago my big crop for one year was dried beans and we grew several great crops of black and white beans during that year and were able to store a good supply, much of which we subsequently used for seed in the years that followed. By growing a lot of one particular food product in a year, we can often grow several years supply of that one food - which will allow us to use our land and resources for other purposes in subsequent years. Some gardens are just not big enough to grow a lot of everything we need every year, but if we can reserve a large portion of our garden to grow one particular crop in an abundant way, we can better utilize the area that is available.

As far as growing food, there are as many opinions as there are growers, and I am still in the learning phase. The main point I want to make, though, is that I know some excellent modernist gardeners who would make poor subsistence farmers. It is one thing to be able to (using ample industrial resources) grow some great veggies or awesome marigolds. It is quite another to purposely work towards providing a majority of the food for your family so that you do not have to buy food at stores - which is the goal and ideal of Off Off-Grid Agrarianism. Be aware that many of those pictures of gorgeous gardens that you see on Internet blogs or catalogs are actually the product of industrialized production using grid water and power - even if they advertise themselves as "organic". So don't be green with envy when you see some suburban "homestead blogger" bragging about their abundant crop and lush garden. When we here in our community see some suburban super-garden, we exchange knowing glances. We know that if the water or the power gets turned off, that person is going to be just as needy and in just as much peril as their store dependent neighbor.

Much less space is necessary for a small subsistence farm than most people think. I am convinced that a pretty large family can live and survive, providing near 100% of their own foodstuffs, on only a few acres *or less*. While our ranch is closer to 25 acres in size, my garden is currently less than 1/8th of an acre. I plan on making more and more land available for tillage every year, but I believe I can provide more than enough *non-meat* food for my family just from this one small garden, using intensive gardening techniques. Someday soon we hope to build a garden that is nearly 1/4 acre. I will keep my current garden as a perennial garden and will utilize the one acre and ½ acre rotation fields for growing some larger crops each year. When we are in full production, any excess crops that cannot be eaten, stored, used for animal feed, will be sold at the farmers market, or bartered with neighbors in our Christian community. My gardens will consist mainly of double-dug beds, used in rotation, and used year-round.

As I mentioned before, any good subsistence farming/gardening plan needs to be combined with ample food storage. Root cellars are a necessity, especially here in the hot south, but just about anywhere. We will also need dry storage, some barns and outbuildings for drying and curing foods, a springhouse, and an icehouse. We just recently finished building our large stone smokehouse, and it is a great blessing. Food preservation/storage and food production are inextricably linked. If you cannot utilize it immediately, store it, or preserve it, you probably should not produce it. Very few things, with the exception of lettuce and a few other garden and salad greens and veggies, are going to be grown for immediate consumption - until we build ourselves a good sized greenhouse. It is a great thing to be able to go directly to the garden for a meal, and I relish such times, but I have to keep in mind that food production is for the whole year and is accomplished for our survival and for our safety and security. Too many people look at their garden as a temporary, seasonal fling - or as a spring and summertime hobby. God provides these things for us because He cares about us and loves us, and our labor is bestowed for His glory alone, and we must always keep that in mind. God's provision in allowing us to work for Him in providing nearly 100% of our necessities constantly puts us in remembrance of Him and His goodness and kindness towards us. We pray to Him to wean us from the "store", and to provide for us completely and sovereignly *right here* on the land. We, like plants, need our rain and food in due season, and we rely on Him for it. A good food subsistence program coupled with a sound storage and preservation plan is our way of being dutiful and diligent according to God's commandments. It is He that has commanded us to till the soil, and to work the land (Gen. 2:15, 3:23), and we all ought to do that diligently as unto a glorious and loving master.

A FINAL WORD ON GROWING ANIMAL FEED

Many people get into animal husbandry and they immediately make some really big mistakes. I receive letters and emails from these people all of the time. They go out and buy the best feed money can buy and they keep feeding those animals from the feed store and they never can figure out why they are losing money and time on the deal. We are certainly not in this for the money, but if I have to keep working a day job in order to feed my animals, then something has gone horribly awry. My animals should work for me, I shouldn't work for them. If I have to toil and slave in a corporate job so I can feed my animals, I have dropped from modern suburbanism (where people work all day to buy stuff from other people to feed and provide for themselves), to sub-suburbanism (where people work all day to buy stuff from other people to feed their animals). Not a good trade-off in my opinion. Our plan must include a program to provide much of the food and supplies for our animals from our own labor and from the ground. I mentioned earlier in this chapter but it bears repeating: back in the Old South where sweet potatoes, turnips, collard greens, and carrots, etc. were major staple crops, most of the crop went to feed the animals! When you read some of the old farmer's almanacs you will find that most small farms in the south fed their animals sweet potatoes, rutabagas, radishes, turnips and turnip greens, and other root crops. Corn didn't become a major feed crop on the plains until just before and after the advent of the Industrial Revolution. Many people automatically run to corn as a staple crop for feeding their animals, but historically, at least in this area, corn was not used for that purpose. The idea of root crops being the primary type of animal feed was so pervasive in history that in England, potatoes (regular white potatoes) were considered animal food and not people food. The English (perennially derisive of the Irish) considered it quite hilarious that Irishmen ate potatoes. There was an old English joke that potatoes were food only for horses and Irishmen. The Irish responded wryly that this is why the Irish are as strong as horses. Anyway, I love potatoes and all these other root crops and I eat them, but I also need to remember that, in most of the world, root crops (and the majority of each crop) were used for animal feed. Root crops grow better with fewer problems and run less risk of a total crop failure than does corn and other above ground seed crops. Also, do not neglect harvesting from the wild when you are thinking about how to feed your animals without store-bought feed. Here in Central Texas, we harvest acorns from the hundreds of oak trees on our land to feed to our pigs. We have, in heavy acorn years, been able to feed them and fatten them for several months just off of acorns from the land. If we were more diligent at it, or if we had already established a good free-range program (we don't free-range them year-around yet) we would have had to buy less and less feed for them.

IN CONCLUSION

There will always be some products we will likely not be able to produce. We cannot produce salt, although we do get salt in our diets from a lot of the foods we produce. We do not have a salt mine on our land, so we buy and store large amounts of salt. We will never be able to produce quite a few of our other necessities but that number is dropping and is far smaller than I once thought. Some of the items I once believed had to be purchased at a store we produce, or are learning to produce ourselves, like honey, soap, pepper, candles, even rope, string, furniture, tools, etc. God created us with minds and with the ability to solve problems. We have to divorce ourselves from the consumer mentality and industrial mindset that has crippled our individual creativity, convincing us that everything around us must come from a store.

Having been deprived for their whole lives of the historical, proper, and expected use of their eyes, and ears, and of their legs, arms, and hands, many people today are not able to function when the productive use of these faculties is required. These things atrophy from lack of use, as do all of our other creative senses and abilities. The industrial system paralyzes men and makes them increasingly dependent on the beast system while simultaneously convincing them that they are better off than their ancestors... and more "advanced". So the blind, mentally atrophied cripple has now been convinced that he is better off than those who came before him; men who could think, see, and work fruitfully to provide the necessities of life. Is there a greater deception than that?

CHAPTER 14
PRESERVING THE HARVEST

"We shall call 'primitive' all tribes that make little or no provision for unproductive days." - (Will Durant – <u>Our Oriental Heritage</u>, Vol. 1 of The History of Civilization)

It is hard for some people to accept that, according to a legitimate and historical definition of the word "primitive", modern industrial man would have to be considered "primitive" when it comes to food storage and preparation. If you do not produce and store a significant portion of your food supply, then you may seem to be better off; you may seem to be more advanced; you may think you are safe and secure; but you are little better off than a primitive scavenger... and probably worse. Most people today are living in a hologram of security.

Why are modernist urbanites fooled into thinking they are an advanced culture? Because they eat three meals a day. Through time, the industrial culture and the JIT system that produces, transports, and delivers food items, has become so consistent that it seems to be impervious to interruption. Because most people have never been forced to miss a meal, they think that food appears magically, and that it will always be there. A simple perusal of history – and the inevitable judgment and destruction of every "advanced" culture should drive a stake into the heart of these misconceptions. Unhappily, most folks today are more hip to technology and whatever is coming out of Hollywood than they are of history. More from Durant...

"The wilder tribes among the American Indians considered it weak-kneed and unseemly to preserve food for the next day. The natives of Australia are incapable of any labor whose reward is not immediate; every Hottentot is a gentleman of leisure; and with the Bushmen of

Africa it is always 'either feast or famine.'"

The Historian Will Durant wrote this back in 1938 when it still paid to tell the truth. His comments would be denounced and rejected as "racist" today - but his point was that personal food preservation was, and is, a sign of advanced civilization (and I mean that in a positive way). Primitive tribes either adapted to a lifestyle including food storage and preservation, or they disappeared. Those who refused to practice the long-term preservation and storage of food supplies quickly died away; from starvation, from war, from genocide, or whatever sociologists want to call the inevitable *eschaton* event that brought about the destruction of their JIT society (technically, we ought to call these primitive tribes "JI societies" instead of "Just In Time" because there was no real "time" element to their supply plans. They were actually "Just If" tribes... they would eat "just if" they happened to catch something, or "just if" they found a dead animal, or "just if" they stumbled upon a walnut tree). Many tribes who would not adapt, and who were not assimilated (who did not pass from hunter/gatherers to farmers), became the slaves of those who did. Slavery was most often, though not always, a result of laziness and stupidity. Keep that in mind. Carelessness for the future amounted to a death sentence prior to advent of the industrial/consumer economy and the hologram of security it has provided. When natural resources were plenteous, and men were few, this carelessness was understandable though sad (we know how it ends). Maybe the feast or famine principle could be winked at among simple tribesmen in deserted lands, but there is no historical doubt that this principle inevitably heralded the end of that particular tribe.

Modern society has now, over the past 100 years, reinstituted the cult of carelessness by allowing men to "prosper" without thinking. Survival thinking is now to be done corporately, not individually. As new "wisdom" makes the old wisdom obsolete (they think), innovation is piled on innovation; all is automated and centralized until, eventually, "survival" is guaranteed and accomplished for the people (as a bulk called "consumers")... so long as they promise not to ever stop consuming, never stop buying, and never question where it is all coming from or to what purpose. Hunting, gathering, sowing, reaping – all of these survival skills – are accomplished by proxy, because the people are far too dainty and sensitive to care for themselves. In effect, the cult of carelessness has reestablished the lie that you can live and thrive indefinitely without thinking about it. Provision, and all of the machinations of it, is a work of specialists and is none of your concern. Your job is to work at your assigned chore, like a cog or widget in a machine, earn "money", and spend it on stuff you do not need and that can do you no eternal good. Heedless consumption is the guarantee of survival, in a Ponzi-scheme of epic proportions.

Ayn Rand, that godless atheist, proposed that the world would collapse if Atlas Shrugged – meaning if the "men of the mind" stop producing. We've learned now that that is completely untrue. The world will collapse when either the machines break down, or the consumers stop consuming... the men of the mind are too greedy to ever stop building machines.

God had, from the beginning, commanded men to work the soil, to till it and to cause it to bring forth by the sweat of the brow: *"Go to the ant, thou sluggard; consider her ways, and be wise: Which having no guide, overseer, or ruler, Provideth her meat in the summer, and gathereth her food in the harvest. How long wilt thou sleep, O sluggard? when wilt thou arise out of thy sleep? Yet a little sleep, a little slumber, a little folding of the hands to sleep: So shall thy poverty come as one that travelleth, and thy want as an armed man"* (Proverbs 6:6-11).

Durant tells us that at some point in history, man figured out that there was a smarter way to live:

"Finally nature taught man the art of provision, the virtue of prudence, and the concept of time. Watching woodpeckers storing acorns in trees, and the bees storing honey in hives, man conceived

-- perhaps after millenniums of improvident savagery -- the notion of laying up food for the future. He found ways of preserving meat by smoking it, salting it, freezing it; better still, he built granaries secure from rain and damp, vermin and thieves, and gathered food into them for the leaner months of the year. Slowly it became apparent that agriculture could provide a better and steadier food supply than hunting."

Man, however, perpetually too clever for wisdom, found a way to bypass such "primitive" thinking. His salt lost its savor...

SALT

"Two intrinsic systems set animal and plant life apart; namely, the muscles that power locomotion, and the intricate nerve network that controls the organism, including the muscle fibers themselves. Sodium is an indispensable part of nerve and muscle function. Green plants have neither nerves nor muscles; so, lacking these, generally they have little use for sodium, over the long or short term." - (Morrison, Philip and Phylis. The Needy Porcupine, Scientific American, March, 2001; page 77)

The Greeks harvested salt from the ocean and used that salt to buy slaves from the slave merchants. These slaves, most of whom had been taken prisoner either as criminals, in wars of conquest, or in military punitive actions, would then be sold to the factories or the mine operators. Some happy few would be bought by private individuals to be used as domestic help. The slaves who went to the cities - to the mines or to the factories and the blast furnaces of industry - were as good as dead. Due to the brutal work, harsh conditions, toxic environment, and questionable food, they were not expected to live very long. Their lives were short and miserable. Those few who were sold as domestic help usually found that grace and mercy had surely fallen upon them. If they were good and hard-working (*"worth their salt"*) they would be received into a family or clan as if they were a member of it. The patriarch of the family worked alongside his slaves doing the same work, and if a slave got injured, was sick, or grew old, he was loved and cared for by the family of which he was a member. The slave had considerable rights, could not be killed by his master, and could flee to the temple if he felt himself mistreated (where he could demand to be sold to a new master). What does all this talk of slaves have to do with food preservation? Nothing... and everything. It lets you know the value of SALT - because if a man was *worth his salt*, then salt was worth the price of a man. That is hard for the modern colonized mind to conceive.

Pre-industrial man had a completely different system of value and living than we do. Salt was money, and salt was life. Like water, without it you wouldn't live very long. Coinage, minted by every village and city-state, had drastically different value from one town to another. Coins were usually debased by local governments in order to gain competitive advantage over other towns or cities in trade. Very few cities (Athens was one) stabilized their currency by government mandate against the debasing of coinage. Athens guaranteed their coins and stamped them with the owl – and an owl became a medium of trade that was "worth its salt". Athens boomed and thrived because their currency was accepted readily. Everywhere else, coins were suspect, but salt was salt. When a man paid with strange coin, he was suspected. When he paid with salt, he was respected. Salt was savor and preservation; it was survival and satisfaction. The Roman soldier was paid his *salary* - money he could use to procure salt and other necessities - and from the importance of having salt, we derive the name for our pay. From salt we also get the word *"sale"*, because many transactions were concluded with salt as money. If something was *salubrious* or *salutary*, it meant that it was healthy, or wholesome. To hail, greet, show honor to, or express greeting to someone else was to *salute*. Meat was salted for preservation, and when the salt went to work on the meat, it drew moisture to the surface of the meat – the meat *salivated*. A *salad* (salted dish) was a dish of vegetables seasoned or sprinked with salt. Our language records the critical importance of salt in our survival.

Salting, smoking, and lacto-fermentation were the first means of long-term preservation of food. We are often mentally enslaved by the little that we know. Although I knew of all of these methods of food preservation, I was convinced for several years that the only workable method of preserving meat for our homestead was the process of cold-weather (winter) butchering and canning of meat. Then, while I was studying preservation methods one day, I learned that in the hottest parts of Africa, villages would butcher whole cattle and preserve the meat by drying it. How could this be? Didn't the meat go bad in the heat? No, it didn't. The villagers would gather together for the butchering. They would bring buckets or other containers in which they had put heavily salted water. As they butchered the animal, the cutters would cut chunks of meat off in strips and immediately drop the meat into the salt water. After a good soaking of several hours, the meat was hung in a large, roofed and screened drying hut. The meat would be dried until it was so dry it was brittle. Then the meat was taken down, bagged in large burlap bags, and stacked in a communal dry room. When the meat was needed, it was distributed in the community. The meat could be re-hydrated and cooked into stews, fried up like steaks, or powdered and mixed into breads and other dishes. Needless to say, I was shocked by this revelation. People had processed meat in this manner for millennia, but I – living in what is considered the most "advanced" civilization on earth – thought that the only way to preserve meat was through a process (canning) that wasn't invented until the early 1800's. I was one step wiser than the "freezer and refrigerator" society, and miles and miles more ignorant than so-called "primitive" man. More research into "primitive" preservation techniques taught me about lacto-fermentation of meats and sausages (actually, you can lacto-ferment just about anything), solar drying, larding, and many other brilliant and simple methods of extending the harvest.

I have just recently begun experimenting in lacto-fermentation. Recently we butchered a cow and I made lacto-fermented sausage out of about 45 pounds of the meat. Now, you might be confused or even "grossed out" by such a technical sounding name, but I learned that "lacto-fermented sausage" is merely the process by which the numerous and delicious "artisan sausages" are made that you can buy at any upscale grocery store. In effect, artisan sausages are made by a *charcutier* (meat artist) who is able, using science and talent, to create delicious dried sausages without cooking. The primary tools of the *charcutier* are salt (and other natural preservatives and spices), smoke, time, artistry, and patience. As I said before, just about any food item you produce from your land can be lacto-fermented. Sauerkraut is just lacto-fermented cabbage. "Real" pickles are just lacto-fermented cucumbers. Most chutney is just some form of lacto-fermented relish. A reader on my blog explained lacto-fermentation simply and succinctly:

> *"Lactobacilli are a naturally occurring 'good' microbe in soil and on the surface of vegetables. Salt is needed to fend off pathogenic bacteria while the lactobacilli grow to a population high enough to shut out pathogens. Traditionally made sauerkraut, relishes, etc. can be made using this method. It is not only a good preservation method, but a way of replenishing the natural flora of the gut, improving digestion and perhaps protecting you from illness"*

Like I have said before, I won't recommend many books in this book – but in this case I do recommend the book *Wild Fermentation* by Sandor Ellix Katz. It is filled with basically all you need to know about Live-Culture Foods, including recipes that work.

THE ROOT CELLAR

I talked about the philosophy behind, and the necessity of, the root cellar back in Chapter 7. Please re-read that chapter for more of the background on the topic. The root cellar is a solution that solves many diverse problems. In fact, when I first researched the root cellar I was distressed because almost all of the readily available information about root cellars was written by Northerners (either from Northern Europe, or from Northern North America), and they almost universally assumed that the problem to be solved by the root cellar *was extreme cold temperatures in the winter*, something we rarely experience around here. Indeed, the root cellar is a delightful solution to the problem of root vegetables freezing and being destroyed by extreme cold. The temperature in the ground is generally stable at between the mid-50's and mid-60's degrees Fahrenheit throughout the temperate zones in the world. Root cellars were originally dug in northern climates in order to preserve summer and fall vegetable crops from freeze damage in unheated store rooms or houses. That's all great... but as a southerner, vegetable damage from freezing was not really my biggest concern. In fact, in my area, other than just a handful of days throughout the winter, vegetables could easily be stored in unheated store rooms (or in baskets under the cabin) *above ground* without the threat of damage from freezing. The problem where we live is heat and not cold. Our problem is that it is virtually impossible to keep stored vegetables and other produce from ruining in the *summer* from the heat. Our problem was completely different from that of northern folks. Happily, the root cellar solution works just as well for both problems (in fact, we often keep our root cellar door open on selected days throughout the winter in order to let the damp, warm air out and to let cool air in). For us, the root cellar also serves as a cool place to get a brief respite from the summer heat; a storm shelter from our often severe spring and summer storms; and a place of relative temperature stability for our fermentation and lacto-fermentation experiments. I repeat here with the utmost gravity: In my opinion the root cellar ought to be one of the first, if not THE first, structures built on any off-grid homestead.

THE SMOKEHOUSE

As you can see, in this chapter I have listed the preservation methods and structures in the order that I think you will need them - if not in order of importance. Salting, curing, drying, and lacto-fermentation processes can be used without a specific structure built for the purpose - and these will likely be your primary methods of food preservation until you can build some of these structures. After the root cellar, we built our smokehouse, and we are so pleased to have it available to us.

Of course, it is not necessary that you build a traditional smokehouse. Meat and other foods (cheeses, etc.) can be smoked using methods that range from very simple and primitive, to very technical and advanced. Many historians now believe that smoking as a preservation method was "discovered" by accident (or providence) as a corollary to drying meats. In the southern areas (of the northern hemisphere), the drying of foods could be accomplished almost all of the year in the sun. In these cultures, smoking as a preservative method was seldom used until much later in the timeline, and then it was primarily used for taste and not particularly for preservation. In northern climates, where it is often wetter and always colder, drying, for much of the year had to be done inside and often near fires. In what would become a common historical process, indigenous peoples in North America (and in Northern Europe) discovered that meat that was hung near fires (often near the tops of tipis or tents, where the smoke was to escape) kept for longer (and tasted better!) than food that was merely dried in the sun. This process of discovery was repeated independently all over the world. Eventually, dedicated structures were built, some small and simple and others very large and more complicated, to more evenly and predictably apply smoke to food for long-term preservation purposes. Dried smoked meats, now an expensive delicacy, were once the common fare of the poor. In Czarist Russia the rich could afford to have whole animals killed for a single meal. The serfs and peasants, by necessity, became experts in smoking and drying meats to preserve them. In a delicious irony, the wealthy aristocracy and nobility ate meats (often broiled or baked) that would be considered more "common" fare today. The poor ate meats that are considered "artisan" or high cuisine today. History is fun, rich in irony, and sprinkled heavily with salt.

Ours is a large and traditional smokehouse. We built it of slip-formed stone walls with a gabled wood roof. It is 12' x 12' and is capable of smoking an entire beef, or many pigs, goats, or sheep at one time. There are smoker plans available in books and online that will allow you to smoke and preserve meat with little to no investment. Your smoker doesn't need to be a large stone building – it can be a barrel or a tent. When I eat my cured/dried/smoked sausage, I wonder at the fact that such a delicious delicacy was actually just a primitive way to store the meat harvest. I used to buy expensive store-bought artisan sausages for special occasions, or just because I liked and wanted them. Now, I need just walk to the "store" room to have better, and healthier, artisan sausage than I could have ever afforded to buy regularly at a corporate specialty grocery.

THE ICEHOUSE AND THE SPRINGHOUSE

I talked a bit about the icehouse and ice storage in Chapter 7, so refresh your memory if you need to, by reviewing that chapter.

The practice of storing winter ice through the summer in specialty structures built for that purpose is thousands of years old. Ice (and cooling) can be one of the largest, and most resource wasting expenses on any off-grid homestead. The ability to store cold, for us, has many, many benefits beyond comfort and the carnal pleasures derived from an icy drink in the summer. I have been planning my icehouse/ springhouse for many years, and, having just recently completed our smokehouse, the icehouse will likely be the next food preservation structure we build on our homestead.

An *icehouse* is a very well insulated building (usually a building within a building), built either below ground, above ground, or in some combination of the two, designed to store ice for long periods of time during warmer periods of the year. A *springhouse* is, ideally (or in a perfect world), a rock or concrete building built where cold water can be diverted into it for the purpose of keeping food cold. Traditionally, springhouses were actually built on, or over, the originating source of a natural spring, where the water was the coldest. In the classic springhouse, a trough of stone or wood was built into the sides of the walls and the cold moving water would fill the trough, circulating through the structure. Jars or crocks of food - milk, butter, etc. could be placed in the water to stay cold. In our area, a springhouse could be built in conjunction with an icehouse so that the melted runoff from the icehouse could be diverted into the springhouse troughs to keep food and beverages cold.

The concept of the icehouse and the springhouse is quite simple, and there are materials and articles available in books and online that will explain the concepts and offer "how to" advice for the building of these homestead structures.

CANNING

Canning, as a process, gets its own subtitle, but don't think there won't be any agrarian-separatist philosophy in it, because there will be. As you know very well by now, this is not a book about how to do things. It is a book about HOW TO THINK. If we think correctly, we will usually do correctly.

In the past, when I have written about canning on my blog, I would usually get some comments from a few people who are a bit confused by what we mean by that. By canning we should really say "jarring" since the term "can" makes people think about tin or metal cans, although most people who do preserve foods "can" in glass jars and not in metal cans. *Canning* usually means "to preserve food for long term storage by preparing it in cans or jars and utilizing heat and/or pressure to kill dangerous bacteria". Learning how to live off-grid can be a constant education in word meanings and etymology (the study of the derivation of words). Preserving food in jars actually preceded the more industrial practice of preserving food in metal cans for mass consumption.

Again, I was shocked to learn that canning is a relatively new food preservation phenomenon, one that was unheard of until the French Revolution. I mean, my grandmother canned and her grandmother probably canned, so I figured that canning food had probably been around in some form or another... forever. How silly is that? The practice of canning is just about 200 years old, thus was unknown for the thousands of years of civilization prior to that. As far as survival skills go, canning is not an automatic default option. It is a relatively new thing.

Long-term storage of fresh food in jars, cans, pouches, or containers, came about because of military necessity, not because some European agrarians needed or even wanted it. Unlike most purely agrarian preservation techniques, the practice of canning came about because of war and the inevitable need to feed moving armies. After hundreds of years of almost constant warfare in Europe, large armies of men moving across lands that had already been stripped time and time again for decades and even centuries by preceding armies, needed food supplies that could be carted along with the army. Feeding an army with food carted along with it was itself a very novel idea. For millennia; through the Classical ages of civilization; through the Dark and Middle ages; up until the turn of the 19th century, an army provided for itself and purchased, foraged, or plundered what it needed along the way. By the late 1700's, there wasn't a whole lot left to steal, and many rural people and villagers had become experts in keeping their "stuff" away from marauding armies. If Europe was going to keep up its fascination with perennial war, a new way of feeding armies would need to be adopted. A French newspaper, motivated by the French government, offered a huge monetary reward to anyone who could invent a way to store large quantities of food cheaply. In 1809 a French scientist noted that food stored in jars and kept airtight, stored a lot longer than those that were not. No one knew why this phenomenon happened for another 50 years until Louis Pasteur proved that microbes were what caused spoilage. After Pasteur it was learned that killing the microbes would make the food stay "good" for a very long time, and the process of "canning" was born.

All of this is to say that a lot of times we off-grid folks default to some process thinking that it is the only way to do it, since our grandparents and their parents did it. Don't get me wrong, I'm all for canning; my family pressure cans food all of the time and we will continue to do so, but canning, if looked at logically and unemotionally, does not fit all of the criteria for sustainability that we have talked about throughout this book. With canning there is always a continuous need for canning jars, lids, and bands, and pressure canning as a practice is subject to disruption if we are unable to replace the pressure canner or its parts if there is a problem with them. Canning, then, falls into the category of "intermediate means". If it is not simple and sustainable without large amounts of outside "store bought" input it cannot trusted to be a workable solution if things go really bad for a long time. So canning remains in the category of "intermediate means" for us. We will continue to can foods and to use canning as a resource as long as we can, but if we become inordinately dependent on canning for our continued survival then we put ourselves at risk. You may purchase and store a large quantity of spare jars, bands, and lids (and we do), and even store a spare canner and spare parts, but in reality if any disruption goes on long enough you will eventually have to abandon canning as a means of food preservation. Canning also destroys most of the natural living "good" enzymes and microbes in the food, which means that some of its nutritional and health value is lost. From my studies, it seems that lacto-fermentation can be a much healthier long-term preservation method than canning.

Ok, so along with canning, we need to learn some of the more "primitive" or sustainable methods of food preservation that I've mentioned in this chapter; like using salt, oils, fats, sugar, honey, etc., along with root cellaring, smoking, curing, drying, and other means of keeping our food for long periods of time. We also ought to consider some of the other ideas in this book, like relying on foods that don't require as much (or any) preservation or storage. Root crops often can be kept in the ground throughout the winter, and, with the addition of root cellars, many food staples can be kept without expensive and time-consuming preservation techniques. We need to consider and study how agrarians in past centuries (before the advent of modern food preservation techniques) were able to survive and thrive without these newer means. There is nothing inherently wrong with technology or progress. Nothing is bad just because it is new (except doctrine, which is always bad if it is new... but that is for another book). But if we constantly weigh every process or product against our scale of separation, simplification, and sustainability, we will learn to go past the easy and immediate answers and look for longer term answers. If you are able to can and store a year or two supply of food for your family, great! Use that year or two to learn the older, more permanent and sustainable storage and preservation techniques, *and* acquire the skill by practice to use them successfully. Then you can feel free to "can" all you like since you will be able to NOT can if you need to. Freezers and refrigerators have been a default option for so many people for so long, that not using them seems strange and bizarre - even to some agrarians. In our family we continue to study and learn the *arts* of smoking, curing, fermenting, potting, etc., and we teach those arts diligently to our children.

"Rid me, and deliver me from the hand of strange children, whose mouth speaketh vanity, and their right hand is a right hand of falsehood: That our sons may be as plants grown up in their youth; that our daughters may be as corner stones, polished after the similitude of a palace: That our garners may be full, affording all manner of store: that our sheep may bring forth thousands and ten thousands in our streets: That our oxen may be strong to labour; that there be no breaking in, nor going out; that there be no complaining in our streets. Happy is that people, that is in such a case: yea, happy is that people, whose God is the LORD" (Psalm 144:11-15).

A SHORT AND PLEASANT RANT

Some of you who maybe really don't care about right agrarian philosophy, but who are more interested in ways to do stuff... you can pass by this small rant if you like. It is polemical. Right philosophy, like right doctrine, divides. The rest of you just buckle up for a second.

What follows is my opinion. Do with it what you like...

You hear a lot in these days of fear and loathing about "preppers", "survivalists", "homesteaders", etc. What is the difference? After a major long-term disaster; the destruction of a civilization or some other horrendous calamity; historically the normal, ignorant, colonized folk die off pretty soon, often taking most of their neighbors with them in a maelstrom of violence, cannibalism, and blood. The "preppers" do a little better than unprepared folk – some of them may live on for months or years – until the "stuff" runs out and their lack of skills and practical know-how, or even real-time practice of those skills, exposes them to reality. "Survivalists" fall into both categories. Some die off in the original surge of violence, when the logical weaknesses and fallacies of their short-term mentality are made painfully evident. Some survivalists, due to their penchant for, or default to, violence, become part of the problem that God sweeps away in the original tsunami of bloodshed. Other survivalists, like some of the "preppers" do make it for quite a while, and are able to use pre-positioned materials along with learned and practiced skills to "survive" (however they define that word). Write this down though:

> *Unless people eventually learn (like their ancestors did) how to really survive and thrive off of the land for long periods of time without the aid and support of the so-called "civilization" that has abandoned them, they will not "survive" in any meaningful sense of the word.*

If you are alive today, it is because at least some of your ancestors, way, way back in the mists of time, were not brain-addled idiots. It remains to be seen what will happen to this generation. One of the problems with the preparedness folk is that they do not see beyond the fundamental errors of the people 'round about them. Whereas the ignorant folk say "I have no need of storing up any goods when there is a nice, clean, shiny store just down the road", the preparedness folk say, "Yes, and I will go to that store now and buy up enough food for *x* years", as if they know that precisely *x* years supply of food will be sufficient. In both cases, the people are relying on the store and the current system. Beyond that, they are differentiated by the fact that the ignorant folk say, "the government will take care of me if I run out of food, water, or shelter", and the preparedness folk say, "Well, I would rather rely on myself, my stuff, and chance". By this I mean that neither of these categories of people desires to make a wholesale change in the very principles and worldview that inform their decisions; neither group desires to be dependent on God and His Word *today*; and neither wants to give up modern comfort and modern security in order to throw themselves on the mercy, and to expect the providence of, a Holy and Righteous God. I use to say this all of the time in my preparedness classes, "If it is a good idea to 'be prepared' in case of the failure of the prevalent world system, then why not start living that life now? If it is logical to learn how to live without a system that we all think is broken (or will break), why not just work towards learning to live without it altogether?"

I've seen it for years. I was a preparedness teacher for years before the Y2K scare of over a decade ago. In fact, I was teaching preparedness at some level before I had even heard of Y2K. I finally gave up teaching "event preparedness" when I realized that people will prepare for events, and they will prepare for hardships, but only so long as their fundamental principles are not challenged. They will accept disaster as a temporary disruption in their lives, but they will not accept the idea that the very fundamentals of their industrial/commercial society are anti-christian, as well as mentally and spiritually crippling. They will not accept that the way they have chosen to live *is* why the system is evil and must eventually collapse. They will not accept that their perpetual 72 degree lives are designed for no other reason than to ease them into hell. They will prepare so long as those preparations guarantee a certain standard of living, and so long as their preparations make them believe that they will not die hungry or thirsty, or from some horrendous calamity, and that someday, over the rainbow, things will return to "normal"; which is to say that they will one day get to return to their lives of colonized leisure and comfort. If you were walking on thin ice, and you were warned, would you spend your time, energy, and money working out a plan to stay on the thin ice, but "survive" if it breaks? Or would it be wiser to get the hell off of the thin ice?

To change the analogy... we can know that different people will stay in spiritual and cultural Sodom for differing reasons. Some will not leave Sodom at all because they are Sodomites. This collapsing culture of wickedness is their home. They like things the way they are. Some will leave (or begin to), but will turn back hoping it is not utterly destroyed because they love it. They are torn because they don't want to leave, but they also know that Sodom (or "The City of Destruction" if you are a _Pilgrim's Progress_ fan like me) is going to be destroyed. They are torn between two lovers (their comfort and their lives) and inevitably they will turn back. However you look at it, preparedness for _events_ alone is a recipe for eternal and spiritual failure.

I am not saying you should not buy food from stores or make use of intermediate means, especially when good, storable food is on sale, or if you have not yet developed a system of food production for yourself and your family. I am saying that you should not rely on a Band-Aid for a bullet wound.

CHAPTER 15

BUILDING

This chapter on building will be shorter than most of the others. I can give you some advice and philosophy and a few of my experiences, but there are more opinions and options on the construction of structures than there are pages in this book. As you can imagine by now, most people (especially urban and suburban modernists, but most people in general) get everything upside down. This chapter will be a short and brutal attempt to turn them right-side up. The enemy of right thinking, as always, is the evil triumvirate made up of the world, the flesh, and the devil. These three forces combine into a martial front we call "worldliness" (the love of the world and of the flesh; 1 John 2:16).

Worldliness is the constant, daily, selling of one's eternal soul in exchange for temporary carnal comfort. The grand plans of many aspiring Agrarian homesteaders crash and burn because of some pre-conceived mental threshold of minimal comfort that the mind both expects and demands. I would say that almost 100% of the objections raised against Agrarian Separatism and Off-Grid Homesteading have as their root the inordinate love of COMFORT, no matter how the questions are disguised or how the objection is framed. When the protester denies that comfort is behind his or her objection, it is still always there lingering as both the primary and final unmistakable truth behind why people won't leave the world behind, even if they admit they should. When someone protests that they are staying in the world for the sake of their children or grandchildren, or because of evangelism (everyone's an evangelist when it comes to modern "christians") and the excuses they make for their love of, and intercourse with, the world, or because they believe that their "sacrifice" will allow future generations to live like God has commanded – you can almost uniformly replace their entire protest with two words... *CARNAL COMFORT*, and you will be a whole lot closer to the truth.

Now, I have no problem with being comfortable. Please don't get me wrong. I like a nice bed and a good meal as much as anyone. That kind of comfort is not what we're talking about here. We are talking about comfort being the *rule* or predominant factor in whether someone decides to do the right thing or not. The issue is that if we make carnal comfort the rule and we never look at what we *should* be doing and how we *should* be living - merely because the right thing *seems* uncomfortable - then we will never be obedient in those things we ought to do. Comfort cannot become the canon (rule or measuring stick) of behavior. God's Word declares that we can work towards comfort after we have done our best, in obedience, to prepare our work and make our fields productive. I have mentioned this verse before:

> *Prepare thy work without, and make it fit for thyself in the field; and afterwards build thine house.* (Pro 24:27)

In the wisdom of God, as we move towards obedience to His Word in how we should live, we ought to be willing to live uncomfortably for a time while we are preparing ourselves and our land for the future. We ought to make our lands, fields, gardens, and animal facilities workable, managing all of it for our future good and for the sustenance of our families - and we ought to do these things first. Then, when God has blessed our endeavors and our obedience to His Word, we should build our house. The excellent and learned commentator John Gill said this about this verse:

> *"and afterwards build thine house; when, though the blessing of God upon thy diligence and industry, thou art become rich, or however hast such a competent substance as to be able to build a good house, and furnish it in a handsome manner, then do it; but first take care of the main point, that you have a sufficiency to finish it; see the advice of Christ, Luke 14:28"*

Of course, many people are going to say that there is no Biblical command for people to live agrarian lives (they have to say that because their wants and lusts demand it), despite what these verses say (Please see the last chapter on *Answering Objections* for more on this topic). They will say that these verses only applied to some other culture, a long time ago - to some backward people that *had* to prepare their fields because they didn't have a Wal-Mart. Some people really believe that modern, urban, consumer-industrialism is just as good and pleasing to God as fulfilling His command to work the soil and take benevolent dominion over the earth... and I suppose if they are willing to discount or disbelieve about half of the Bible and just about all of the parables they might have a point. God says that we ought to live in such a way that we produce food from our own fields, and my point is that we ought to expect and even foster some discomfort at the beginning of our journey to proper home ownership. If our countrymen had followed this advice we would not have a mortgage crisis today; we would not have a banking crisis today; we would not have a credit crisis today. The average worldling today is unable and unwilling to feed themselves or provide for themselves by themselves. They do not, and will not, grow food or husband animals for their food and care. Yet they live deliciously in mortgaged, cracker-box castles, eating dainties that have been poisonously grown and covetously marketed, and being cared for by a paternalistic beast that juggles the means of survival just well enough to make all this seem right for a time.

BUT WHAT SHOULD YOU DO?

When choosing to move off-grid, you should remember the rules of survival:

Separation
Simplicity
Sustainability

Start simply, even if it means you might be uncomfortable for awhile. My family of 6 has been living in a cabin of less than 500 square feet, with a small 1976 camper as an addition, for more than 5 years as I write this chapter. My bedroom is the size of many modern walk-in closets. It is possible to do what I am teaching you to do. If you will make sure your initial setup fits these three critical rules, you should do well.

John Gill points out that we ought to expect God to reward our diligence in doing our duty. I am convinced that if the Lord wills that we prosper here on our land that I will be able to build a substantial house some day when my fields and animals are prepared properly. I believe that the house I will one day build (if the Lord wills it) will be nicer, more sustainable, more permanent, much more well-built and solid than any I might have built in haste with very little (or borrowed) money. So my advice to you is to expect, and even embrace, discomfort in the beginning. Live with less and prove what is good and right. By that I mean that you should try to live without all the stuff, and when you realize that you can do so, you will have proved to your own satisfaction that you don't need it. More than 75% of the stuff we did not sell before we came here, but put in storage, we found out we didn't need after all. My advice for many folks today is to sell everything except the few items you are absolutely sure, without doubt, that you will need. Sell it all and then buy what you *know* through study that you will need. I am convinced that most people already have the resources they need to begin their off-grid journey, but the money is locked up in junk they don't need, rarely use, and shouldn't own.

Building an off-grid life, for many of you, will likely start with the soil... and not much else.

I have made many mistakes in my off-grid adventure and I am willing to admit those mistakes and pass the wisdom on to you. If I had it all to do over again, I would start with the dirt and a shovel. I would dig a hole for my root cellar as my first building project. Whatever your first project is, remember the three rules and keep it simple. Always remember that food and water are primary, and ought to occupy your time and mind for a long while before you ever begin to think about long-term comfort. So long as our mind considers the world to be a safety-net and a crutch, we will not have a right view or mindset. We ought to think that food and water production and storage are critical to our survival, because they are, but a nice place to lay our heads is not critical at all. Imagine this (and I mean this - close your eyes and imagine it!)... If you were cast onto your land with nothing but some basic tools, how would you prioritize things? Would you spend your time on carnal comforts? Or, would you spend it digging, tilling, and planting? Survival is often the product of the right use of the imagination. Now, this part of the book is about building, and I suppose I ought to get to that, but I wanted to make sure our minds were right about the subject first.

SO... WHAT TO BUILD?

Remember that this is the part of the process that will take the most time, will require the most of us, and will last the longest with us. Where and how you choose to build - these are going to be decisions that stay with you for a very long time. If you choose to build in a modern style, and then a few years later you think you might want to use your farm for historical, "agro", or "eco"-tourism, then you are going to regret building your modern style buildings. If you choose to build in a place or direction that isn't well thought out, and then you learn later that you didn't have all the information and that there are multitudes of things you didn't consider, then you are going to regret many of your decisions. This is why I believe that God would have us live on our land for some time, working the soil and producing food, etc., before we build our permanent home. That way we can see the way the wind blows, how the water pools and drains, and myriad other important realities that will one day effect how we live our daily lives. In these parts (Central Texas), back in the old days, the folks would dig a root cellar as their temporary living quarters while they prepared their fields, pens, sheds, and barns. The house would come to be much later. That idea, as we have shown, is a very good one. If you have the means you might want to build a small temporary cabin, or you could purchase a small camper or tent to live in while you prepare your fields and out-buildings. I started in a tent then went to a small cabin. In any case, get to know your land for a year or two before you build permanently. You will make better decisions in the long run.

Our first "structure" was a chicken coop built from a castaway, mostly rotting, deer blind we found on the back of the property. I put a new floor in it, built it up on "stilts" and used some old fencing to fence in a rudimentary chicken run. Next, I built a second coop that would also serve as a grain and feed storage. After that, we put in our garden and a corral as we were building our small "temporary" cabin. Our cabin was designed as a temporary dwelling (we hoped to only use it for 5-7 years) and has grown a bit to help us do the things we need to do. Our intention all along was to eventually make our cabin into a dry-storage/pantry after we move out of it. We started our root cellar in the first full summer after we arrived here on the land, even before we had finished our temporary cabin. We had the root cellar ready to use at the beginning of the next spring. Today, we are blessed to have hundreds upon hundreds of pounds of storage and preserved foods in our root cellar. That root cellar is our "store".

I have received dozens of questions about the building of remote/off-grid cabins. While I do have many ideas about the subject, and I have learned a lot about what to do and what not to do, you need to remember that this book is about maintaining a sane and intelligent philosophy and process in going off off-grid. My advice in building a cabin is going to be limited, but your research will need to be expansive. Small is fine, especially if it is temporary. You really want to go for inexpensive, but not dangerously cheap. *Never go into debt to build a structure in which to live*. There is no need to. Debt is a freedom killer and the enslaver of all who enter therein. Going into debt for land, although it is not ideal, is at least understandable. This debt, if it is short term, is not a comfort issue, and it may be the only achievable method a person can devise to get out of the world in a timely manner.

I cannot, however, conceive of any situation where anyone ought to go into debt for housing. Live in a structure you *can* afford until you are able to build the structure you would like. Try to use resources that are free or very inexpensive. We have found folks willing to let us tear down old houses and other buildings if we will just remove the materials. From these materials we have built all sorts of things, including a storage shed and a farrowing shed for our pigs. Just yesterday a man in our community told me that he had just finished a sheep shed, and it cost him all of $16! One of our neighbors in this community has built most of his large barn from scavenged, free materials. The basic philosophy, though, is to spend some time anticipating your needs. You should always plan for things like water catchment and storage, etc. as you plan your design. Think about where you are going to put the stuff you need, and how to get rid of the stuff you do not need. Think about the weather, seasonal changes, sun track, where you want to sit when it is hot in the morning, and where you will sit when it is hot in the evening. How can you (or do you want to) direct the breeze through your building? How much light will you need? Where would be a good place to put a wood-burning stove? Can you build your structure so that most of your light can be natural light? All of these questions need to be studied in light of how much we can (or would like to) spend.

I am convinced that I can build a good sized (but maybe partially unfinished) cabin, with a sizeable water catchment and rainwater storage, for less than $10,000, and that is using mainly *new* materials. I know I can do this because I have already done it. If one were able to procure a large amount of free, cheap, or salvaged materials, the cost would be significantly less. I am fairly positive that we don't have anywhere near ten grand in my current cabin, and we built it in increments, as money, supplies, and labor were available. That is something that you can do too.

As I have said many times, I would build below ground first. My first structure would be a root cellar, and I would live in it while I build a second, larger root cellar (larger than this current cabin). Then, if I needed to put a small one-room shack over my underground structure, I would do so. This plan would do the following for me:

1. It would be much easier to manage the temperature swings, and to stay cool in summer. Our expense for cooling "stuff" for the first year we were on the land probably added up to well over $200 a month for the first few months, and may have been over $2000 for that year. This cost would be almost eliminated if we had built underground, and that money could have gone to future building instead of to waste. Even now, as I write this portion on this 17th day of March, it is 83 degrees and I have two ceiling fans (solar powered) going at full blast to cool the cabin. I would have no such need in a root cellar or basement cabin.

2. The root cellars would be handily accessible from a permanent house I plan on building in the future. The house I build someday, if the Lord wills it, will incorporate a large underground or partially underground living area for the *coolness* factor.

3. There would be no need for us to leave the cabin and slog through the mud to the root cellar when severe weather threatens. We could put the children to bed and not worry about having to get up and traverse the hazards to get into the root cellar if a tornado were to be coming.

When I do build a permanent house, if the Lord wills, I will incorporate all the things I have learned through practical experience, and I will know much more about my land and about how to do things correctly. I will know more about wind currents, temperature changes, sunrise and sunset at different times of year, rain runoff, etc., and I pray the Lord will continue to give me wisdom and good ideas right up to the time when I finally start to build my house.

Returning to our point, if we do not look at off-grid living as a complete system, with a philosophy that guides our decision making, then we will fly to and fro without any real purpose, and quite often we will be working at cross-purposes with ourselves and with our future plans. Take the time and use your mind and your creativity to envision how you want to live, and how to go about it. All of the rest of your building plans, then, will fall into place, and will only require the materials, the know-how, and the motivation to get them done.

Now, don't you feel better?

Remember, you need to not only consider when you will build, where you will build, and what will be the size and purpose of what you build; you also need to study and consider many different building methods, or, *how* you will build. As I said in the beginning of this chapter, there are as many building methods and philosophies as there are pages in this book. You can build your off-grid home above ground, banked, partially underground, or fully underground. I have read and studied methods of building with earth, straw, bricks, cob, wood, papercrete, tires, tin cans, cord wood, cement, stone, or a hundred other materials (or combinations thereof)... pretty much everything but diamonds and donuts. Don't limit yourself to modern books either. Folks in our community have found literally hundreds of books from past generations with many, many good ideas about building. Never forget history. If people lived in your area before there was grid electricity, municipal water, and a JIT food system, do your research and find out how they did it. History is not only interesting, it is fun. Constructing your off-grid home is one of the most exciting parts of the whole adventure, and it will say a lot more about you than you can possibly imagine. I hope I have convinced you that living an off off-grid life is achievable. It has been done for thousands of years, and it can be done today. Inspiration is often accomplished by the burning down of our idols and the wholesale destruction of our errant notions and false conceptions. Decolonization is about being set free from the brainwashing of the culture that has colonized us. What we say is far less important than what we do. What does your life say about you?

CHAPTER 16
ANSWERING OBJECTIONS

You can never answer every objection, especially when you live in an age when most people worship the God of their own mind. As you can imagine, over the years I have heard just about every objection to off-grid Agrarianism that you can imagine; first from my family and "friends", who didn't like the aims and goals of my life; then from our religious acquaintances, who were convinced that for anyone to attempt to live exactly like their own great-grandparents they would have to be in a dangerous and wicked cult. In reality, and maybe subconsciously, they discerned that our peaceful and separatist way of life condemned their worldly one. In any case, I have heard objections from the sublime to the bizarre. Most are pretty knee-jerk and predictable, others, though rare, are actually well thought out, seriously intentioned, and lovingly offered, however erroneous. Maybe you have several objections in your mind right now. Congratulations if you have read this far!

In the following selections and writings I deal with most of the common questions and objections to the lifestyle and philosophy that I advocate. I have written quite a bit about my philosophy over the years, so here I offer to you a cross section of some of these articles, answers, sermons, etc. I hope you will find them helpful. The articles are not substantially edited from their original form, so they may include small portions already included elsewhere in this book. This chapter is specifically designed to provide answers to the most common objections, so it was necessary that I not edit out any small portions, even if they might be repetitive, if the material was necessary for answering the question.

* Questions and objections specifically about Christian Separatism as a doctrine I hope to deal with extensively in my next book (if the Lord wills it) - *Christian Separatism.*

AGRARIANISM VS. URBANISM

The Bible teaches that mankind, in his most perfect state, was created and is designed (and has a primary duty) to dress the garden, to till, manage, and overcome the land, for the pleasure and provision of man and for the Glory of God. In our view, then, man's duty, apart and above all other duties, is to manage the Creation for God's glory, because *"The earth is the LORD'S, and the fulness thereof; the world, and they that dwell therein"* (Psalms 24:1). The first hint of any commandment or duty given to man in the Bible is from the first chapter of Genesis:

> *"And God blessed them, and God said unto them, Be fruitful, and multiply, and replenish the earth, and subdue it: and have dominion over the fish of the sea, and over the fowl of the air, and over every living thing that moveth upon the earth"* (Genesis 1:28).

In a deeper explanation of this command, we find more details in the second chapter:

> *"And the LORD God took the man, and put him into the garden of Eden to dress it and to keep it"* (Genesis 2:15).

Question: Wasn't that all prior to the fall? Man was expelled from the Garden. And were not the Agrarian commands nullified by the flood?

Prior to the fall, the duty of man was primarily the management, dressing, and keeping of the Garden of Eden. Man was given *"dominion over the fish of the sea, and over the fowl of the air, and over every living thing that moveth upon the earth"*. Here we have solid evidence that man was designed to have his primary duties in agrarianism and animal husbandry. Specialization and urbanization did not exist for quite some time, and only entered into the human system by way of the sinfulness and rebellion of mankind.

After the fall, God re-institutes His divine command that mankind work in the soil:

"Therefore the LORD God sent him forth from the garden of Eden, to till the ground from whence he was taken" (Gen. 3:23).

So the fall did not eradicate the command of God concerning the primary work of man.

Cain and Abel, for a time (around 130 years or so according to Ussher) obediently continued on in their Agrarian pursuits. One was a gardener (Cain), the other kept flocks (Abel). No city was built until after Cain slew Abel and received the condemnation and curse of God (Gen. 4:17). What was this curse?

"When thou tillest the ground, it shall not henceforth yield unto thee her strength; a fugitive and a vagabond shalt thou be in the earth. And Cain said unto the LORD, My punishment is greater than I can bear. Behold, thou hast driven me out this day from the face of the earth; and from thy face shall I be hid; and I shall be a fugitive and a vagabond in the earth; and it shall come to pass, that every one that findeth me shall slay me" (Gen. 4:12-14).

Cain's curse was that he would henceforth be banned from pursuing the Agrarian life that God had commanded. As a villain, the ground would not bring forth her product to him. Henceforth he alone, as a criminal, was commanded to be a nomad and a vagabond. His punishment was that he was banned from Agrarian pursuits! Cain cries out to God, *"My punishment is greater than I can bear!"* He has real fear, and a conscience that continuously attacks him for his sins. He is now estranged from the earth. He expects that he will be killed along with his progeny, but God tells him that because He wants him to face the seriousness of what he has done, no man will be allowed to kill him. So what does this criminal, this murderer, this arch-enemy of God do? He rebels against God again and decides to build a city (a citadel, a fortress for his own defense). God says "be a nomad", so, in rebellion, Cain settles down into a city of his own construction and names the city after his son Enoch. According to John Gill, Sir Walter Raleigh identified this city as *Henochii* an antediluvian city thought to be east of the location of the original Garden of Eden. Always keep this in mind... cities were invented by a murderer in order to defend the wicked from justice and to hide the rebel from God.

As man grows more and more wicked, and as the urbanite spirit of Cain overtakes mankind, God destroys it all with the flood. After the flood, Noah and his family depart from the Ark. God re-establishes his plan for man (Gen. 9:1, 9:9) and again gives man dominion over the animals of the earth (Gen. 9:2). Noah and his family obey God, and Noah *"began to be an husbandman, and he planted a vineyard"* (Gen. 9:20). Noah's understanding was that the command to take dominion over the earth, to multiply, and to grow crops and husband animals, was still in effect after the flood. The spirit of Cain, though, would again and again re-infect man, and through his covetousness he would inevitably be drawn back to the cities.

The command for Agrarianism was established before and after the fall, and before and after the flood.

The parables of the New Testament go on to re-establish mankind's agrarian responsibilities, and also recognize man as the steward of God's possessions. Man, as steward (a steward, or bailiff, in an agrarian culture was a foreman or manager of a farm, Luke 12:42-43), will eventually give a reckoning and account to God who is his absentee landlord. Man was to be a tenant farmer, with God as His master: *"Blessed is that servant, whom his lord when he cometh shall find so doing."* (Luke 12:43) The earliest believers, instructed by the parables, inextricably linked our responsibility as farmers and land managers to the final judgment and the return of the One righteous landlord. The divine plan for man to steward and work the land was designed not just for our sustenance and provision, but to instill in mankind the working design of God's sense of order, function, and beauty. Our minds were designed by God to be *trained* at a very young age by agrarian behaviors. Working the land and the animals gave man a sense of *dominion*, but always a limited sense of dominion. Whereas a man could certainly improve his odds of a plentiful and bountiful crop by hard work and planning, the results were always left at the foot of God who alone was and is sovereign over all conditions, weather, war, plague, etc. Biblical Agrarianism (and Biblical Agrarianism alone) trained man in the godly balancing act of submission and dominion.

Question: Isn't Agrarianism just another economic "system", whereby man works to make a living?

Agrarianism was never a system devised whereby man would primarily "make money", or "earn a living". We work because we are commanded to. If we are His, God promises us a "living". Tolstoy said, *"God gave the day, and God gave the strength. The day and the strength are sanctified by God, and labor is its own reward."* Agrarianism is a system of *obedience*. Agrarianism was beneficial in that man could, though Biblical methods, hard work, and honest obedience, receive of the providence of God – IN ORDER TO keep himself and his household separate from the ways and means of the godless world. Living an "off the grid" lifestyle should not instill in us pride or a sense of self-sufficiency, but should reassert a humble worldview, making us totally dependent on the grace, mercy, providence and sovereignty of our God.

It is interesting to note that our assertion that God trains minds through Agrarianism can be judged by even a cursory view of Biblical history. Where mankind thrived in godliness and righteousness, we also find an Agrarian society – and it is only in these types of societies (like in the Waldensian Alps prior to the Reformation, or in Germany and Switzerland in the 1500's) that we ever find theology and Biblical knowledge being purified. In contrast, wherever urbanization exists, we find the judgment and wrath of God upon that people. By contrast, in those "seats of learning" where specialization and urbanization are the way of life (say... Rome, or Athens, or Paris, etc.), we find nothing theologically but liberalism and apostasy. This is not to say that Agrarianism creates good theology, rather, that Agrarianism is the only proper seed-bed for good, Biblical theology. When the mind is trained in an urban/specialized setting, it becomes so much more difficult for that mind to embrace the mysteries of God that are unveiled in the types, shadows and parables of God. The Bible is an Agrarian book that rejects and condemns urbanization and specialization, and it is written to an Agrarian people. Biblical Agrarianism tends towards separation from worldliness and towards a dependency on the Providence and Sovereignty of God. Un-Biblical urbanism tends towards unification and independency *from* God, and dependency *on* the beast system of finance and commerce.

The shadow pictures (types/antitypes) of sin, separation, reconciliation and redemption can only be properly understood from a foundational knowledge of the agrarian/urban contrast. When a man lives in harmony with God, we find him in an agrarian/pastoral setting, dependent on God and not primarily on wicked neighbors, city dwellers or questionable forms of commerce. When man rebels and rejects God's ways, we find him gathered together with like-minded rebels in cities (The City of Cain, Babylon, Rome, Athens, etc.). In the divine illustration of salvation and redemption, God pictures His own children as wheat seed, which must fall in "good ground" (well prepared and managed soil), in order to germinate and bring forth fruit. From this we learn that God's children should be found as workers of the soil. They are spread out in good land, thinned by the Sovereign gardener, and nourished and pruned in order to bring forth good fruit. In contrast, when seed falls among the thorns (meaning a crowded, weed-filled place), with all manner of wild plants competing for sustenance, that seed is said to be "choked" by "the deceitfulness of riches". Most urbanites today, especially those who claim to be Christians, would deny that they are being choked by the deceitfulness of riches, and yet their continued reliance on specialization in an urban setting for survival contradicts their claims. Any urbanite today must find himself in league with the ungodly in order to survive, whether it be in a neighborhood or at the workplace, the city-dweller must be in unity and union with apostates and professed unbelievers on a day to day basis. Why? Well, *in order to make a living* you will be told (or from the bolder rebels you will hear that they are actually "evangelizing" the heathen. That is why the 83% of Americans who call themselves "christians" are in the world, living just like the world... they are there to evangelize!) This in itself denies the providence of God in giving good gifts and provision to His children.

God promised to deliver His people from such a land of bondage and dependence, into a land of Agrarian paradise:

> *"And I am come down to deliver them out of the hand of the Egyptians, and to bring them up out of that land unto a good land and a large, unto a land flowing with milk and honey..."* (Exodus 3:8).

Now God promised that He would give His children a good and productive land, and that all they had to do was to go in and "possess it" (which is to say, subdue it, till it, and manage it as good stewards according to the perennial command of God), but the children were rebellious and preferred their urban ways (yes, the children in the desert were really urbanites, city dwellers, etc. They did not grow food or plant crops. Their food was provided JIT without their participation). They had become specialized and feared the job ahead of them in overcoming the land.

"And Moses sent them to spy out the land of Canaan, and said unto them, Get you up this way southward, and go up into the mountain: And see the land, what it is; and the people that dwelleth therein, whether they be strong or weak, few or many; And what the land is that they dwell in, whether it be good or bad; and what cities they be that they dwell in, whether in tents, or in strong holds; And what the land is, whether it be fat or lean, whether there be wood therein, or not. And be ye of good courage, and bring of the fruit of the land. Now the time was the time of the firstripe grapes. So they went up, and searched the land from the wilderness of Zin unto Rehob, as men come to Hamath. And they ascended by the south, and came unto Hebron; where Ahiman, Sheshai, and Talmai, the children of Anak, were. (Now Hebron was built seven years before Zoan in Egypt.) And they came unto the brook of Eshcol, and cut down from thence a branch with one cluster of grapes, and they bare it between two upon a staff; and they brought of the pomegranates, and of the figs. The place was called the brook Eshcol, because of the cluster of grapes which the children of Israel cut down from thence. And they returned from searching of the land after forty days. And they went and came to Moses, and to Aaron, and to all the congregation of the children of Israel, unto the wilderness of Paran, to Kadesh; and brought back word unto them, and unto all the congregation, and shewed them the fruit of the land. And they told him, and said, We came unto the land whither thou sentest us, and surely it floweth with milk and honey; and this is the fruit of it. Nevertheless the people be strong that dwell in the land, and the cities are walled, and very great: and moreover we saw the children of Anak there. The Amalekites dwell in the land of the south: and the Hittites, and the Jebusites, and the Amorites, dwell in the mountains: and the Canaanites dwell by the sea, and by the coast of Jordan. And Caleb stilled the people before Moses, and said, Let us go up at once, and possess it; for we are well able to overcome it. But the men that went up with him said, We be not able to go up against the people; for they are stronger than we. And they brought up an evil report of the land which they had searched unto the

children of Israel, saying, The land, through which we have gone to search it, is a land that eateth up the inhabitants thereof; and all the people that we saw in it are men of a great stature. And there we saw the giants, the sons of Anak, which come of the giants: and we were in our own sight as grasshoppers, and so we were in their sight" (Numbers 13:17-33).

For the wickedness of the people we see that God curses the whole nation (all those over the age of 20 except Joshua and Caleb) to perish in the desert, never to see the true land that overflowed with milk and honey. But why did Caleb and Joshua see what no others would see?

"But my servant Caleb, because he had another spirit with him, and hath followed me fully, him will I bring into the land whereinto he went; and his seed shall possess it" (Numbers 14:24).

Joshua and Caleb saw what was good in the land. What was it? They noted that the land was rich and would produce crops and fruit and abundance. Did they say, "This will be a good land for building a city whose top will reach up to heaven?" No! They showed their brethren *"the fruit of the land"*. They said "this land will produce bountifully for us". What did this tell us about God's intention for His elect people?

Caleb (and later we see him joined together with Joshua) had *"another spirit with him"*, and God said of Caleb that he *"followed me fully"*. Do you understand the importance of this as it relates to separation? Most who hear these messages, but who still will not separate themselves from the wicked, and who still live in cities, and who still will not live a life directed by a truly Biblical Worldview, are not able to SEE the good land, because all they can see is giants and problems and things that cause fear (when they are not too busy evangelizing, of course). When people contact me about "getting off the grid" they are often afraid because they don't think they can subdue the land and they don't know how they will survive. They see with carnal eyes and do not see the providence and promise of God as if it were already completed. They do not see with the eyes of faith.

God's children were designed and created to live in Agrarian communities, knit together by a common worldview and common faith. They were to be a shining light, set on a hill (not a bunch of dim lights scattered throughout the darkness). This shining light was to be their evangelism! Whereas there was always "micro-specialization" (every man did not have to produce 100% of what he consumed) in that some individuals and regions produced some particular items for sale to other individuals and regions that might specialize in another product, it is evident that most of the people were expected to provide for most of their own needs. Each family should produce the bulk of their own food and supplies from their own homestead. Farmers never produced just one crop, or one type of product, expecting to make enough money from the sale of his goods to buy the rest of the things he needed to survive. This concept left too much to "chance", "luck", and "fortune" (all pagan deities), and did not rely on the Providence of God through the obedience of faith. Proper farm and land management techniques (crop rotation, multiple and cross-beneficial crops, etc.) were passed down from the Patriarchs through their families and descendants – until inevitably the children rebelled, sold or abandoned the land, and moved into cities where specialization and segmented labor would "insure" temporal survival. This, you see, is the curse of Cain.

When the Puritans and Pilgrims left the crowded and corrupt cities of Europe in order to experience religious freedom in the New World, we find that they re-instituted many of the traditions and laws of ancient, Agrarian Israel. It is true that the Puritans were already theologically sound, but we must confess that the "good ground" where the Puritans were led by God to plant their farms and families insured that the Biblical Agrarian model brought forth great temporal and spiritual fruit for many generations to come... *We exist today on the fumes of their faithful labors.*

Where the people began to gather together (once again) into large cities; where they began to be more urbanized and specialized (such as in New York and Boston); we also see the slow absorption of anti-christian doctrines. Just as the rural/agrarian system is the proper seedbed of good theology - the urban, specialized, worldly system that exists in cities is the best seedbed for liberal, manipulative churches teaching anti-christian creeds.

Note where the "food" of a man is supposed to come from, and think about it as a sign of how our spiritual "food" (The Word of God) comes to us:

> *"He watereth the hills from his chambers: the earth is satisfied with the fruit of thy works. He causeth the grass to grow for the cattle, and herb for the service of man: that he may bring forth food out of the earth; And wine that maketh glad the heart of man, and oil to make his face to shine, and bread which strengtheneth man's heart"* (Psalms 104:13-15).

Spiritually, God puts forth those things necessary to bring our spiritual food forth for our service. But who will understand the Word of God? When man has put aside the Agrarian system and knowledge that showed us how God brought our physical food to us, how is man to understand the spiritual antitype (or fulfillment) of this type? So much of God's Word and so many of God's mysteries are hidden in the Agrarian understanding. Is it any wonder that we are a people starved for wisdom and understanding (just as our bodies starve for natural nutrition)?

Question: But can you really say that city living is evil?

The modern economic system is actually crumbling around us, having been built on nothing and suspended by mythologies and lies. The economies of commerce that feed and support the large urban centers today (and even most midsize and small towns) is a system built on lies and worldly "good faith and credit". When that system collapses, more than 90% of any modern nation's population will likely suffer and starve; either that or even *more* wicked and statist means of provision will have to be brought forth in order to feed and sustain a great majority of consumers who have neither the desire nor the skills to produce and survive.

Many people read the commandments in the Bible to *"come out from among them"* (2 Cor. 6:17), *"come out of her"* (Rev. 18:4), and to separate from the world, and they think, "Listen, I don't go to bars, and I don't do drugs, and I don't go out and party, and I don't spend my money foolishly... so I *have* separated from the world"; but in their rationalistic replies they show how foolishly and ignorantly they have failed to discern the plain teaching of the Bible. It is our mutual *dependence* and interdependence upon the world and worldlings that evidences whether or not we are a Biblically separated people. Listen, if all the wicked worldlings immediately perished or were stricken with some serious malady that caused them to be unable to continue in their jobs – the cities (and all those who rely on them) would collapse and perish. It is your dependence on the world that is at issue here, not whether or not you partake in *all* of their habits.

God's people must be separated and dependent on God alone instead of dependent on the world that is perishing around it. Spiritually, we must recognize that *"Abram dwelled in the land of Canaan, and Lot dwelled in the cities of the plain, and pitched his tent toward Sodom"* (Gen. 13:12). I pray to God that He is still sending angels to pull His children out of cities and that He still strives with those He plans on blessing. In the Bible, we see cities and city-dwellers *overthrown* (Gen. 19:25), *destroyed* (Gen:19:29), and *terrified* (Gen. 35:5); the children of Israel were forced to build cities for an evil Pharaoh (Ex. 1:11); God gathered the people together into cities to punish them (Gen. 47:21, Lev. 26:25); God promises to lay the cities waste (Lev. 26:31, 33); God exhorts Joshua and the children of Israel to smite all the cities with the edge of the sword.

In one of the most telling types/shadows of all of history, as the Roman armies surrounded the wicked city of Jerusalem, God had his people (the Christians) flee the adulterous and rebellious city for the surrounding countryside and the safety of the caves of Pella. In the perfect picture of what we are each to do in our own lives, when we see the wicked city, rebellious to the core and surrounded by enemies, we are to flee from that worldly city before it is destroyed. You see, if we belong to God, we *are* the righteous city of God, the New Jerusalem (Rev. 3:12, 21:2), a city set on a hill, the betrothed Bride of Christ, purified and adorned for His purposes. Separate yourself O Holy City of God! You must separate yourself! Return to the garden in the physical, and you will return to the garden in the spiritual. Rely on the Providence of God, and God will give you the fat of the land - a land overflowing with milk and honey. If you would desire to understand spiritual mysteries, then you must be willing to reject carnal fears. The giants are NOT too big, and the land will not swallow you up. Our God is a mighty God, and, as an absentee landlord He will soon return for a reckoning. YOU will give an account as to your stewardship of the land. I pray that God will lead you out of Sodom before that reckoning comes.

Question: I see many "farmers" who seem to be just as worldly and dependent on the world as any city dweller. How, then, is Agrarianism different substantively from Urban Industrialism or the modern Consumer State?

PURE AGRARIANISM VS. MERCANTILE AGRARIANISM

I have already in this book described the differences between Pure Agrarianism and the industrial so-called "farming" that is actually just another part of the Kingdom of This World. See Chapter 8 for more details, but here is a small snippet:

"When the farmer stops growing his own food, and instead puts all of his land and resources into growing a single 'money crop', then he begins to rely inordinately on the system, and he begins to feed the system that will one day destroy him. As this type of system develops, eventually the farmer doesn't even know where his food is grown or who grows it. In fact, he is not a farmer at all... he is an 'industrial producer.'"

So it is a mistake to look at industrial producers, who are part of the whole industrial system that I condemn, and use them as a tool to attack or judge true Agrarianism.

Let me start by saying that I prefer any Agrarianism to modern Industrial-Consumerism, and that my comments here are not designed to deflate, attack, or dishearten anyone who is engaging in any Agrarianism anywhere.

I appreciate Agrarianism wherever I find it, but I did want to delineate between what we mean by "Biblical" (or "Christian") Agrarianism, and what we would call "Mercantile Agrarianism". Mercantile Agrarianism is a form of Agrarianism that developed late in agrarian cultures, usually as the last dying step before Industrialism. Mercantile Agrarianism was _not_ Agrarianism in its purity, but was really the last gasps of Agrarianism as it was given over to a new system of covetousness and greed. In its purity, an agrarian society consisted mainly of homesteads and farms where family groups (or colonies) produced most of their means of survival (food and supplies). Though there was often trade and barter, commerce and exchange, the primary means of survival for each family or colony was in farming, husbandry, and gardening. There have always been craftsman and tradesmen in Agrarian societies, but even these craftsmen and tradesmen provided most of the means of their survival for themselves - from the land. There were specialists, but specialists lived and thrived within the context of the overall agrarian culture. In the later stages of an agrarian society, if the people do not remain watchful in order to protect themselves and their worldview, the tradesman and craftsman gives way to the merchant. The merchant begins to exercise control over the society, and Agrarianism gives way to Mercantilism. Now, trade becomes the central truth and reality of the culture and from there moral compromise, mass production, "economy of scale", and industrialism become inevitable. From there, the merchant driven society becomes a consumer driven society; the merchant is, in turn, overthrown by the corporation, the market is overthrown by the superstore, and, as we have seen, the tradesman and craftsman is replaced by the mind-numbed laborer. A self-sufficient middle class of producers who once sold to the merchant is replaced by a middle class of consumers who produce nothing for themselves, but who serve to be consumers of those goods owned and sold by the rich and mass-manufactured by the labor of the very poor. These middle class workers are constantly bombarded with messages that intend and serve to increase consumption, usually marketed on the altar of "comfort" or "leisure", so that they might keep the system afloat by an ever increasing appetite for flesh satiating goods and gizmos.

The danger is always there, even on the small scale... even in the family group, agrarian colony, or community. When our desire for a simpler, separated, and God-centered life begins to give way to the desire for profit, comfort, or leisure; when we begin to seek our sustenance from the merchant instead of from the ground; when we settle for a "picture" of agrarianism instead of the real thing - then the collapse of our system is inevitable. In Mercantile Agrarianism, the "agrarian" is satisfied to live on a small portion of land (in many cases less than an acre), living (for the most part) like the industrial/consumers who live around him, but convinces himself that he is different from them.

Question: Just about everyone is part of the system. If you participate in the system, even in the smallest way, aren't you just a part of it?

I know that there are some who will insist (for selfish reasons of rationalization) that if anyone, anywhere, ever, participates, in even the smallest way with the modern industrial/commercial system, then they too must be cogs in the world system, but this is not the truth. It is understood that there will always be some level of concourse with the society, even in the perfect Christian Agrarian culture, but we must not allow mere necessary contact (or even "evangelism") to become an excuse for defending actual intercourse with an idolatrous society. So in Mercantile Agrarianism (no matter what it calls itself) you may see two extremes: on the one hand you may have the suburban gardener, or a small land-holding entrepreneur, for whom Agrarianism is a hobby, or maybe a profit-center, but not an over-arching philosophy and way of life. On the other hand you may have a commercial agriculture capitalist (a businessman) who raises some cash crop that is to be pumped into the industrial society that supports him. If the market dries up or crashes he may lose the farm and everything, or he may rely on the government to get him through to the next bull market. Both types of Mercantile Agrarians buy the bulk of their goods from the merchant, and they produce very little of what they consume. Their agrarianism is utilitarian, but we dare not call it "Christian" or "Biblical", and it is important that we know the difference between Mercantile Agrarianism and truly Biblical Agrarianism.

Question: Isn't Agrarianism and Off-Grid living just a lifestyle choice?

I believe that Agrarianism is not just a "lifestyle choice" or a "good ideal" for Christians. I believe the Bible commands it (see Gen. 2:15, 3:23) and that the entire Book is written in agrarian terms to an agrarian people. Many (actually most people) do not understand the Bible because they are living worldly lives contrary to it. This doesn't mean that I expect everyone to live like I do, or to immediately put on a camel-hair coat and go sit in the desert, or to start plowing fields and raising carrots; this is why I have carefully defined what Agrarianism is, and why Christian Separatism is so critical a principle for Agrarianism

(Christian Separatism will be covered in the next book, Lord willing). Just as the Amish and many Mennonites believe that Christian Separatism and Agrarianism are fundamental to the very core of their Christianity, our fellowship believes the very same thing. Most Amish and Mennonites are kind of idealized for their way of life and for their separatism, precisely because they aren't writing books about it or on the Internet blogging about it. Be sure that if they were, many people would feel condemned by what they *actually* believe - which is why many people feel somewhat condemned by what I write. I write what I believe and everyone is free to read and heed it, or to reject and ridicule it. Some do the former, and most do the latter.

Let me paint a quick picture for you... If you were riding through Amish country and you saw an Amish man plowing his field using horse power, you might say to yourself, "There is something I can appreciate. There is a man living separately according to the dictates of his conscience. There is a lifestyle that is admirable; a man who puts God, faith, and family above the love of the world". You may develop a warm feeling and a strong affection for this old and proven way of life. Then let us say you stopped your vehicle and made conversation with this man. You might be shocked (if he is honest, and you are diligent in your questioning) to learn that he considers you "the English" (the Amish name for anyone who is not "plain", meaning he considers you *a worldling* and *a persecutor*), and that he believes that "the English" are lost and reprobated and that most of them will be damned. The Amish man loves peace and quiet, so he may not tell you what he thinks of you – because of this most people will never be mad at him. My fault is that, in openly declaring what I think is right and good, people are naturally going to interpret by that what I think is wrong and bad. Well, there goes the pretty postcard picture of the Agrarian Separatist, don't you think? The difference between me and the quaint Amish man is that you know what I think.

Question: You've told us what you think about Urbanism. But Jerusalem – the City of God – is (and was in Bible times) a city. How can God be anti-city when He has focused so much of His story in one?

Jerusalem was in no way comparable to a modernist, industrial city of today. Jerusalem during the time of Christ was "one of the biggest cities between Alexandria and Damascus, with a permanent population of *some 80,000...* The years from A.D. 1 to A.D. 33 happened to be a high point for the holy city. It was, says Eric Meyers, professor of Judaic studies at Duke University, 'a great, great metropolitan area and home to the lavishly restored Jewish Temple, a world-renowned wonder. It was prosperous and cosmopolitan'". (Time Magazine article by David Van Biema, Andrea Dorfman, Jonathan Calt Harris, Said Ghazali, Eric Silver, Haim Watzman)

Just so we get this straight, Jerusalem was a city of just 80,000 people (basically a large town in today's terms) that was destroyed by God, precisely because it was wicked and fundamentally anti-Christ, only about 40 years later. If Jerusalem was just a fine city with some wicked people in it, God would have destroyed only the wicked. But he didn't do that. He gathered the wicked into it and destroyed it and them together. That God raises up cities is not denied by us. God also raises up Kings – but He said He did so because the people were wicked and would not be led by Him alone:

"Then all the elders of Israel gathered themselves together, and came to Samuel unto Ramah, And said unto him, Behold, thou art old, and thy sons walk not in thy ways: now make us a king to judge us like all the nations. But the thing displeased Samuel, when they said, Give us a king to judge us. And Samuel prayed unto the LORD. And the LORD said unto Samuel, Hearken unto the voice of the people in all that they say unto thee: for they have not rejected thee, but they have rejected me, that I should not reign

over them. According to all the works which they have done since the day that I brought them up out of Egypt even unto this day, wherewith they have forsaken me, and served other gods, so do they also unto thee. Now therefore hearken unto their voice: howbeit yet protest solemnly unto them, and shew them the manner of the king that shall reign over them. And Samuel told all the words of the LORD unto the people that asked of him a king. And he said, This will be the manner of the king that shall reign over you: He will take your sons, and appoint them for himself, for his chariots, and to be his horsemen; and some shall run before his chariots. And he will appoint him captains over thousands, and captains over fifties; and will set them to ear his ground, and to reap his harvest, and to make his instruments of war, and instruments of his chariots. And he will take your daughters to be confectionaries, and to be cooks, and to be bakers. And he will take your fields, and your vineyards, and your oliveyards, even the best of them, and give them to his servants. And he will take the tenth of your seed, and of your vineyards, and give to his officers, and to his servants. And he will take your menservants, and your maidservants, and your goodliest young men, and your asses, and put them to his work. He will take the tenth of your sheep: and ye shall be his servants. And ye shall cry out in that day because of your king which ye shall have chosen you; and the LORD will not hear you in that day. Nevertheless the people refused to obey the voice of Samuel; and they said, Nay; but we will have a king over us; That we also may be like all the nations; and that our king may judge us, and go out before us, and fight our battles" (1 Sa 8:4-20).

It is just as wrong to say, "There are earthly kings, so they are good", as it is to say, "There are earthly cities, so they are good". God allows many judgments to come upon people because they disobey Him. But let us not forget that the term "city" in the Bible age didn't even mean what it means today. The term "city" comes from the word "citadel". Originally a "citadel" was a fort designed for military defense. The village grew up *outside* of the citadel, and supplied agrarian produced materials to those who worked in or defended the citadel. Eventually, the walls of the citadel were extended to include the village and the temples that had grown up to provide for it. The cities of Israel were centers of trade and commerce, but relatively few people actually lived in them. It emphasizes the point when you realize that over 2 million Israelites came out of bondage in Egypt, and here in 33 a.d., 1500 or so years later, we find only 80,000 people living in Jerusalem, the main city in Israel.

We find that Jesus and His disciples walked to and from Jerusalem from the surrounding countryside, just as most of the people travelled to Jerusalem without living in it. Jesus spent most of his time headquartered in Bethany, a small agrarian village outside of Jerusalem. Jesus went to Jerusalem to warn it, to plead with it, to weep over it, and eventually to pass judgment on it. Jerusalem was not just a center of trade and commerce along an important trade route from Asia to Egypt and between the interior of the East and the Mediterranean Sea, but it was also obviously an important religious center as well. I have said many times that in an agrarian society, there likely will be towns, villages, and even cities. There always have been... all the way back to Cain. All of this is a moot point though, since we know that the Industrial Revolution didn't happen until the late 1700's. Prior to that, there was NO society that was not primarily agrarian.

Next, we need to point out that the "cities" in the Bible were *walled cities*. They were places of defense. They were necessary "citadels" for the defense of the people from marauding and invading armies. The people, for the most part, did not live in the cities. They went to the cities to trade and to worship, and they went there when an enemy invaded the country. When the Assyrians and the Babylonians and eventually the Romans invaded Israel, the people knew they were coming for some time. Only in the final days, as the armies approached, did the masses of country folk run to the cities. Notably, as the Roman army approached, the Christians, heeding the words of Christ, headed the other way.

So:

1. The word "city" did not mean what it means today. The city was a place for the trade, barter, and transit of Agrarian products. It was a religious center, but primarily it was a place of defense.

2. The city was an agrarian marketplace - there was no industrialism as we know it today at that time.

3. The city was destroyed by God. God gathered the wicked into the cities to destroy them (as tares, bound together for the fire), and commanded His children to flee from them or perish in them.

Question: I am old (weak, single, married, blind, handicapped, poor, rich, a prisoner, a widow, etc.) and I cannot move towards Off Off-Grid Living, even if I wanted to. What should I do?

I believe that in most cases, where God grants a will, He also grants a way, but it is obvious that no one - outside of the miraculous will and actions of a Sovereign God - can do what they really cannot do. If you are actually and really unable (meaning incapable) of doing something, then obviously you are unable to do it. There is not much to say about that. There only remains prayer, research, study, diligence, and obedience in as far as you are able. I do not believe that most people who say that they cannot be obedient are really *unable* to do what they think they should do. Usually they are just *unwilling*. The human mind is able to rationalize anything, and the modern colonized mind is the most perfect "rationizer" in history. However, it is possible that there are many categories of people who are actually, because of their circumstances, unable to be obedient to what they believe they ought to do. This is more a commentary on the corruption of our society, and on the slavery it engenders, than it is on the practicability of

Agrarianism or Off Off-Grid Living. Unhappily, there are very real consequences for sin, both personal and national, and one of those consequences is that our society and culture is such that many people are inextricably entangled in the web. This means that either God will give us the means to obey Him as we truly desire to do in our hearts, or He will destroy the culture and the society with many stragglers still in it. We pray for His mercy. Our prayer is that God's long-suffering towards His people will allow many, many more people to extricate themselves from their current situation – and that the Lord will help them and strengthen them to move OUT of the City of Destruction.

IT IS GOOD

It is an unhappy reality that I am generally forced to spend almost all of my teaching time answering objections, and so little time showing people how Off Off-Grid Living is not just necessary... it is GOOD! When we talk about "survival", it is often necessary that we talk about the negative aspects or realities that make prudent actions or changes necessary. But this emphasis on the negative often leaves people feeling as if they are being forced or pressured into doing something undesirable. With Agrarianism and Off Off-Grid Living, that is not the case. The benefits and joys of independent and free living so far outweigh the negatives (hard work, diligence, etc.) that the two are not even comparable. In fact, what so many people consider negative in the Agrarian life, most Agrarians consider huge positives! Urbanites pay money to "work out"; they pay money for all of their utilities; they pay money for their food; and they have to go to jobs they generally dislike in order to have the money to pay for many of the things that Agrarians get for free. We are currently building a treadle water pump for our pond. This treadle pump will allow us to pump water from our catchment pond up to our gardens and to our animals. Basically, the treadle pump we are building looks a lot like a commercial "stairmaster" stair-climbing exercise machine. I was joking around the other day and I said, "After we get it installed, we can charge city-folk $30 a month to come out here and work out!" This just illustrates the

346

point. Ours is a lifestyle of joy and freedom and 24-hour God-centered worship in the heart of His Creation. We get to feel His earth, watch His providence, and experience His grace and mercy directly – without the multitudes of predatory middle-men who do nothing but insulate us from the face of God. We are in touch with the wind, the rain, the seasons, the cold, the heat, and the manifold mysteries of God's divine plan for man on earth.

Freedom has become just a by-word today. It is an empty slogan. It has no real meaning in the context of modern urban life. Freedom can mean "some political leeway" or "lack of the direct and palpable application of chains", but it cannot mean what it truly means in a Biblical context. In our community, we believe that our freedom entails the freedom to glorify God according to His will and commandments, and the freedom to partake of His bounty in the Kingdom of God – separate from the slavery and bondage of the Kingdom of This World. The world may see us as "backward" and call us "dumb, plain, hick farmers", but I assure you that we don't hear them over the rattle of their chains.

> *"Then said the man (Christian), 'Neighbors, wherefore are you come?' They said, 'To persuade you to go back with us.' But he said, 'That can by no means be: you dwell,' said he, 'in the city of Destruction, the place also where I was born: I see it to be so; and dying there, sooner or later, you will sink lower than the grave, into a place that burns with fire and brimstone: be content, good neighbors, and go along with me.'"* (Pilgrim's Progress, by John Bunyan)

Freedom cannot continue to be an empty slogan or a by-word if we are to spiritually, and even temporally, prosper in the land given to us to husband for God's glory. If you are not free to glorify God by obedience, then you are not free. Breaking the chains of slavery can look daunting, but, in most cases, it involves the revolutionary act of saying "no" to the power on this earth that has colonized our minds and traded in the souls of men. "Just say no" takes on a whole new meaning in this context.

> *In a long enough timeline, the survival rate for everyone goes to zero. Obedience in life, then, is the act that most glorifies God. Without it, survival is just a delaying tactic.*

"Be content, good neighbors, and go along with me."

SUGGESTED READING

Surviving Off Off-Grid was never intended to be a "how to" book. Some of you may have noticed that many of the topics usually included under the banner of "survivalism" are not included in this book (for example: wilderness survival, retreats, guns, and defense). The following materials are offered for your instruction, and to give you a very quick introduction into many of the survival arts. Although many (or most) of them contain philosophies and a worldview that are contrary to my own, I have still learned much from them, and I believe that you may too... MB

Writings of a Deliberate Agrarian, by Herrick Kimball. ISBN 0972656472

Living the Good Life, by Helen and Scott Nearing. ISBN 0805203001

How to Survive the End of the World as We Know It: Tactics, Techniques, and Technologies for Uncertain Times, by James Wesley Rawles. ISBN 0452295831

Perennial Vegetables, by Eric Toensmeier. ISBN 9781931498401

Wild Fermentation, by Sandor Ellix Katz. ISBN 1931498237

Successful Small-Scale Farming, by Karl Schwenke. ISBN 0882666428

Charcuterie, by Michael Ruhlman & Brian Polcyn. ISBN 0393058298

Preserving Food without Freezing or Canning, (many authors). ISBN 9781933392592

Tom Brown's Field Guide/Wild Edible and Medicinal Plants, by Tom Brown, Jr. ISBN 9780425100639

Primitive Wilderness Living & Survival Skills, by John & Geri McPherson. ISBN 0967877776

Home Production of Quality Meats and Sausages, by Stanley & Adam Marianski. ISBN 9780982426739

Root Cellaring: Natural Cold Storage of Fruits & Vegetables, by Mike Bubel & Nancy Bubel. ISBN 0882667033

Build it Better Yourself, from Organic Gardening Magazine. ISBN 0878571337

OTHER BOOKS BY MICHAEL BUNKER:

Swarms of Locusts: The Jesuit Attack on the Faith, by Michael Bunker (2002). ISBN 0595252974

CONTACT

Michael Bunker constrains most of his communication to *"snail mail"* (traditional post). Please write him a letter if you have questions, comments, or suggestions. Michael does keep a very small, very intimate email alert list. To receive Michael Bunker's e-mail alerts, which are rare but do include notifications when new sermons or podcasts are posted, and updates on Michael's ministry, ministry trips, etc., please send an e-mail to: *editor@lazarusunbound.com*

To listen to Michael Bunker's "radio podcast thingy", please go to *www.audiobunker.com*. You can subscribe to Michael's podcasts on iTunes.com

11531668R0020

Made in the USA
Lexington, KY
12 October 2011